TALAT MAHMOOD

The Definitive Biography

Sahar Zaman

Cover design by: Hunar TV Edited by : Samar Raeesuzzaman

FOR MY SON, KAZUO IMAD

(Kazuo Imad, great-grandnephew of Talat Mahmood stands in front of the legend's portrait painted by artist Amit Srivastava)

Contents

AWARDS

- **'Popular Choice Award 2024'** by Auther Awards presented by Times of India and JK Paper Ltd – "To encapsulate the life of a man often described the 'King of Ghazals', though he was much more than that, is no easy task. For daring to undertake this endeavour, Sahar Zaman deserves our applause. As his grandniece, she has skilfully depicted the life and era of Talat Mahmood. Congratulations for adding yet another feather to your cap."
- **'Biographer of the Year 2024'** by Bollywood Film Journalists' Awards presented by Power Brands – "The book is a rare treasure and a labour of love penned down by Sahar Zaman."

REVIEWS

- "Sahar Zaman details the actor-singer's life and art like never before." - **Times of India**
- "Sahar Zaman has penned a heartfelt biography which combines journalistic rigour with the flair of an expert raconteuse." - **The Hindu**
- "The author lives up to the challenges on researching Talat Mahmood's life and maintains a delicate balance while writing about family" - **Hindustan Times**
- "An unmissable read about the legend" - **All India Radio**
- "Deeply researched book, loaded with anecdotes"-**CNN News18**
- Sahar Zaman has done great service to Indian film history by writing this book. It holds evidence not just of her deep admiration and love for her granduncle, but also of her thorough research to gather facts, milestones and events from his life. - **Satya Saran, The Indian Express**
- "The book explores unknown aspects of yesteryear singer's professional and personal life" - **The Wire**
- "You would wonder what's Talat's connection with the Army and the NDA? It's in the book!" - **Times Network**
- "The acclaimed author and grand-niece of Talat Mahmood, Sahar Zaman's book provides intriguing insights into the life and legacy of the musical maestro. A spectacular celebration marking the 100th birth anniversary of the legend." – **The Pioneer**

-

- “Sahar has done an excellent job to mark Talat Mahmood’s centenary by penning this biography with exclusive details.”- **Doordarshan News**
- “She looks at the singer's life, from a rebellious teen who wanted to sing for films to one who promoted new talent in his later years.” - **The Print**
- “To encapsulate the life of a man often described the ‘King of Ghazals’, though he was much more than that, is no easy task.” - **The Week**
- “Forget Drake and The Beatles, discover Talat Mahmood’s timeless music journey through Sahar’s book.” - **The Quint**
- “We must thank Sahar for writing this book because it’s an important chapter in the history of our cinema.” - **Satya Hindi**
- “The book reveals why Bal Thackeray gave him a rose, why Noorjahan offered him a blank cheque.” - **The Lallantop**
- "The biography reveals not just the dizzying heights of Talat Mahmood’s stardom but also his simplicity as a family man, a nationalist & a fund-raiser for social causes." - **Sahitya Tak**
- “Author Sahar Zaman writes about a lesser-known aspect of his busy calendar of global concert tours”. - **ABP Live**
- "A volume written not just with abundance of facts and details but with a lot of intense involvement & passion." - **Tehelka**
- “The book is a great service to all music lovers interested in the Golden Era phase of our film music industry” - **The Federal**
- “Sahar presents a remarkable gift to fans and music enthusiasts” - **The Daily Guardian**

ADAPTATIONS

- Music recital by actor Harsh Chhaya & singer Sudeep Banerji at the Nita Mukesh Ambani Cultural Centre
- Theatre show by thespian Sohaila Kapur, titled ‘Talat Mahmood: Reluctant Hero, Superstar Singer’
- Dance recital by Moving Souls Ltd.

FOREWORD I

It was an evening of cool breeze and gentle calm when Sahar first spoke to me about writing the biography of her grand-uncle, Talat Mahmood. It came as a sudden surprise to me because one hardly talks about this legend today. His velvet voice has soothed many hearts during an age when more time was given to human emotions, when the genteel qualities of a human mind was appreciated and when one was allowed to reflect on the experiences of life with eloquence and finesse. He added pure gold to the Golden Era of films that he belonged to.

When his grand-niece, Sahar, mentioned his name, the sweet memories of Talat sa'ab (sir) came rushing back to me. It made my evening even more beautiful. He has mesmerized me with both his voice and his personality. There is a desire to understand what made him so sweet and soft spoken. He was very warm and affectionate but carried the persona of royalty. His voice reflected all these aspirational qualities and that makes one curious about knowing more of him.

It made me very happy that Sahar has taken this upon herself to write the journey of a man who is one of the most exceptional people that I have ever met in my life. I have met so many singers and artists but none like him. He was one the biggest stars but not much is known about his life. There was a time when everyone would want his Midas touch in their songs.

For Sahar to be both a journalist as well as a family member, will surely add to the credibility and authenticity of this definitive biography. Youngsters today should certainly read about him and be inspired about how to be both a good human being and a good artist. I promised Sahar that for Talat sa'ab, I will always be available for any kind of help that she requires from me. And since she is related to him, I feel the same love and fondness for her.

I remember the first time I met him in the early 1960s when I used to work as a casual (non-permanent) artist in the radio at AIR Cuttack. Talat sa'ab was part of a tour sponsored by AIR where top artists would visit radio stations across the country. That's when he noticed my talent and encouraged me to come to Bombay.

(The author with Pt. Hariprasad Chaurasia)

When the world first heard me play my bansuri (flute) in films, it was with Talat sa'ab's voice. How can I ever forget him?! He was the first singer that I recorded with after I moved to Bombay. It was for the film Jahan Ara (1964). I got a call to play the flute for the song 'Phir wohi shaam'. Music director Madan Mohan ji had called me to Famous Recording Studio located in Tardeo. When I reached there, I saw Talat sa'ab standing in deep thought in front of the microphone. I was struck in awe and delight. His voice carefully caressed the poignant sound of my flute and became one with the spirit of the song. It's an unforgettable number which has become a cult classic. It's also a song that made my studio dreams come true because I recorded with one of my favourite singers.

His behaviour was so silent and soft, always lost in his thoughts of music. I wanted to talk to him more but wondered how I could strike a longer conversation with him. After we finished recording the song, he asked me where I was staying and offered to drop me back to my hotel. I was surprised with the humility of such a big artist. After that, I would often drop by his house. His wife Nasreen ji would give me evening tea and delicious snacks. They were a very loving couple. Watching them made me think that they would never quarrel. My wife also grew very fond of them and we both remember those lovely moments that we got to spend with them.

These were some of my observations on his personal life. But even as a professional, I was enchanted by his disposition. Those were the times when artists would give space and time to reflect on their music. I felt that he was a very reserved person and whenever he spoke, he only spoke about music. This was the reason why his work remains a class apart to date. With his behaviour and diction, he seemed like a Maharaja (Great King). He opened up to me for a while and would talk to me about his hometown Lucknow as well. In those moments, I felt close to him, like a family member.

Sahar has shown me the same love and respect, promising that the first copy of this book will be handed over to me. I am very touched and wish her all the very best.

Pt. Hariprasad Chaurasia, Padma Vibhushan
(Indian Classical flautist and film music director)

FOREWORD II

(The author with Dr. Shashi Tharoor)

Rarely does history witness the birth of an artist whose sole ambition is to serve the cause of art, enabling it to transcend divides and enshrining it in the hearts of all. Talat Mahmood was one such artist: a virtuoso ghazal singer who, with his honeyed and dreamlike voice, allayed the agony of a turbulent India. A tender trailblazer, Talat came to embody the artist's fervour when he — at the early age of sixteen! — defied the dictates of his conservative family and began to sing in his hometown of Lucknow. With the All India Radio as his launchpad, Talat rendered the ghazals of Daag and Mir in his velvety cadences, eliciting effusive acclaim. This exalted him to the dizzying heights of Calcutta and Bombay, from where there was no turning back. In a journey that mirrored the political evolution of India and the efflorescence of the Hindi Film Industry, Talat established himself as a phenomenal singer and masterful actor. Here was a "singing star" whose fanbase far exceeded the ghazal aficionados of the subcontinent, including in its sweep admirers in the US, UK, West Indies, and East Africa, where he extensively performed long before international tours of Indian singers became a concept.

In this incisive biography, Sahar Zaman — a renowned political journalist and the grandniece of Talat Mahmood —brings to life the story of an unassuming man who lived to serve his art.

Today, nearly a century after he was born, Talat is revered as the foremost pioneer of the "filmi ghazal," and his endless list of disciples includes such doyens as Jagjit Singh and Mehdi Hasan. But Talat was not just a maestro: he was also a fierce patriot who remained in India after Partition; and who, through his poignant inflections, brought to the commonfolk the mellifluous delicacy of Urdu poetry. In recognition of his invaluable artistic contributions, Talat received the Padma Bhushan in 1992.

A biography of his had long been due: and now, at last, we have this exemplary volume by Sahar Zaman, who simultaneously imbues the narrative with the rigour of a seasoned journalist and the inquisitive affection of a family member.

This brilliant book on India's first "King of Ghazals" is essential reading for all connoisseurs of the genre.

Dr. Shashi Tharoor , Chevalier de la Legion d'Honneur
(Best Selling Author & Member of Indian Parliament)

FOREWORD III

(The author with Sonu Nigam)

It was the 1st of April, 2000 at the Studio 4D in Worli, Mumbai. I was called to record my first song with Lata Mangeshkar ji by A. R. Rahman for the movie 'One 2 ka 4'. I watched everyone's musical Goddess on the microphone for the first time until she met me after getting done. As I got up to touch her feet, she suddenly uttered that there's something by me that I sang on my then popular TV show 'Saregama' that she loved tremendously. She goes on to say, "Aapne Talat Mahmood ji ka gaana 'Phir wohi shaam wohi gham wohi tanhai hai' gaaya tha... Ooof kitna sundar gaaya tha (You sang the song by Talat Mahmood sa'ab, 'Phir wohi sham wohi gham'...Uff, you sang it so beautifully)."

Can there be any better and bigger endorsement of my regard, study and studentship of the great Talat Mahmood sahab (sir) than this? Lata ji picked up this from the hundreds of songs I must have sung over the 5 years I hosted that show! Such is my and my family's love for Talat sahab. I truly feel you have to reach a certain level of wisdom to get a glimpse of what he was, rather is. Uniqueness, that is unparalleled. The texture of his voice, his poise, his class, his quintessential combination of tremolo and vibrato, his pitch perfect rendition and his pathos is a case study for any sincere student of music. I have also noticed that he is undoubtedly the only singer that is the most difficult to copy if one tries to sing in his style. It's almost impossible to sound like Talat Mahmood.

I was introduced to these qualities of his voice by my parents. They used to tell me about him and his journey like tales are told to children. I remember my father telling me that music composer Anil Biswas *ji* selected him for his unique tremolo, but when he came to the recording, he masked the tremolo by singing in a straight voice. He apparently was not confident if that was going to work for him or not. Anil *ji* then insisted that he maintain his uniqueness and the rest they say is history.

Apart from this, we find some anecdotes about him in magazines. Some of it is unverified hearsay over the years. To have an authentic biography by someone closest and most credible, is something that I was looking for for a very long time. To document the greatness of a man who everyone says was a gentle soul with a class of his own, is like a treasure for music aficionados like me.

Thank you, Sahar for taking up this mammoth task. Long live the great Talat Mahmood sahab.

Sonu Nigam, Padma Shri
(Playback singer and music artist)

PREFACE - MY BAMBAI NANA

(The debonair Talat Mahmood)

LABOUR OF LOVE

(The author at the debut concert of Jashn-e-Talat)

The energy backstage felt very different from what I had experienced in other events and television shows. As a journalist, reporting behind-the- scenes on big shows is very different as opposed to being the curator of one such concert. In this particular case, I was not just the curator, but also promoter, founder, investor, ideator, production manager, marketing executive and presenter – all rolled into one whizzing head!

The green room door was pushed ajar by my friends while my make-up artist was still giving the final touches to my face. My saree's *pallu* was still being pinned in the right place. And my hairdresser was yet to spray my top lock of hair in place. But there was no stopping the rush of my excited friends and supporters who couldn't stop pulling at my hand to congratulate me. "You did it Sahar" , "Congratulations, finally " , "What determination Sahar".

Confused and worried, I looked at my watch. These gushing responses even before the show starts? I peeped out from backstage towards the audience and realized that all the seats were full. The aisles were beginning to crowd up and many people started sitting on the floor. My husband, Dhiraj, who was my most patient pillar of support in this madness, rushed into the green room. "We have no choice but to start RIGHT NOW", he said with emphasis. "The audience is getting very restless and it's already houseful. The organizers are trying to put in extra chairs but there are at least 20-30 more people waiting outside the gates." The maximum capacity of the hall is 350 seats but this was certainly more than the upper limit because it felt like a sea of people, taking up every possible space, including the chairs inside the production control room right at the back. Certainly, no one had anticipated these footfalls, no one was prepared for this rush.

We were to start at 6.30 pm but the hall was already packed by eager music lovers by 6pm in the heart of Delhi, at the India Islamic Cultural Centre. This was unexpected by Delhi standards where people usually walk in fashionably late. I instructed my first set of performers to be stage-ready 20 minutes before time. I had five minutes to calm the audience. The backdrop of the stage had a 20x16 feet poster of our tribute show. It said "Jashn-e-Talat by Sahar Zaman" with a large vintage photograph of Talat Mahmood dressed in a tuxedo, with his chin gently resting over the violin placed on his shoulder. It was an image taken from his film 'Dil-e- Nadan'. As I walked on to stage, the spotlight shone on me, blinding me for a few seconds. I greeted the audience with an unprepared speech. I am used to speaking without a script in my LIVE news bulletins, but this speech on stage was about my grand-uncle Talat Mahmood, not the country's current affairs. I didn't think about what I would say but it all came out perfectly crisp in extempore.

"We are all here for the love of Talat Mahmood. To celebrate his timelessness. Be it Dilip Kumar standing between fluttering curtains for 'Shaam-e-gham ki qasam' or Sunil Dutt consoling Nutan over phone with 'Jalte hain jiske liye', Talat Mahmood still pulls at heartstrings. And in that he remains an ever-green star. Every Supporting Partner's logo that you see on this Jashn-e-Talat poster is all for the love of this gentle legend. You are sitting here within these packed aisles and your excitement is touching. Thank you so much for showing your support and love tonight…" I said all of this and walked backstage while sporting a band-aid on my nose – a zit that chose to firmly plonk itself in the middle of my face amidst all the stress caused by executing the first ever Jashn-e-Talat concert. "It's a *nazar- battu*", laughed a friend, to ward off the evil eye! It was a labour of love, after all. But one that stretched me beyond my comfort zone and expertise. As I heard the thunderous applause to my speech, I wondered how many such applauses Talat Mahmood himself would have received, show after show. My mother Romana, had told me a lot about the mob frenzy that he would face in the prime of his career, but this tribute show was decades after his passing away. It was evident to me that his fans and music lovers are still as enthusiastic, even today.

That night was a mix of Ghazal singers serenading the audience with their favourite Talat songs, young dancers performing a Bollywood salsa to his peppy numbers and a Kathak performance to his traditional singles. Thus came the birth of Jashn-e-Talat, with a bang. A celebration of his life, that eventually led me to write this biography.

NATIONAL VELVET

Talat was the one and only velvet voice ever known in the country. Like dew drops on a fragile leaf or a slender blade of grass, his voice was a source of enchantment for generations of music lovers. How does one describe it best? It was lilting, it was caressing, a soft cadence. It felt delicate and vulnerable with the sheen of a gossamer at the break of dawn. It had a sensitive rendering that elevated pathos to dramatic heights.

His songs were not a nine-day wonder. They are for eternity. Every anniversary of Talat Mahmood causes a rush of dedicated music shows on radio, articles in print and tribute concerts in remembrance of the unique musical sensibilities that he brought to mainstream cinema. It's a testimony to how he silently continues to live on in the hearts of true music lovers.

And that's the power of my Bambai Nana. Yes, that's what I used to call him, pragmatically coined by my brother, Samar, when we were kids. "Since he lives in Bambai (local name for Bombay/Mumbai), let's call him Bambai Nana".

I remember him as a cute grand-uncle with twinkling eyes who would be excited to treat us and make sure we had the best time while visiting Bombay. One of my most special memories is when I met him in Delhi after he received the Padma Bhushan, one of the highest civilian honours bestowed by the Government of India. We celebrated at his hotel room while watching one of his old films playing out on Doordarshan, 'Sone Ki Chidiya'. You will read more about such personal insights in greater detail in the course of the book. What I liked most about him was his simplicity. Despite his huge stardom and pioneering success, I don't know how he managed to remain so humble.

For the uninitiated, Talat was a big name in the Golden Era (1950-1970) of Hindi films in Bombay. He was the voice of Dilip Kumar who epitomised tragedy in the song 'Ai dil mujhe aisi jagah le chal'. When Sunil Dutt wooed Nutan over the phone with 'Jalte hain jiske liye', it felt as if you were at the other end of the receiver. And when Bharat Bhushan played the role of Mirza Ghalib decoding the mysteries of the heart with 'Dil-e-nadan tujhe hua kya hai', Talat poured his heart out in each written word, making the poetry sparkle like diamonds when encased in his soft, velvety voice. His charming manners and good looks got him cast as the main hero in a dozen Hindi films opposite Nutan, Mala Sinha, Suraiya and Shyama. Little wonder he was called the 'King of Romance' or 'King of Hearts' by some fans.

I recently came across a European website where a designer was selling T- shirts and mugs printed with Talat Mahmood's face. One of the taglines of the T-shirt said, "I don't need a therapist because I have Talat Mahmood".

I was amazed by the impact of his voice across generations and nationalities even today. After all, he was introduced to the American audiences as the Frank Sinatra of India. You listen to him just once and he will remain on your playlist as your friend and confidant forever. It felt he cared and he sang only for you, "I hear you. There..there…"

THE BIOGRAPHY

The idea of writing Bambai Nana's biography came to me while I had been organising different concerts of Jashn-e-Talat across India. Curating these music shows is not part of my profession. I belong to the world of journalism where I am trained in news gathering, reporting, television shoots, anchoring bulletins and hosting political debates. It's a world of breaking news, sharp deadlines and endless days. So, Jashn-e-Talat was a very challenging side hustle which I emotionally chose to take up alongside a full-time journalism career and a growing-up child.

It was befitting when the British Council listed it as a contemporary festival to watch out for. The combination of vintage music in the contemporary context was unheard of.

Inching closer to his centenary year in 2024, my wish was to have this exclusive work of non-fiction in the hands of music lovers across the world, to enjoy and marvel at his pioneering journey. This is my gift in lieu of all the love and pride.

It's the story of an artist whose career cuts across the history of India. From being a pre-independence celebrity to being Independent India's film star. Coming from an educated and cultured Muslim family that supported our freedom movement, this is a musical journey in which the birth and evolution of India is closely entwined.

The biography explores his indelible mark on the Golden Era of films by taking you behind the scenes of moments from the recording studio, personal friendships with colleagues and the impact of his stardom. I feel blessed to be his grand-niece where members of my family have dug into their archives of old letters, diaries and incidents to revisit his young days and help recreate exclusive insights. My brother Samar, an aficionado of old film songs, has been the constant 'fact-checker' of dates, names and events in his life.

This is an attempt to discover Talat as a person and rediscover his music. But it does not claim to be a music analysis of his work. That task is best left to the people who are well-versed in the rich heritage of India's classical and folk traditions.

The names of the cities Calcutta (present day Kolkata) and Bombay (present day Mumbai) have often been interchanged with respect to the timeline in the book.

Throughout the book, I have often referred to him by his first name, Talat. Please be assured that this is not to be disrespectful to him under any circumstance. It's only for the convenience of the reader.

MOULD BREAKING MULTITASKER

I have researched and found out so many more aspects of his career that I choose to define him as a gentle mould-breaker. He refused to fit into one box and was a constant pioneer in what more a singer could be. If multitasking is a term which is in vogue with GenZ today, Talat was already doing it in his lifetime.

Apart from his thriving career in Bombay's Hindi film music, his parallel career in non-film ghazals since the 1940s earned him another popular title, the 'King of Ghazals'. He gave record-breaking sales to music labels and often experimented with Western sounds of the guitar and drums to be used in Ghazals with traditional poetry. Today, the independent music industry in the genre of Ghazals across South Asia rests largely on his shoulders. He had a life-long dedication to the class of Urdu poetry and had the masses feel familiar with the language through his finesse and appeal. You will be delighted to read personal insights in the book about how later legends such as Mehdi Hasan and Jagjit Singh chose to become Ghazal singers only because they were die-hard Talat fans.

There is a lot to mention about the early years of his career in Calcutta in the 1940s when he was picked up as a young talent by the then giant of the music industry Pankaj Mullick. This is where he first struck gold with "Tasveer teri dil mera". The Ghazal broke all records, selling more than a lakh copies in those days which was unprecedented. That's when Mullick put him up on an unexpected challenge to learn Bengali and start his career as Tapan Kumar. From being an expert of Urdu, Talat had to quickly learn a brand new language which he knew nothing about. But his honey dew voice was completely in sync with the sweetness of Bengali.

He soon became an important figure in the movement of Modern Bengali music. The country's biggest studio of the time was in Calcutta. The New Theatres signed him up on contract as singer and actor. Even today, people are surprised to know that Bengali was not his native language.

FIRST GLOBAL PERFORMER

In the course of my research, I realized that in the peak of his career, Talat was the first ever Indian playback singer to start world tours in 1956. He ended up charting the path for other singers and colleagues who followed suit. His world tours helped ascertain in which cities the Asian Diaspora was willing to sponsor tours and buy tickets for Hindi film music concerts. Right through the 1970s to '90s, Talat turned to concerts full-time.

In those early days, he already had a New York agent. He was often the first artist to perform for local Indian-American clubs across the United States of America and the United Kingdom. The first generation of Indian immigrants would long to have someone visit from India and play them the music of their homeland. Many of these immigrants became rich businessmen and established cultural clubs that started inviting singers from India. Inevitably, as the very first of the popular singer post-independence, Talat set the ball rolling for his friends Mukesh and Manna Dey, after which Lata Mangeshkar, Mohammed Rafi, Kishore Kumar and others followed suit. The careers of many concert organizers got established through this. It has been a delight for me to get in touch with some of these overseas clubs who remember Talat with great fondness as someone who generously performed for them.

He was a unique global icon that many cannot comprehend today. President Nasser of Egypt was his fan. So was King Zahir Shah of Afghanistan, who especially requested him to sing for his wives. The Indian Embassy in the Kingdom of Saudi Arabia made special arrangements for his concert, in a country where music and films were strictly frowned upon.

I have also reflected on the misconceptions propagated by many that leaving for world tours and acting as main lead in films dented his singing career. To set the record straight, the only tour that he took in the peak of his singing career was in 1956. The rest of his concert career was from 1968 onwards, when he was beginning to face a dwindling number of film recordings but an increase in non-film recordings.

Regarding his films where he acted in, he naturally sang in them as well. Yes, he admitted to having been tired when he would shoot all night and then be present for song recordings in the morning. But did he lose out on singing assignments? Only because of preconceived notions of filmmakers, he suffered a 20 percent loss in the number of songs in 1957 and '58. But again, the early 1960s got him some of the biggest hits of his career. He has always categorically denied ever turning down songs for the sake of acting in films.

ACTIVIST & FAMILY MAN

With Talat's continuous travel and exposure to Western music labels, he developed a fine understanding of their royalty rights for singers. This is where Talat, the activist, stepped in. In the 1960s, he took charge of the Playback Singers Association as the Secretary. There was already a buzz about the right to royalty fees for playback singers in film songs. In his official capacity, Talat led the way, along with his friends Mukesh, Kishore Kumar and Lata Mangeshkar, to mark the first ever mike-down protest by singers against the music labels. While speaking to insiders, I have been given to understand that this was a defining moment for the cause in the industry.

Apart from his professional milestones, I touch upon Talat, the person – as a son, a husband, a family man and a supportive parent. While he was mostly viewed as an introvert for the outside world, at home he was jovial and quite often the one pulling a prank. Readers will be amazed to learn about new facets of his personality. What was he as a young child in Lucknow, his ambition as a young teenager and who helped him through those trying years where he had to make a choice between his father's house or his music career. What was the mystery of his family which was educated and culturally engaged in some aspects but was curiously conservative on other issues. There were moments when his singing had to be kept under wraps but his siblings and aunt helped him sail through.

What emerged with Talat's trailblazing decisions was a man who set an example for the family on how to live life on his own terms. It's been a blessing for me to be a journalist and a family member both. My professional training on news gathering, access to members of the film industry and family sources make it an apt combination to write this book.

Yes, there were moments where I felt that should I be so brutally honest or should I not give out too many details. So it's been a tightrope walk of constantly striking the right balance. The best biographies in the world are said to be those when the protagonist is treated like a real person with all shades of black and white and everything else in between.

How to live a life dedicated to music and love - that was his motto. But for all these details and more, read on!

CHAPTER 1 - THE CHARM OF LUCKNOW

(Talat Mahmood as a young child)

BIRTH IN A CULTURAL HOUSEHOLD

The India of 1924 under British Rule was set to witness a new thrust to the independence movement. Mahatma Gandhi who was imprisoned in 1922 for a sentence of six years was hurriedly released after only two years because of an emergency medical operation. Gandhi had fallen ill in 1924. He was suffering from appendicitis and was in great pain. The government of the British Raj was alarmed. Under no circumstances could they afford a sympathy wave if Gandhi died in prison. An urgent operation was arranged and the government thought it best to release him and keep him free.

With two years of Gandhi in jail, the Non-cooperation movement which demanded India's independence from British rule was at a low ebb. Many Congress leaders were either imprisoned at the time or facing a low morale. When Gandhi was released from prison, he decided to galvanize the movement once again and spend time in bringing about Hindu-Muslim unity and the removal of untouchability. He travelled all over India. His influence among the people was steadily growing. Gandhi had not given up the idea of non-violent resistance to British rule. He was merely waiting for the right time.

It was at this right time in our history, that the birth of a gentle hearted and sweet-voiced child took place in the city of Lucknow. He was the third child and youngest son out of six siblings born to Rafi-un-Nisa and Manzoor Mahmood. He was named Talat, a Turkish and Urdu word which means 'pleasant face'. In the Holy Quran, it means the one who is spiritually ascending. Personalities with the name Talat are believed to be generous and caring individuals who like to use their artistic talent to better the world. They are elegant, sophisticated and stylish in behaviour and appearance. It's uncanny how each description of the name befitted this new born boy in the Mahmood household.

This was a conservative Muslim family that gave a lot of importance to education, cultural engagements such as classical music and Urdu poetry, and held a voice in the freedom struggle of India. They lived in a large house which was a C-shaped plot out of respect for protecting a huge Peepal tree below which people had placed idols for worship. The area of the tree was left out of the private plot to allow the public to freely continue worshipping under the tree.

Talat's young neighbours, two brothers Akbar Khan and Puchey Khan (Sohail) describe the place from their childhood memories. "The street name was Nariyal Gali and their house number was 40. Our house number was 41, so we were right opposite them. Both these homes belonged to my great grandfather, Mohahmmad Adil Khan. Talat's family were renting the place. You might be able to locate the house even today. But the street's name has been changed to Batashe Wali Gali in the Aminabad locality of Lucknow", recalls Akbar.

It was a sturdy structure built in 1886 from the slender and tough red colour Lakhori bricks on the inside, with Martin Burn tiles on the outside. The majestic gate of the house gave it a Rajputana (royal) look. It had a heavily carved set of two wooden doors with geometric patterns. The top panel of carving bore two fish facing each other which was the insignia of the princely state of Awadh, used for good luck. The massive facade of the house had tall walls with high arches blending into multiple mehrabs, slim pillars and tiny jharokhas. The main gate of the house would open into a big courtyard, the left side had a big area which were the Mahmood family's private quarters. This is where they had their bedrooms and separate washrooms. Outside these rooms was a central courtyard with trees and led to a flight of stairs on the right side. This was meant for male visitors and was called the Mardaana (men's room). This, of course, indicates that the family followed a purdah (separation by veil) system, where women of the house were not allowed to openly interact with men from outside the house, and gender segregation was followed.

"Further down the verandah, there was the Bawarchi Khana (kitchen). I still remember the qorma (Lucknowi mutton curry) that was cooked in their house. It's the best that I've ever had. It was light on the stomach and full of gentle aroma", adds Akbar.

Around twenty years ago, the sturdy Peepal tree made way for a two storey temple called the Ashtha Bhuja Durga Mata Mandir (temple for Goddess Durga). The C-shaped plot was split into two independent units by the successive owner, thus changing the postal address and the original construction permanently. Today, just a part of these twin houses has survived. All the mango and guava trees that used to be inside the courtyard have been chopped off as well.

Manzoor Mahmood ran a curio store in Nazirabad which was close to their home. This was a huge shop of electronics and collectables. Since electricity had just arrived in the city in the 1920s, there was a new demand for fancy lamps and chandeliers. Manzoor had given his shop the poetic name of 'Barqee Ajayabat' (Electric Wonders). He was a collector with good taste and showcased some specialized pieces in his shop. It sold cut- glass cabinets with crystal wine goblets, lamp bases made of iron statues, porcelain tableware sets, etc. All of these were pieces made in Europe, mainly England. He mostly sourced this from different places in Bombay.

"He was such a cultured man who raised his children by instilling in them tastes for music and literature. My aunts were friends with Talat's sisters and they used to come home for different occasions. I have fond memories of his sisters singing nath (songs in praise of the Prophet) during the annual Milad celebrations (Prophet's birth anniversary). And during the rainy season, the house would come alive with our traditional 'saawan ke jhule' (swings that are hung up from mango trees in the courtyard). They had beautiful voices and would regale my aunts with some famous folk songs of that time which were sung to celebrate the rains", recalls an excited Puchey Khan.

Talat's father was known for his booming voice. He was closely following India's independence movement and was taken up by the power of Gandhi's charisma and holistic approach on Indianness. He would often sing patriotic songs during protest gatherings against the British in the 1930s. In those days, a lot of these meetings happened without the microphone but his voice managed to reach every person present there.

Talat's other brothers - Hayat Mahmood and Kamal Mahmood, sang well too. Elder brother Kamal Mahmood had a strong voice similar to their father. But Talat's voice was different and gentle. They were all die hard fans of the superstar singer-actor K L Saigal. All brothers would compete with each other to sing his songs in a voice that sounded closest to Saigal. Inevitably, Talat would win!

THE POWER OF MAHLAQA BEGUM

(Talat's beloved aunt, Mahlaqa Begum, was a rare, liberated woman of her times (Courtesy: Zaheer Kidvai))

Despite this culturally engaging atmosphere at home, Talat soon realized that beyond a point, it was relatively orthodox. He noticed this difference when he shifted to his aunt's house in Lucknow. As was prevalent in those days, the boys of the house were brought up by the paternal aunt instead of their mother.

Along with his two brothers, Talat was brought up by his phuphi (father's sister) Mahlaqa Begum in the 1920s. She was a beautiful, vivacious and fiercely independent woman who could best be defined as a rare trailblazer for her times. She decided to utilize the large courtyard of her house for baithaks/mehfils (cultural gatherings in music and poetry) with the popular poets, singers and musicians of that time. A young Talat grew up in this culturally rich atmosphere and soon started maintaining a diary of his favourite poets. When he showed it to his aunt, she was surprised by his choice of selections. She then allowed him to sit in these mehfils at her courtyard so that Talat could hear the best of the artists at her home. The list of artists who sang there included greats such as Roshan Ara Begum, Gangubai Hangal, Bade Ghulam Ali Khan, Narayanrao Vyas and Hirabai Barodekar. The star poetess of those times, Attiya Faizi (who had headed the country's first Music Conference as Chief Guest), was a frequent guest at home. She was Mahlaqa's close friend. There was always a buzz in the air when she hosted fancy dress parties with her famous friends. Under the shadow of Mahlaqa Begum, the young Talat was richly instilled with values of art, culture and some form of gender emancipation as well.

"At the age of 25, she had bravely written the Foreword for a book titled Alam-e-Khayal (A World of Imagination) written by Shouq Kidwai. It was about a woman's love and longing for her husband. You can well imagine how controversial this would have been labelled for a conservative Muslim society of Lucknow at that time where women barely looked outside their veil and the confines of their home! Under Mahlaqa's guidance, Talat first understood how the nuances of Urdu poetry and light classical music were magically brought to create the most romantic genre of music called Ghazals. As a boy when Talat would sing some Ghazals at home, he would sing them in a classical style. It was Mahlaqa who first brought it to his notice that Ghazals are sung in a soft classical style where feeling the emotions of the poetry is as important as the musical notes", says her grandson, Zaheer Kidvai, beaming with pride.

Talat used his holidays like a sponge to absorb everything that Mahlaqa's house of wonder could offer. For the rest of the year, he and his brothers were sent to study at the sprawling campus of the Minto Circle school and hostel in the city of Aligarh.

The aesthetically-designed school boasted of Indo-Islamic architecture lined up with palm trees and surrounded by a circular lawn. Founded in 1875 by social reformist Sir Syed Ahmed Khan, this heritage school is under the Aligarh Muslim University (AMU) and was a leading elite educational institution with several other notable alumni such as Nawab of Pataudi, poet Javed Akhtar, actor Naseeruddin Shah, former Vice President of India, Hamid Ansari and many others, in the following years. Today, it goes by the name S.T.S. School.

The school provided a holistic approach to modern education and literature in both Urdu and English. It also ensured that its students were exposed to music, poetry, theatre and other aspects of culture. It is here that Talat went on stage for the first time in his life to sing a song as a young teenager. His friends knew that he enjoys poetry and music, so they were cheering him on as he held the microphone. His choice of ghazal was Ghalib's 'Nuktacheen hai gham-e-dil', the version that was sung by his lifetime favourite actor- singer K L Saigal for the film Yahudi Ki Ladki (1933). Before I move ahead on what happened to Talat on stage, let's understand who was the legendary Saigal that this young boy idolised to the point of worship. Kundan Lal Saigal was considered the first superstar of the Hindi film industry before India's independence. His voice took British India by storm. People would buy his latest records and tune in to the radio and find themselves mesmerised by the unique poignancy of his deep baritone. He was the benchmark for most of the singers who followed him.

Back in school, when Talat stepped on stage, he was shy and timid. He sang the first few lines and suddenly froze with stage fright. All the cheering changed to booing. He forgot the lines, he forgot the music and ran bawling down the stage. When he met his aunt back home, his teenage mind dramatically decided to give up his dream of being a singer. "I can't do it, it's not in me", he said in anguish. Mahlaqa Begum knew there was too much talent in her nephew to allow him to remain hurt and scarred about a small incident. She consoled the sweet boy and reminded him of his diary of Urdu poetry. The wisdom in these writings will help you in life, she said. "One day, the world will see the greatness of your voice once you learn how to bring these words to life, with all your heart". She knew she was looking at a special gem who had to be nurtured with care.

NEGOTIATING THE DREAM OF PROFESSIONAL MUSIC

The final year at Minto Circle School was up to class 10. In those days, it was called Matric Level. After that, he was back in Lucknow to complete class 11 and 12 at the neighbourhood school called Aminabad Intermediate School (1939-40). It was also an uptown English Medium school but it felt relatively small and restrictive after the beautiful vista of the Aligarh campus.

Today, his name is a matter of pride in the list of exemplary alumni from the school. "On Republic Day celebrations at school, we not only make tableaux of important people in the history of India but also include Talat Mahmood's tableau since he is an important name from the history of our school", reveals Sahab Lal Mishra, the current Principal of Aminabad Intermediate School.

When Talat was back home with his brothers, they would together bring the house down, flaunting their science experiments to their young sisters. They would catch frogs from their courtyard, dissect them and demonstrate a LIVE science lesson for their younger sisters, who would often be horrified about it. The experiment that really helped though was to get rid of house lizards. They would paste tobacco at the end of a long stick and wrap it with white lime. For some curious reason, the lizards would eat it and fall off the walls, unconscious. But unlike his studious brothers, Talat was not interested in school since all that he ever wanted to do was to train himself as a singer. The reputed Marris College of Music was next to their house, so Talat's preferred destination was not far away from home.

But Talat's father was against his wish of taking up music as a career. As long as it was a hobby, it was okay. But making a profession out of singing was frowned upon. Mahlaqa Begum persuaded Manzoor to let Talat live his dreams, especially when the boy has such talent and sincere interest in music. He softened a bit when his sister pleaded in the boy's favour. Manzoor reasoned with Talat and set him up on a challenge. "If you complete your studies in school with a good grade, I will allow you to study in that music college." Manzoor had also been persuaded to call a music master at home so that Talat wouldn't lose practice. "The master would always say the boy's surr (rhythm) is very nice. He was given his own harmonium for riyaz (practice). Sometimes, it would be sent to the shop called Allan Sahab and Company for repair. This is the same shop that was owned by music composer Naushad Ali's uncle. His family was not very well off, so he would often work at his uncle's shop as a young boy", reminisces once again, his old neighbour Puchhey Khan. Destiny and showbiz brought these two powerhouses of music talents from Lucknow together in the Bombay studios years later!

In these last two years in school, Talat was actively involved in cricket as well. His nephew Rishad Mahmood recounts a memorable incident which his father (Talat's elder brother Kamal Mahmood) would often speak about. "The cricket team of the Aminabad Intermediate School got selected for a tournament in Calcutta. Kamal was Captain of the team while Talat was the Vice Captain. They had 8 matches to play in Calcutta. After the third match, they found out that Saigal was in town for a recording. They bunked the next matches, to wait outside the studio everyday to meet their idol. It was hilarious because both the Captain and Vice Captain were missing from the field. Then one day, luck shone on them. As Saigal walked out of the studio, both the boys held Saigal's hand and started kissing it.

Talat gushed that he always practises at home to sing in Saigal's style. The legend was amused. He asked Talat to sing a few lines. He sang Saigal's song, 'Dukh ke ab din beetat nahin..'. Kamal stepped in to inform Saigal that he has a singing voice too! He was surprised to meet these singing brothers from Lucknow. Since Saigal himself could not complete his school education, he had strong advice for the boys. He asked them both to complete their studies first and then pursue professional singing, if they wanted a career in music."

STARTING YOUNG AT A.I.R.

The All India Radio (AIR) which had opened its recording studio and station in Lucknow in 1938, offered a new opportunity for aspiring young singers. In 1940, when he was 16 years old, Talat decided to meet someone in charge of the music department at the radio. He believed this to be a fair way of trying his luck. But his first day in the recording studio turned out to be a disaster. In Talat's own words, he was ignorant of the basics to the core. All he knew was his own voice and understood little about coordinating it with the music instruments. He was out of sync with the tabla or the harmonium. After causing a laugh riot amongst all present in the recording, he was handed over to Munna Khan, the music instructor at AIR, who was in charge of training this young teenager for a duration of six months before trying his luck at recording again. One of his first radio recordings was –
'Chhaani jo khaak humne uss but ki rehguzar mein,
Apne ko kho ke baithe paayayeh umar bhar mein'

(In my perfect pursuit of the callous one,
I plunged deep, and life was done)

This was precious time away from studies. These initial years for Talat often remained a continuous hide and seek between his father and his music. It was decades later, at an interview to the Urdu magazine 'Shama' in 1981, that he spoke about it in detail. His younger sister (my grandmother Laila Kidwai) was a trusted confidant who had the painful task of listening to a lot of his adventures but keeping entirely mum about them! So dedicated was she, that one could never say how much she really knew even till the siblings were well into being sexagenarians! When this magazine interview was released, it was then that she admitted to knowing all about it.

Talat's radio recordings of the early 1940's were a blessing. Remember we are talking about pre-independent India where opportunities were very limited and restrictive. By recording at the Lucknow AIR station, his voice could be heard at the transmissions in Delhi, Lahore, Bombay, Madras, Peshawar, Rawalpindi and Karachi. He would earn five rupees per recording. This amount wasn't a pittance in those days. One could easily buy groceries worth one month for that amount. But he wasn't doing this for money, of course. Recording his voice at the radio gave him the required technical skill for a studio and an understanding of how he sounded over the microphone. Soon enough, he became a sought-after recording artist not just as a unique voice but for an exemplary command over Urdu. He could effortlessly sing couplets of Ghalib and Iqbal or the poetry of Mir Taqi Mir and Daagh. This deep understanding and perfect diction in Urdu remained a constant plus in his entire career.

One of India's greatest Indian vocalists, Pandit Bhimsen Joshi, recalls this period in Lucknow. "When I went to Lucknow, it was with a desire to learn Thumri and other light classical forms. I spent one or two years there when the top artists of the time were Begum Akhtar, Siddeshwari Devi and Rasoolan Bai. And you know Talat Mahmood? He is also from Lucknow. I used to like listening to him too. And it was during that time, under British India, where I was a staff artist at the All India Radio."[1]

Somehow, Talat seemed to have made a peaceful pact at home. It appears that recording for the radio was mildly acceptable. But working in commercial films still remained an absolute red-line . His grades in school were good and it was time to push the envelope and remind Manzoor of his promise. Talat was expecting his father to allow him to study Hindustani Classical Music in Marris College (now known as Bhatkhande Music Institute Deemed University) in Lucknow. As a man of his word, the father kept his promise. Talat's joy knew no bounds. His journey in professional music had just gotten better.

CHAPTER 2 - THE TEENAGE STAR

(Talat became a recognizable voice at barely 16 years of age)

HISTORICAL LEGACY OF BHATKHANDE

The Marris College (Bhatkhande Music Institute, Deemed University) in Lucknow has a rich legacy. It was Founded in 1926 by Pandit Vishnu Narayan Bhatkhande who was an Indian musicologist. His biggest contribution was that he got down to writing the first modern treatise on Hindustani classical music which was otherwise propagated only through oral traditions for centuries. He reclassified ragas (a collection of musical notes) into a new modern system which forms the foundation of how Indian classical music is taught today! He prepared course material which entailed a logical format written in books from which students could learn music. He released a series of textbooks which continue to remain the foundation of Hindustani classical music. Not wanting to ignore the Carnatic Classical Music of South India, he decided to kickstart the All India Music Conference which provided a common platform for the North and South to discuss their classical music. For the first time, Indian classical music was brought into a structured education system inside a college.

It had a strict set of entrance tests to be able to study music there. This is evident from the quality of artists that the college produced. A few names from the institute's exemplary list of notable alumni across generations includes music director Roshan, India's first female music composer Saraswati Devi, violinist V.G. Jog, singers Anup Jalota and Shanti Hiranand, and other names from today like Neeti Mohan and Amit Mishra.

While the college was established in 1926 , the building used for it was a historic structure. That's the thing about the city of Lucknow. Heritage goes back to as long as you keep peeling the layers. The building was built in 1850 by the last king of Awadh, Nawab Wajid Ali Shah. And Lucknow used to be the capital of this princely state. He was a big patron of the arts and culture. He himself was a poet, writer and Kathak dancer. He would love to keep himself in the company of paree (fairies). These fairies were no mythical beings but in reality, were young girls and women who were being trained in light classical music and Kathak dance. They were also being taught social etiquettes to present themselves as the perfect courtesans before the Nawab. He provided them palatial quarters to stay in called the Pari-khana (House of Fairies). The architecture of these quarters were based on the Mughal style with stylized arches, pillars, domes and a large marble- floored courtyard. It was connected with a marble bridge over a canal that formed part of the char-bagh gardens where the courtesans performed.

Today, part of that Pari Khana is the building used by the Bhatkhande Music Institute. When I visited the campus, I felt that nothing could have been a more artistic and inspiring place for a promising music college of modern times. Talat Mahmood had often spoken about the admission process he faced there. He said that he was always bad in theory and was certain that the written test would make him fail. But it was the vocal assignment that made him shine. Undoubtedly the confidence of recording songs for the AIR added to his confidence. The panel of teachers had rarely heard an aspiring student sing an alaap (opening piece) like he had. For reference, he would say, it was an opening piece similar to what he had sung for Dilip Kumar in the film Shikast (1953) for the song 'Sapnon ki suhani duniya ko'. The judges were stunned to hear him. They overlooked his dismal marks in theory and quickly passed him for admission. Clearly, this wasn't a talent they wanted to go waste.

From 1941 to 1943, Talat had the most adventurous years in college. He learnt classical music from one of the most celebrated Gurus (teachers) in music, Pandit S.C.R. Bhat, who had dedicated his entire life to the cause of Hindustani music. His honesty and large-heartedness made him one of the most revered Gurus who trained many reputed musicians like K.G.Ginde, Dinkar Kaikini, C.R. Vyas, Indudhar Nirody, Zarine Sharma, to name a few.The word spread fast that Marris Music College had a new star student who was already popular and familiar to radio listeners. Before that, one didn't know where to place this voice. His nephew Rishad Mahmood would often hear his dad talk about how Talat got mobbed on his way to college one day. "He was once stopped by a group of young girls including Quratulain Haider who later went on to become a celebrated Urdu writer. These girls wanted him to sing them a song right there on the road. Talat pleaded that he was getting late for his class but the girls made sure they were treated to the pleasure of his voice in person. He finally relented and actually sang a few Ghazals on the road. Delayed to college by hours, when Talat finally reached there, his master had already called up home to complain about Talat bunking the day!"

FIRST RECORDING WITH H.M.V. LABEL

Recording label HMV would often come hunting for new talent on campus. Talat was unmissable for them and they decided to take him to Calcutta (Kolkata) to cut a few singles. You might wonder why Calcutta? Well, in those days Calcutta was the hub of the entertainment and music industry. Not the present day Bollywood in Bombay (Mumbai). It was Calcutta which was the financial capital of British India. It had all the big studios, the big stars of the time, the best recording equipment and the big money for it. So the prospect of both HMV and Calcutta calling meant that Talat was literally hitting the jackpot for his next big step. He signed a contract of three songs for thirty rupees with HMV in 1941 at the tender age of just 17 years.

Arriving in Calcutta to record at the famous HMV studios in Dum Dum would have been an intimidating experience for a young teenage boy. The sprawling complex of rows of single storied recording studios and the trademark red chimney already carried an illustrious past. The more the chimney smoked, the more successful the music industry. The smoke would result from the melting of vinyl used to manufacture the 78RPM records.

This is where British India's first ever recorded singer, Gauhar Jaan, had her voice immortalized on the ribs of the vinyl plates. This is where other famous stars like KL Saigal and Devika Rani recorded their songs. It's where the great Nobel Laureate Rabindranath Tagore recorded his poems. And where copies of radio broadcasts of many speeches by leaders of the freedom movement, Jawaharlal Nehru, Mahatma Gandhi , Subhash Chandra Bose, etc. were made. Dum Dum was in the process of being an icon of India's music legacy for 80 years.

As Talat sat outside one of the studio rooms under the shade of the tree, waiting for his turn, he kept his eyes locked on the large black board in front of him. It was the time table for the day's recording schedule written in chalk. You had to find your name against an allotted time slot and studio number. He promptly sprang up from his bench when it was his turn. The first song that he recorded was called 'Sab din ek samaan nahin tha' (All days were not alike). Written by Fayyaz Hashmi and composed by Kamal Dasgupta, this was also the first full song penned by the poet. The pair were to record many more landmark songs in the coming years.

'Sab din ek samaan nahin tha, Ban jaaungaa kya se kya main
Iska to kuchh dhyaan nahin tha Sab din ek samaan nahin tha'

(All days are not the same How I will scale success
I would have never thought All days are not the same)

K L Saigal's deep impact on Talat can be heard in this recording, where he tried keeping his voice thick in a low baritone with a nasal sound. The other side of this record had Talat's second song 'Tum lok laaj se darti thi' (You were afraid of social norms). You will find it difficult to believe, but these recordings are still so popular that you can find both these songs listed on Youtube and other music streaming platforms with a million hits.

Visiting Calcutta didn't just mean recording for the HMV but meeting other music greats as well. This is when Pankaj Mullick came into Talat's life. Mullick was a known singer and music composer of that time. He was a pioneer for introducing playback singing in Indian cinema and a significant name associated with the biggest film studio in Calcutta called New Theatres. He heard Talat recording 'Sab din ek samaan' in the Dum Dum studios. "This song is about your impending success, Talat", quipped Pankaj Mullick. The teenager smiled shyly in response. Mullick was eager to sign him up for New Theatres. But given that he had only come for a few days break from college and his father would have been furious about commercial singing, Talat requested the music genius to wait for another three years till he finished his music studies! Imagine, such was Talat's confidence and such was Mullick's eager wait. He had taken an instant liking to the soft spoken boy. Both of them kept their word to meet three years later.

In the same trip, Talat was spotted by filmmaker P.C.Barua as well. He was in the midst of making his film Jawab (1942) and offered Talat a role in it. But alas, Talat had to turn it down for the same reason of his father's apprehensions about commercial cinema as well as his own conviction of completing his music education at Bhatkhande first.

CHAPTER 3 - THE CALCUTTA YEARS

THE MIGHTY COMMERCIAL CAPITAL

"Phuphi (Aunt Mahlaqa) always encouraged my singing. She would never stop me from going to Calcutta. This is an opportunity of a lifetime for me", pleaded Talat.

"Don't use Aapa's (elder sister) name to persuade me. I have always made it clear that I'm not in favour of commercial singing. This cannot be allowed in our family", shouted Manzoor. He put his foot down and gave Talat an ultimatum - it's either the family house or his music. The two men could not see eye to eye on this matter. Talat decided to leave his father's house and pursue his music dream. He made up his mind and informed his father that he will not set foot inside home again unless he makes it big as a singer.

With a suitcase full of clothes, sweet memories of Lucknow and the wrath of his father, Talat landed in the big city of Calcutta. It was 1944, soon after he completed his course in Marris Music College. This time, he came prepared to stay in the city. He was a 20 year old adult. Handsome and more confident about his voice. He was eager to meet Pankaj Mullick again and show him how he had grown as a singer. The years at Marris College helped him find his own identity. He was still very much a Saigal fan but no longer his clone. Talat was now comfortable in the original vibrato and velvety quality of his soft voice.

When he arrived in Calcutta, there was everything promising about the air he breathed in there. It was very different from the laid back royalty of Lucknow. This city was the hub of power. The roads were broader, the transport with local trams was much better, buildings were bigger and everybody seemed more professional about work. The city meant business. After all, it was the financial capital of British India. It didn't take much time for Talat to immediately fall in love with the place. There was also the comfort of having his elder brother, Hayat with him this time, who was already working in Calcutta at the Orient Airways. Hayat's son Shehzad Mahmood has the most enchanting tales from that time, "The two bachelor brothers used to stay in lane 11 at Park Street. They were very close to each other. And both were very fond of pets. It was really funny how they kept a dog and a monkey together. The dog was Charlie and the monkey was Freddy. He was kept to clean Charlie's fleas but Freddy had better ideas. He would sit on Charlie's back and go for their morning and evening walks everyday. They were an absolute delight for the neighbours."

The cultural scene at Park Street was very different. It was mostly for the British and visiting American G.I.s with films screened from Hollywood and jazz music performances. The cosmopolitan culture offered newer insights to the brothers but for food, they relied on something that would remind them of their Awadhi cuisine of Lucknow. Something that came close on the heels of that aroma and taste was the Nizam's Restaurant's signature dish. "Their favourites were the Nizam's kebab rolls. They would call it 'jannat ka manna' (food from the heavens)", adds Shehzad.

K.L. SAIGAL - SHOWER OF LUMINANCE

On the work front, Pankaj Mullick was delighted to hear from the shy boy that he remembered from three years ago. He called Talat to the recording studio of New Theatres. It was the biggest film production unit in showbiz during those days.

"Come, there's a recording of Saigal tomorrow. Would you like to hear him sing in the studio?", asked Mullick.

"How can I not like to hear him in person? Absolutely, yes. Thank you", gushed Talat.

He couldn't believe that he would actually get to see his idol in action. The last time he had met Saigal was as a school boy, waiting in line, outside the studio. This time, he would get to hear him sing in person. Saigal was there to record a song for his next film 'My Sister' and the song was 'Aye katib- e-taqdeer'(O' writer of destiny). The music for the film was composed by Pankaj Mullick. It ended up being the fourth highest grossing film of the year and the song was an exemplary display of Saigal's unparalleled talent in crashing down to the lowest pitch soon after hitting the highest notes.

It was a voice drenched in emotions which could neither falter in notes nor ethos. The recording of songs in those days used to be in one single take with a LIVE orchestra. Every musician, conductor and singer had to be in sync. There were no options of copying and pasting parts of the song over a digital timeline of a computer system during post production. A retake meant that the song had to be performed right from the start and up to the last note, with the entire orchestra. Talat describes being present at this recording as the most surreal moment of his life. He says he was unable to understand what hit him. He felt transcended to another dimension. A moment so spiritual that he poetically called it "noor ki barish" – shower of luminance. [2]

THE 'TASVEER' PHENOMENON

The word 'tasveer' means photograph. It's a word that gave Talat many hits in his career. Mullick wanted to record a certain Ghazal in Talat's voice. He knew that he was the perfect voice for it.

Mullick's grandson Rajib Gupta explains his knack of recognizing the right voice for the right song. "He used to be a great believer in the uniqueness of each voice and believed that one should choose songs to sing that best- suited one's voice. He always maintained that one should express the emotions of a song to the best of one's ability. That was what made a song touch the listener's heart."

Talat's voice not only touched the listeners heart but stayed in it for decades to come. Mullick had also predicted that it would be Talat's biggest debut hit. How perfectly correct he was with his prediction.

'Tasveer teri dil mera behla na sakegi,
Ye teri tarah mujhse to sharma na sakegi'

(How can your photograph evoke any emotions,
How will it shy away from me like you do)

It became a smashing hit and made Talat an instant celebrity at the age of 20. It also cemented the frequent partnership of Talat singing to the music of star composer Kamal Dasgupta and the poetry of Fayyaz Hashmi. It sold more than one lakh records at the time of its release and continued to be in big demand throughout his career. This kind of a record breaking sale for a non-film song was an extremely rare feat in those days. The yardstick for a big hit in those days was to sell 300 records. Obviously, 'Tasveer teri...' exceeded much beyond every expectation. More than the record sale, it was Talat's voice that took the country by storm.

Many years later, his close friend and singer Manna Dey had said that he became Talat's fan after hearing him in this song. "No one had ever heard this style of expression in love which was soft and gentle. I was bowled over to the point of envy since I could not replicate Talat's unique style."[3] The way he sang the first word 'tasveer' with a smooth flow despite the twists and emphasis is impossible to replicate by many singers. Musician Kamal Dasgupta kept the song in a steady rhythm so that it gave the feeling of a secret love in hushed tones.

'Main baat karunga to ye khamosh rahegi
Seene se laga lunga to ye kuch na kahegi
Aaram wo kya degi jo tadpa na sakegi
Tasveer teri dil mera behla na sakegi'

(She will remain silent when I talk to her
She won't say a word when I hug her
What comfort can she give if she can't make me suffer
How can your photograph evoke any emotions)

Poet Fayyaz Hashmi scored an ace with his poetry. But there was one word in the song that he was unhappy about. For 20 years, Fayyaz lived with that word unchanged in his song. When technology progressed, many old 78RPM records had become obsolete. Therefore, Talat decided to re-record some old hits in 1965. It included ''Tasveer teri'. Fans who didn't have the original, could buy a copy of the 1965 version. This version finally had the pivotal word in Fayyaz's poetry that he had always wanted. Talat's late son Khalid Mahmood had the details of this nugget on his Youtube channel. In 1944, Talat sang -

'In honton ko Fayyaz main kuch KEH na sakoonga'
(I will be unable to say anything to these lips)

In the 1965 re-recorded version, Talat sang -
'In honton ko Fayyaz main kuch DE na sakoonga'
(I will be unable to give anything to these lips)

As the story goes, Fayyaz Hashmi had taken a promise from Talat that if he ever re-recorded this song he must change this single word because that's how he had wanted his poetry to sound. Fayyaz had left the country and shifted to Pakistan after the Partition and Independence of India, but Talat made sure to respect his friend's request. It's not known why the word was changed in the first place but one can only surmise that saying something to the lips would have been more suited to the conservative tastes of the 1940s instead of directly giving something to the lips!

As 'Tasveer teri..' struck gold for Talat for his debut commercial hit, allow me to share my experience with this immortal song as well. As a young teenager myself in 1996, I recall standing on stage at my school competition and singing this Ghazal song from 1944. Many kids in the front row were yawning, laughing and others got up from their seats. There was a strong influence of western music in my growing up years in Delhi. My classmates and I heard and sang the latest English pop. And if you ever had to sing Ghazals, it only meant Jagjit Singh or Pankaj Udhas. I was wondering why had my mom selected Talat nana's boring Ghazal for me to perform, which I was certain would make me lose the trophy now! But further down the stage, I could see my school Principal Mrs. Usha Ram, smiling at me and the special judges called from outside, sitting along with her and listening to me in rapt attention. One of them was Urdu literature connoisseur Shyam Banerji. When they announced the winners, I topped the competition and won the trophy!! Shyam Banerji told me he was astounded by my choice of song and performed very well! Was it the charm of the Ghazal or the voice? In my case, I can safely say that the magic of this Ghazal was my good luck charm.

Later the same year, we went to Bombay for our summer holidays. My mother proudly mentioned to Bambai Nana that I sang 'Tasveer teri...' in school and won the trophy too! His eyes lit up in a twinkle. She asked me to sing a few lines for him but I would dare not bore him with my mediocrity.

PANKAJ MULLICK CREATES TAPAN KUMAR

After the smashing hit of 'Tasveer teri…', Pankaj Mullick wasted no time in asking Talat to start singing Bengali songs in 1944. This came as a surprise to him and a new challenge as well. Here he was, already having perfected his Urdu and working on polishing his style. But now he was supposed to learn a new language, understand the nuances, be perfect at pronouncing it and emote the right feelings. Talat was game for the challenge.

"I hope I can do justice to Bengali, I don't know the language at all", said Talat.
"Don't worry, Kamal Dasgupta will help you with all your doubts", assured Pankaj.

He recorded his first Bengali album for HMV in 1944. 'Shono go sonar meye' (Listen, golden girl) on side 1 and 'Jobe esechhile tumi priyo' (When you came to me my dear) on side 2. The music was composed by Kamal Dasgupta and the lyricist was Pranab Roy. This also marked the birth of a new singer who became part of the Modern Bengali music movement. His name was Tapan Kumar. Both Pankaj Mullick and Kamal Dasgupta decided that this name will be more acceptable to listeners in Bengal. So therefore, in the initial years of his career, whenever Talat sang in Bengali, it was recorded in the name of Tapan Kumar. Mullicks' grandson, Rajib Gupta, reflects on this aspect. "There is no specific reasoning behind the renaming but it is apparent that it has to do with dedication. It is something which he expected from all artists he came in contact with. Pankaj Mullick had a penchant for giving unique names to people, including singers", he explains.

Back home in Lucknow, Talat's younger sister Laila was appointed to slip in his new 78RPM at home and make their father listen to it. Laila showed it to her father saying that this new singer Tapan sounds really talented. When Manzoor heard Tapan Kumar, he immediately recognized that it was his son. "The boy has lost his mind. He is now commercially singing in Bengali too?", roared Manzoor.

The record was a hit, so Kamal and Talat came together for another set of two songs for HMV in 1945. The songs from this record were - Duti pakhi duti teere, majhe nodi bohe dheere (Two birds across two banks as the river flows slowly) and Ghumero chhaya chandero chokhe (The shadow of sleep in your eyes

Little did Talat realize that he was going to become an integral part of the songs movement which was called 'Modern Bangla Music'. The genre of this music was built with experimental notes and non-traditional lyrics. It was different from classical music which gave more importance to musical notes and less thought to lyrics. Whereas Modern Bengali songs gave much more importance to the verbal expression of human emotions in their lyrics. The composition of music was less dependent on Indian classical notes and more influenced by Western styles with a variety of rhythms and beats. It was undoubtedly a genre which originated in Calcutta given the access to English music and American jazz. It was a city which was bustling with English officers under British India combined with visits by American G.I.s during World War II. This is when the uptown area of Park Street became a major hub of Western culture where evenings were pulsating with LIVE jazz performances in clubs, the theatres were screening the latest English films and the restaurants served the best of European cuisine.

SINGER-ACTOR AT NEW THEATRES

(Talat's twin appeal of a velvet voice and charming looks)

In those days, contracts with singers were not exclusive to one single label. Since Talat had given some hits in Bengali, Pankaj Mullick signed him up for three years with New Theatres from 1945-1948. This was a significant climb because the New Theatres studio was a pioneer in making landmark films in both Hindi and Bengali cinema. Under the guidance of Mullick, it was also the first production house to establish playback singing as an industry in India. The studio was located in Tollygunge, about 8 kilometres away from where Talat stayed at Park Street. In those days, it would take about an hour to commute by taking the public transport like the local trams and buses.

Talat would spend days at New Theatres, absorbing all the history that had already been created by this novel experiment which added a thrust to the film industry. With the start of the talkies, the sound of the film dialogues, music and songs would be recorded live on the site of the shoot along with the actors on cue. Therefore, a lot of actors of that time used to double up as singers too. But New Theatres started the advent of recording studios where music and film songs could be recorded separately in a closed sound-proof room. The studio space of New Theatres was a huge compound with a set of mill buildings with high ceilings . With shoots and recordings buzzing around, it created an excitement in the air that lured many into the world of films. This is the banner under which cinema greats like K.L. Saigal, Kanan Devi, P.C. Barua, Prithviraj Kapoor, Bimal Roy, Nitin Bose and Pankaj Mullick had a chance to polish their talent and become stars. Barua's film 'Devdas' (1936) starring Saigal remains one of the most iconic depictions of the lovelorn protagonist despite several other newer versions of Devdas featuring Dilip Kumar, Prosenjit and Shah Rukh Khan, down the decades of Indian cinema.

'Rajalakshmi' (1945) by filmmaker P.C.Barua was Talat's first film of his career as playback singer. He had two songs in the film which included 'Jaago musafir jaago' (wake up, o' traveller, wake up). But this was the year of new experiences and experiments in life. Barua wanted Talat to act on screen for this song as well. Talat couldn't refuse but he couldn't contain his excitement either. He came to the sets clean shaven and squeaky clean for the camera. Once into the make-up room, he realised he had to play the role of a sage with a long beard stuck on his face with glue. "I could barely move my face or open my mouth. Each time Barua asked me to lip-sync for a close up shot, I would be in excruciating pain. My torment lasted for 3 days, till the shoot was finally completed", Talat would often laugh out loud while recalling this incident. That really burst his acting bubble, he used to say.

In 1946, Talat sang another two Bengali songs for the film 'Saat Nambar Bari'. These songs ruled the airwaves for a while and once again reinforced the legend of Tapan Kumar, who continued to gain more and more acceptance in Modern Bengali music. These songs were 'Kotha noy aaji raate' (Not tonight) and 'Ke daake amay seki tumi' (Who seems to be calling me).

New Theatres was keen to not just have Talat as a playback singer but also cast him as the main lead in a romantic role on camera as well. The studio was churning out some of the country's biggest hit films but it faced a unique struggle of finding a suitable face to be cast opposite Talat for acting assignments. His boyish looks made him look too young in front of his female co-stars. With no films at hand, they continued paying Talat a salary of fifteen hundred rupees per month while they tried finding him a suitable 'young looking' co-star![4] But this year saw a slowdown for the entire industry per se. India's independence movement was at its peak and so was the divide-and-rule policy of the British. Calcutta was witnessing its worst and most massive Hindu-Muslim communal riots ever in 1946. It came to be known as the 'Great Calcutta Killings' that left more than 4,000 people dead and 100,000 residents homeless within 72 hours. It was caused by the impending division of Bengal on religious grounds in the build up to Partition and Independence. The situation would often be volatile and curfews were beginning to get more frequent.

The following year, the film industry faced a big blow. It lost their biggest superstar. Talat was inconsolable after hearing about the passing away of K.L. Saigal, whose alcoholism had damaged him beyond recovery. He died at the young age of 42 on 18th January 1947 due to cirrhosis of the liver.

"I was not trained under Saigal but he was my *ustaad* (master). Just listening to him was a lesson in music", Talat once said while reflecting on his idol. Even as he learnt to develop his own unique style and stopped imitating him, Talat always maintained that there was never a greater singer than Saigal. Talat recalled how he was fortunate to meet him often during his days in Calcutta and while his nerves finally eased up in the company of his idol, Saigal would often crack some jokes to him too. He felt strongly about defending him too. "Of course, he drank but only in the evenings. To say that he was drunk all day is completely false. But it's true that he would get into the mood to sing and record his songs only after a few drinks", expressed Talat.[5]

Professionally, Talat literally stepped into Saigal's shoes. The New Theatres signed him up for a role opposite Saigal's top co-star Kanan Devi. She was fondly remembered as the first singing star of Bengali cinema. She was New Theatre's most bankable artiste and had already delivered several hits with K.L. Saigal. The name of Talat's film with her was 'Tum aur Main' (1947). Apart from romancing Kanan Devi on-screen, he playbacked for a duet in the same film, 'Purwai pawan lehraye o jiya jaye' (My heart skips a beat with the cool breeze). This was a song to celebrate the monsoon season as people would swing in the mango orchards and listen to the birds sing. The film got a lukewarm response at the box office.

The average business of Talat's films didn't affect his presence on thc airwaves since he maintained a steady flow of non-film recordings. These included both Ghazals and Bengali songs. Singers like Talat Mahmood, Pankaj Mullick and Hemant Kumar were often invited for concerts to perform their popular numbers. During this time, he learnt the importance of having two parallel careers in music, one for films, the other for non-film and Ghazal recordings. In these early years, he tied up with Fayyaz Hashmi to record a Ghazal, 'Do Kaafir Aankhon Ne Maara' (Those eyes that left me wounded). This was his debut as a music composer as well. He composed it in a very traditional style but decided to keep one part of the misra (stanza) with a slow tempo and sped up the second part of the misra.

INDIA'S INDEPENDENCE & PARTITION

It was 1947 and independent India was starting its first chapter in history. Talat Mahmood was one of the few celebrities of pre-independent India who transitioned smoothly into being a film star of independent India as well. But after 1947, things changed drastically. The nation was broken into three pieces and many artists were scattered between India and Pakistan (East and West). His own family faced a similar dilemma. But there was enough clarity in his mind that his future lay in India. India was the country of his choice and this is where he would dedicate his art and talent to. The unprecedented achievement of Independence after years of struggle and perseverance should have been marked with absolute joy. But the air was also thick with the pain of Partition across the country. It was impossible to escape the chaos and horror of it. The euphoria of India's independence with Mahatma Gandhi's phenomenal success of a non-violent movement came with the colossal flipside of Partition. The creation of Pakistan made it incumbent for most Muslim families to make a hard decision of where to stay and why. Talat Mahmood's family was no different. As a prominent Muslim family of Lucknow who were passionate about India's freedom struggle, the choice seemed simple. A secular India is what they strived for, so therefore a secular country was to be their final choice. But even such simplistic sounding decisions demanded a rollercoaster ride of emotions, loyalty and legacy of belonging. While Talat, his unmarried sisters and his parents were certain about staying back in India, his brothers eventually moved to Dhaka and Karachi in a few years. But these decisions were more governed by the career choices they made rather than any ideological belief. Talat and his elder brother Kamal Mahmood were barely a year apart. They had the same interests in music and cricket. But Kamal had another interest which he shared with his father. It was gardening and lavishly maintaining their sprawling garden in their Lucknow home. When Kamal decided to stay back in Karachi for work, it meant that he would not be able to come back to water the plants. While a lot of emotional arguments took place between father and son, eventually the father said in anguish, "But Kamal, who will water my plants, Talat doesn't have a green thumb like you!" Such was the fracture within families.

TRUE PATRIOT OF SECULAR INDIA

Talat was surrounded by neighbours, extended family, cousins and friends who were packing their bags to shift to Pakistan, for whatever reasons that suited them. Emotional persuasion to be together as a family and choose a country of Islamic faith for social security amidst communal riots made for a tough argument in favour of picking Pakistan. Today, it is difficult to understand the enormity of that decision but I take great pride in members of my family who stayed back in India for their staunch secular values.

I remember reading an online article written by a retired officer in 2019. He blindly accused a few famous Muslims of abandoning India and moving to Pakistan during Partition, including Talat Mahmood. I was shocked how such a hate-mongering ill-informed article passed through the editors as an opinion piece! As I happened to work in the same extended media network, I made a few calls in the concerned department about this atrocious article. In a few hours, the corrections were made. I wondered what if I didn't work in that network? What if I had never read his article? His lies would have remained online forever and could have soon been used as reference by others. It's so easy today to build a smokescreen of falsity despite established facts about a frequently- reported celebrity. It's shameful how the name of a national legend, who was honoured with the Padma Bhushan as well as a Commemorative Stamp by the Government of India, was being sullied by a bigot to suit his hate-driven politics, decades after the legend's death.

On the contrary, let me share with you this delightful incident of how much people loved him and wanted him to stay back in India. Talat's nephew Zaheer Kidvai recalls that he was seven years old when his father decided to leave for Pakistan in 1947. They took the train from Calcutta to Bombay before taking the ship to Karachi. Many family members had come to see him off including Talat Mahmood. "When people saw Talat uncle, they rushed towards him and he was soon surrounded by people. When he went running to see us off as we climbed onto the train, we heard people shout - 'That's Talat Mahmood, is he going to migrate? Hold him back, don't let him go.', exclaims Zaheer.

Amidst all this heartburn, Talat recorded two songs in 1947. One was dedicated to communal harmony called ‘Jai Hind, Allah-u-akbar’ and the second was ‘Bharat maata ke do pehlu’. Like a true patriot, he became a significant pillar in the history of India to help establish the film and music industry of the nation.

To keep his mind away from all the trauma, he immersed himself in work and continued recording more Bengali songs with eminent composers like Durga Sen, Nirmal Bhattacharjee, Subal Dasgupta and Robin Chatterjee. These were all names that firmly established the new identity of Modern Bengali music, along with Tapan Kumar. Try listening to two of these from 1948 -

1. Adho raate jodi ghum bhenge jay (If you wake up in the middle of the night)
2. Takhano jageni prabhatero shuktara (The morning the sun didn't rise)

Of course, leading Bengali composers continued to tap into the goldmine in Tata’s throat for ghazals. Chitta (Chittaranjan) Roy, known for his felicity with Nazrul geeti (songs written by the iconic revolutionary poet Kazi Nazrul Islam, who took Roy under his wings as his protege), composed two iconic ghazals for Talat in 1948, with poetry by I.A. Minai, a banker by profession but also a man of literary tastes, being the grandson of legendary poet Ameer Minai -

1. Nazar bulbul ki kehti hai (The eyes of the nightingale speak)
2. Gham-e-Zindagi ka ya rab (The sorrows of life, my Lord)

FALLING IN LOVE

(Talat with the love of his life, Nasreen)

Apart from the love that he got from his career's first ever dedicated set of fans in Calcutta, there was another invaluable love he found in the city of joy. That of a life partner.

I have a very amusing experience to share regarding what his fans believed about Tapan Kumar. He had perfected his Bengali accent so well that many admirers felt that he was born and brought up in Calcutta. How could he not be a Calcutta boy? That's the only explanation for his rasgulla-like sweet voice. And this, I learnt from personal experience. Once when I was sitting in the office and compiling my evening news report, my colleague started humming a Tapan Kumar song. He animatedly described how he has been to the neighbourhood where Tapan was born, where his family lived and how he is actually friends with some old folks of his family. I widened my eyes in disbelief and burst out laughing.

"What so funny", he said.
"You mean Talat Mahmood?", I asked.
"Yes, but what's so funny?, he said, flustered.
"There's no way that he was born and brought up there",

I dismissed him entirely.
"What do you know about Talat Mahmood? Are you some authority on him?".
"I'm not an authority but I can assure you about his lineage."

Well, as trained journalists, we don't give up on an argument easily. My colleague was unrelenting. I had never spoken about my relationship with Talat Mahmood at work. No one knew. No one was told. But to correct him, I had to eventually inform him that Talat was my granduncle. My Bambai- nana. A relative so close that it's impossible to be mistaken about his origin.

"But…but I've met his family there", he gasped in disbelief.
"Of course he has family there, from his wife's side", I patted his shoulder in comfort.

And that brings us to the second gift that the city of Calcutta gave him. The love of his life, Nasreen Mahmood. They met on the sets of New Theatres. It was a film set romance. Though they never worked together in any film, she was a young actress empanelled with New Theatres as well and that's how their paths crossed. Her maiden name was Latika Mullick and as a young girl she was already being cast as the main lead with established actors. Her film Dotana (1945) was opposite acclaimed actor Jahar Ganguli and that made her a noticeable face for the audience. She was a huge fan of Talat Mahmood and was overjoyed to meet him during one of his recordings. It was a whirlwind romance but neither spoke about it in detail at home. I remember amidst their tiffs of a cute old couple, she was always very caring towards him. I was told that once when he fell sick as a bachelor during his time in Calcutta, she and her mom nursed him back to health by cooking soothing soups and broths for him. Whenever they were asked about their romance, all they would manage is a blush and giggle away.

"During his Tapan Kumar' days, the house at 11 Park Street became a very famous address. Local Calcutta news had already started reporting about their romance. Lunches and dinners were happening together. But of course, in the company of his elder brother, who was also engaged to get married to my mother soon", informs Talat's nephew Shehzad.

Back home in Lucknow, his father finally embraced his son's career choice and couldn't hide the pride he felt in listening to his songs. While walking down the crisp footpaths of Lucknow, if he heard the radio playing Talat's song, he would stop by to listen and inform passersby that that's his son's voice. Like a good father's responsibility, he started the process of looking for the most beautiful bride for Talat in good Lucknow families. "My son is a handsome star. He is surrounded by beautiful women in the studios. So his wife should be as beautiful. He deserves the best girl."

Little did Talat know that his love-life would start the brewing of another storm at home.

THE TRANSITION YEAR

1949 came with some renewed hope for his acting career. It was a role opposite Bharati Devi (a rising star of the talkies and later, a Golden Era legend). Talat was happy being the singer-actor for this film, 'Samaapti' (1949). Everything about the cast, the production and storyline sounded very promising. The high budget of the film made a lot of news. At a time when films were barely made for sixty thousand rupees, the producer spent a fortune of eight lakh rupees! But again, as luck would have it, the film sank without making any business. It was quite literally in the true sense of the word 'samaapti' which means the end of things!

The debacle of 'Samapti' left Talat nervous about his future in films and music. The only love that he had a burning passion for all his life was his music. He recorded his next song with this dejection, the lyrics of which reflected his frame of mind. The song 'Hay Bhalobasha Seki Aleya' (It's either love of fire) was written by Pranab Roy and composed by Subal Dasgupta. He was a sensitive mind, who poured his heart out into his voice. The hurt was transparent in his expressions.

He decided that it's time to take the next bold step for his career. It was the right time to shift to Bombay and try his hand in the upcoming film industry there. Even as he shifted cities in life once again, he never forgot his original fans. He would continue coming back to Calcutta to record Bengali songs till the 1970s. His total number of Bengali songs (film and non-film combined) were about 50. His experience in Calcutta also opened up his mind to record songs in other regional languages apart from Bengali. In due course of the book, you will read about how Talat sang in at least 16 different languages that added to his large repertoire of music. Before heading out for Bombay, he was invited as a guest artist along with another star singer, Feroza Begum, to record their voices for Dhaka Radio. This marked the inauguration of the Dhaka Radio Shortwave services by them. It was launched exclusively for playing only Modern Bengali songs that Tapan Kumar was an integral part of.

CHAPTER 4 - BOMBAY DREAMS

A SLOW START

Talat had spent a fruitful time in Calcutta , recording for big banners, churning out hit songs and being a well known name. But Bombay (present day Mumbai) was beginning to create waves with films being made by production houses like Bombay Talkies led by filmstar Devika Rani and her husband Himanshu Rai. Social themes were given huge importance in films those days. The most popular example by Bombay Talkies was Achhut Kanya (1936) starring Devika Rani and Ashok Kumar. It was one of the first films to address the outrageous practice of untouchability and caste discrimination. Celebrated actor and filmmaker V. Shantaram also started his own production company and studio called Rajkamal Kalamandir in Bombay. Once again, social concerns were the prime focus for this studio too, including Dr. Kotnis Ki Amar Kahani (1946) and Do Aankhen Barah Haath (1957).

The reason why Bombay was becoming a new hub for film production was that big investments were shifting to the coastal city. The economic decline of West Bengal was primarily triggered by Partition and Independence. The creation of East Pakistan (present day Bangladesh) caused an immediate dent to the market of films made in Calcutta. Several big banners were deeply hit. The New Theatres struggled for a few more years after independence. Eventually, it dramatically shut down after completing its 100th film in 1955. This caused a talent drain to Bombay. Established names like Bimal Roy, Ashok Kumar, along with many others shifted base to Bombay, signing up contracts with other studios and banners. Looking at all this, Talat made a similar calculation.

It was in 1949 once again, that Talat packed his bags and shifted towns for the sake of his art and music. But this time, he wasn't a novice starting from scratch. He wasn't unknown. He arrived in the city of dreams with a reputation, name and success in the music industry. This new city was big and boisterous. It was pulsating with life. The cool breeze of the Arabian Sea added to its charm and sense of grandeur. The buildings designed in the Art Deco style lent a fresh look of modernism to the city. This was particularly significant for the film industry in Bombay trying to establish itself as the new hub of production and the final destination for anyone who dreamt of being connected to films. The Metro, Eros, Regal and Liberty cinemas were signature examples of this style of architecture that were showcased as the might of an industry involved in the soft power of making films. Talat was already a known name for the Bombay film industry folks. Many had heard his Ghazals recorded in Calcutta, others were familiar with his Bengali songs recorded in the name of Tapan Kumar. Who could forget the phenomenon of 'Tasveer teri dil mera'!! Once in Bombay, Talat decided to permanently drop the Bengali nom de plume and make a fresh start with only his original name.

He managed to squeeze in three songs recorded in Bombay. He had barely spent half a year here after shifting from Calcutta. But unfortunately, these songs proved to be forgettable. One was 'Dil pe kisi ka teer-e- nazar'(Someone's eye on the heart) for the film 'Rakhi' (1949). The other two were 'Jo beet gaya so beet gaya' (Time gone past never comes back) and 'Din beet chale' (Days go by) from the film 'Swayam Siddha' (1949).

THE VIBRATO DILEMMA

It was not directly told to him by any musician in Bombay but he was getting to hear from other people in the industry that his trademark vibrato was not being appreciated here. This could have been loose talk by rivals to discourage him but it was having an effect on Talat's sensitive mind. It left him with dashed hopes. Bombay was the final stop for any Hindi film artist in the industry. But if Bombay wasn't willing to embrace you, who else would? As is the human tendency of boxing people in silos, the city of dreams didn't spare him from it's characteristic struggles. Suddenly the most unique aspect of his voice, the 'vibrato' - the quiver - was being used against him. The vibrato happens when the voice alternates in a very subtle and gentle manner between two close pitches in quick succession. Many professional opera singers in the world train to achieve a vibrato because it immediately adds warmth and expressive layers to their performance. While technical experts believe that no one is born with a vibrato, the natural in- born vibration in Talat's voice was actually a rare gift. Ironically, this was the time when Talat decided to control his vibrato and get rid of it !!

His next stop in Bombay was the Hindu Colony in Dadar, inside a compound of five buildings, out of which one building's second floor was home to the power couple of Hindi cinema in those times - Ashalata Biswas and Anil Biswas. The wife was a successful actress and businesswoman who ran the Variety Production film banner. And the husband came to be known as the Bhishma Pitamah (the supreme commander) of the film music industry. That's because he was there practically from the start of Talkies cinema with the advent of music recordings. His daughter Shikha Biswas explains that he was making music in the Bombay film industry since the mid 1930s.

"He had partly set the template for songs in films. That would mean the prelude and the interlude with the introduction of new instruments. Earlier, the music was directly picked up from theatre, therefore the only instruments used in songs would be the tabla and harmonium. And the sounds were mostly folk and rustic. But as music in films started becoming an important aspect, there was more space to experiment and create new styles", says Shikha Biswas. "He re-styled the system of operatic music with the then prevalent harmonium-tabla by bringing along a team of Anglo-Indian musicians well-versed in Western instruments. So there was an entire orchestra of 12 pieces that was never before used or heard in films. Significantly, this also created the template used in popular Hindi film songs to date."

Many wondered why you would require 12 pieces when all one needs is just two instruments. But that's what the master musician showed people. While music recordings were mostly done on-site during the LIVE shooting sequences of the actors, Biswas brought in the system of recording music inside the studios in Bombay in 1937. While this style was prevalent in Calcutta, Bombay was still catching up with this new technology. In 1950, Anil Biswas was already at the peak of his career when Talat dropped by his home. He already had several iconic songs to his name when Talat met him, especially two from Kismet (1943) - 'Door hato ae duniya walon Hindustan hamara hai' (Move away o' world, this is our India) and 'Dheere dheere aa re baadal'(Gently flow in the clouds), with Ashok Kumar and Amirbai Karnataki. Biswas always liked a good challenge to try out something new and make it acceptable to the masses.Talat's vibrato perhaps reminded him of the opera and this was a quality he was eager to exploit. But how the two men met is not without drama either.

GODFATHER ANIL BISWAS

Biswas had his music room inside his home, where he would meet music colleagues and often compose tunes there. When Biswas met Talat, he was struck by this tall, handsome and fair young man. In a miscommunication between the two men, Biswas thought Talat had come to be an actor, so he sent Talat across to the other room where his wife functioned as the head of her film production company. It seems Talat didn't like the idea of his singing being overlooked in this manner, so he immediately left home. As he was leaving, someone else entered the house and asked Biswas - "Isn't that Tapan Kumar whom I just saw leaving your house?"

"No, that's not the famous singer Tapan Kumar", gasped Biswas. "He's a young lad who introduced himself as Talat Mahmood from Lucknow. I thought he came here for a screen audition."

He soon realized his mistake when he found out that Tapan and Talat are the same person. He quickly dashed out to his balcony to check if Talat was still down the lane waiting for a cab. But alas, Talat had already left. Biswas called up all music directors and left them a message, "Please send Talat Mahmood across to my home if he comes knocking at your door. I want to meet him."

An amused Shikha Biswas adds how the chase continued. "It was music director C. Ramchandra who eventually managed to send Talat back to meet with Anil Biswas. But since Talat felt he was already turned away and thrown out of the house, his Lucknow sensibilities were very hurt. It took at least 9-10 phone calls to get him back!".

Talat would also enjoy retelling this dramatic incident all the time. "I had just moved to Bombay and I was sharing an apartment with director Nitin Bose in those days. Since I knew him from Calcutta, it was comfortable moving in with him in Bandra. While Anil da (brother) was in Dadar. When I met him, he said, 'You are still to record a single song in Bombay and you already consider yourself such a big star that you do not pay heed to my call?' I always admired his work but I found him to be equally loveable. He was so different from the others."[6]

After the much anticipated meeting, it was time to create some magic. He was certain that he wanted to maintain Talat's vibrato in the song. The Dilip Kumar starrer film Arzoo (1950) had already completed production. Anil Biswas was the music composer for the film but he was keen to use Talat's voice in this film itself. He persuaded the film's director to put in one extra song. Dilip Kumar had to be asked for extra dates to shoot this last minute song. The final cut was a phenomena which the industry calls an iconic number of the Tragedy King.

(Talat Mahmood (right) with music composer Anil Biswas and his wife, Ashalata Biswas)

'Ae dil mujhe aisi jagah le chal, Jahan koi na ho'
(O' dear heart, take me to a place Where there isn't a single soul)

It became such a huge hit that it came to be known as Talat's debut in Hindi films, even though it wasn't. Within a year of moving to Bombay, Talat made it in the city of dreams. The song became an anthem for the lovelorn and one of the biggest hits of the year. It was the only song given to Talat in the film but it became a soul defining song for the entire album as well. The poetry by Majrooh Sultanpuri in the song felt like shattered pieces of glass piercing your senses when sung by Talat. The broken-hearted who wants to dissolve into oblivion without a trace in the world.

'Jaa kar kaheen kho jaaon main
Neend aye aur so jaaon main
Duniya mujhe dhoonde,
Magar mera nishaan koyi na ho'

(Let me be lost in some place
Let me slip into a deep slumber
As the world starts looking for me
There shall not remain any trace of me)

On the personal front, this song sealed the partnership of Biswas and Talat as life long friends as well. As Shikha Biswas recalls, "Talat uncle would always say - Asmaan pe hai khuda aur zameen pe Anil da (There is the Lord up in sky and my brother Anil down here in this world). They had an unspeakable spiritual bond which lasted much beyond their active film careers. He would always come home for our Saraswati Puja celebrations and be there for our informal music gatherings and parties at home. I remember when my younger brother was getting married, he was with my dad, personally sending wedding invitations, just like family does."

Undoubtedly, Anil Biswas' faith in Talat took his career on a new trajectory. He became the voice of the Tragedy King, Dilip Kumar. The actor's haunting eyes with subtle grief stricken expressions were in complete sync with Talat's soft whispers of despair. His velvet voice that gently nudged and caressed every heart became Talat's trademark style. It was a defining moment in Talat's career which made sure his graph in Hindi films was always looking north for the coming 15 years.

MEGA HIT WITH NAUSHAD

(Music composer Naushad (left) with Talat (right) and actor Manmohan Krishna (centre))

The Dilip-Talat partnership was used to the hilt by music director Naushad as well. Their film Babul (1950) was released the same year and almost the entire album with eight songs for Dilip Kumar was sung by Talat Mahmood. The master musician exploited every note of Talat's voice to fresh sounds. "He met me when I was composing music for the film Babul. He had just come from Calcutta and Yusuf sa'ab (Dilip Kumar) was very happy with the way his voice suited him on-screen", recalls Naushad [7]

The most popular hit from the film was a romantic duet 'Milte hi aankhen dil hua' sung by Talat and Shamshad Begum but there were other gems in the album where Naushad flaunted Talat's prowess. In the song 'Nadi kinare saath', Talat's voice is heard in a barely recognizable base pitch. I can't recall ever having heard this note in Talat's voice and yet, it was beautifully rendered. The song was an interesting coming together of Mohammad Rafi's vocals used for the fisherman on-screen, while Talat and Shamshad Begum's voices were used for the lead pair Dilip Kumar and Munawar Sultana. Written by Shakeel badayuni, these lines below were rendered by Talat -

'Naye jamane, naye tarane
Le ke javani aayi

Sun sun jisko nach uthe dil
Aisi kahani layi
Sham suhani aayi'

(New times, new experiences
With the coming of youth
The heart skips a beat
Such are the tales
With the coming of sunset)

In the opening line of another song from this film, 'Chod babul ka ghar', the beauty of Talat's velvet touch with a skillful handling of notes can be heard naked without any music instruments at all. The happy and flirtatious number 'Husn walon ko' added a new dimension to the Dilip-Talat partnership. Talat's voice sounded as suitable on the actor's happy face too, apart from the popular sad song 'Mera jeevan saathi bichhad gaya'. The film Babul further sealed their inseparable association and created an effortless transition from the actor's speaking voice to his on-screen singing voice of Talat. In addition to that, it became an album which showcased Talat in all moods and all possible notes that his voice could handle.

There were expectations that this would also lead to many more albums of Talat with Naushad but music lovers were left disappointed about that aspect in the coming years.

VOICE OF DILIP KUMAR, THE TRAGEDY KING

(Long lasting friendship of Talat and Dilip)

At this point, I will step away from the chronological order of Talat's films and weigh in on this special friendship of the two men. Down the years, there were several hits that they enjoyed together.

When the character Devdas sat among the trees and vented his broken heart with the song 'Mitwa Laagi Re Ye Kaisi Anbujh Aag…' the moment belonged to Talat Mahmood as much as it did to Dilip Kumar. Theirs was an actor-singer partnership that the film industry had scarcely seen before. Given that this was the early 1950s and partnerships like these hadn't begun to take root.

Dilip Kumar's spectacular career of six decades can be broken down into different chapters. And each chapter had role defining songs. If we look at the first chapter of the Golden Era (1940-1960s), Dilip Kumar's mould- breaking roles got him the title of 'Tragedy King'. The legend's passing away in 2021 had got me reminiscing about my old family stories about him, fondly recollected at family occasions and such like. As the curator and willy-nilly researcher for the Jashn-e-Talat concert series, I have tried to study and understand many facets of Talat's life and times. One of these happens to be the partnership that became the highlight of the careers of both Talat Mahmood and Dilip Kumar. The 'Tragedy King' phase of Dilip Kumar's career was inseparable from the voice of Talat Mahmood. When Dilip Kumar appeared singing 'Ae Dil Mujhe Aisi Jagah Le Chal', it epitomised the anguish of his performance with the pain in the vibrato of Talat Mahmood's voice. Or when the Tragedy King expressed love and happiness, it was Talat's velvety voice that lifted the actor's screen-mood. The song 'Dil Mein Samaa Gaye Sajan' is a great example of that. When Dilip Kumar's screen-persona sulked in love, Talat's voice was there in 'Shaam-e-gham Ki Qasam'.

A few decades later, when the industry recognized the talent of the great singer, Jagjit Singh, as the next tallest Ghazal singer that the country had seen, he always spoke about the impact of Talat on his life. "When I was in school, I started learning music and watching Hindi movies. The greatest hero in those days was Dilip Kumar and the greatest voice was Talat Mahmood. In my initial days I started following Talat's singing. A soft spoken man with soft singing. There is no vulgarity either in poetry or his singing. Totally, a gentleman's voice, I must call it."[8]

As Dilip Kumar's preferred voice on-screen, the entire album of Madhumati (1958) was booked for Talat Mahmood. But to everyone's shock, Talat asked Dilip Kumar to help out his friend, Mukesh, and allow him to sing all the songs for Dilip. This compassionate gesture endeared Dilip Kumar even more towards Talat. The Dilip-Talat partnership also came from their similarities. Their friendship blossomed with their mutual love for Urdu and Persian poetry, interest in English literature, their gentle dispositions, sensitive minds and the subtlety with which both approached their respective art forms. There were similarities in their struggles in the face of family pressure against joining films. The friendship also extended to their families. Dilip Kumar's sisters became friends with Talat Mahmood's younger sister Laila. Family lunches and long drives together were therefore common.

On the professional front, Dilip Kumar's intense immersion in his on-screen personas left him exhausted. These were days of deep realism in films and he was at the forefront of depicting all that was wrong in Indian society at that time. Doctors advised him to take a break from intense cinema and try lighter roles with some comic relief. Consequently, the two men's professional paths separated but they remained friends till the very end.

Dilip Kumar was thrilled when Talat Mahmood began his own acting career. He was there to grace the premiere of Talat's acting debut as the main lead of Dil-e-Nadan (1953). Much later in 1986, he especially came to launch Talat Mahmood's comeback album 'Ghazal Ke Saaz Uthao'.

And while marking Talat's 70th birthday celebrations in 1994, Dilip Kumar sweetly paid his tribute, "Talat stood out both in romantic and dramatic songs. The films we did together were immensely successful because his voice enhanced the tragedy inherent in the characters I played. Aggression was not Talat's cup of tea, he combined the qualities of a good singer and a perfect gentleman." [9]

As the third generation of Talat's family, I decided to re-establish contact with Dilip Kumar's family, reaching out to his wife and celebrated actress, Saira Banu. She endeared me with her openness and prompt responses to my messages. I have personally been in touch with her and in my conversations with her I realised her singular love and dedication to Dilip Kumar especially in his final years. It was most touching and it made me marvel at the selflessness of a woman who was a remarkable trailblazer in her own right.

What was also touching was the great care she took in nurturing the memory of his old friendships as she shared with me pictures of the two legends, some of which even I didn't have in our family album. In his last few years, her husband was not in a condition to talk about any details but she clearly recalled the fondness that he had for Talat. Because of this, she made it a point to remember my granduncle and our family in her prayers on special holy nights. I was almost in tears when she asked me the names of Talat's other family members who were friends with Dilip Kumar's family, for her to include in her prayers.

He once made the biggest statement that an actor would ever make for his playback singer. He was asked about which song in his career that he lip synced for was his life's theme?

"Aye Mere Dil Kahin Aur Chal by Talat Mahmood in Daag. Though Mohammad Rafi and Mukesh rendered brilliant numbers for me, Talat Mahmood was the true musical speaker of my soul", expressed Dilip Kumar.[10]

It was an era that not just built great partnerships but even greater friendships. A lot of these incidents will be mentioned in much more detail during the course of the book.

CHAPTER 5 - THE UNSTOPPABLE 1950S

THE MOST WANTED VOICE

Apart from two Dilip Kumar films, the year 1950 included about 35 songs sung by Talat, some of these from unreleased films. But the big bang arrival was established. The gentle giant made his mark with big actors on-screen as well as the established composers.

Raj Kapoor sang to Nargis in an endearing tone 'Armaan bhare dil ki lagan tere liye hai' (My heart full of desire is only for you). From the film Jaan Pehchaan (1950), it was Talat's first song for the blue-eyed actor. It was also his first duet with the bubbly Geeta Dutt who was the voice for Nargis in this song. The film industry works on the tastes and opinions of many people. This duet was first recorded in the voices of Kishore Kumar and Asha Bhosle. But acclaimed sound recordist Robin Chatterjee, who was also the co-producer of the film, did not like it. So it was re-recorded in the voices of Talat and Geeta. These inside details were narrated by Asha Bhosle herself during the reality show 'K for Kishore' on Sony TV (2008). She explained how she and Kishore faced early setbacks in their career but were determined to make it big. Replacing and changing singers for the final version of the song is a flaw that the film industry has had forever. Nearly every singer to date has faced this but it continues to be done in the name of creative licence.

After singing for Dilip Kumar and Raj Kapoor for these hit numbers in 1950, how could Dev Anand be left behind? Talat did playback singing for the trio which further cemented his presence. The film named Madhubala (1950) was the first time an actress carried the title of the film from her name. It starred Madhubala and Dev Anand together and was much awaited to see the two stars on screen. Talat sang a light hearted duet with Shamshad Begum,

'Jawaani ke zamaane mein jo dil na lagaayega peechhe pachhtaayega
(Those who don't fall in love in their youth will regret it later)

This was a very different song for Talat's usual style. The lyrics were a fun banter between the two with a heavily layered chorus track.The song doesn't have much recall value but was popular for the time. As always, Talat was never fully dependent on his film hits. He continued to saddle two parallel careers with elan. His non-film singles and albums were a constant in his active years. Poet Fayyaz Hashmi and composer Kamal Dasgupta once again come together with Talat in 1950 for this Geet -

'Soye hue hain chand aur taare
Aaj ki raat andhiyari
Tum baithi ho paas hamaare
Soyi hai phulwari'

(The moon and stars are asleep
The night is dark tonight
As you sit here next to me
The night is asleep as well)

The recording goes into placing an echo effect to Talat's voice. This exemplifies the stillness of the night and the privacy of the lovers lost in their own space. After his experience with Bengali songs, Talat would no longer shy away from singing songs in other languages which offered a niche following in regional cinema. This year, for the first time, he recorded for a Punjabi film. He sang two songs for the film Mutiyaar (1950) and this included a duet with well known Punjabi singer Surinder Kaur. She was credited for popularising the genre of folk in films and was fondly called the 'Nightingale of Punjab'. Their song together was –

'Aa chan wey, aa chan wey
Badli de pichhey, chori jhaatiyan na pa'

(Come my love, come
Don't steal glances from behind the clouds)

If 1950 seemed like Talat was unstoppable, the coming years will make you wonder how it was humanly possible for him to pack in all his recordings, shoots and world tours.

1951

'SHUKRIYA AYE PYAR TERA' (THANK YOU FOR YOUR LOVE)

1951 was a landmark year for the country. After gaining independence in 1947, India's promise to democracy had to be tested. For the first four years, India functioned with an interim parliament headed by Pt. Jawaharlal Nehru. In 1951, we conducted our first ever General Elections. The Indian National Congress (INC) won a landslide victory, with Pandit Nehru becoming the first democratically elected Prime Minister of India. The generation of freedom fighters who became part of the first government of India held an exceptional place of reverence and respect in the minds of people. But traditionally, politics has always been kept away from the film industry. The world of films continued with their focus on romance, social strife and often glorifying the daily struggle of man. They addressed social issues of poverty and casteism strung into the omnipresent theme of romance.

The class divide faced by a struggling artist was addressed in Talat's next film. In 1951, people got to see the handsome face of Talat Mahmood on screen in a cameo. Even though he had acted in a few films before, those were shot in the production houses of Calcutta. Aaram (1951) was a big banner film of a Bombay production house starring Dev Anand, Madhubala, Premnath and Talat Mahmood. This is where Talat played a cameo, the singer himself. Dev Anand plays a poor artist who manages a successful opening show and is newly engaged to his love interest played by Madhubala. At this point in the story, the leading pair celebrate their love and success. Talat, the singer is called in to dedicate a song to their celebrations. Dressed in a white tuxedo with shy mannerisms, he sings,
'Shukriya aye pyaar teera' (Thank you for your love...)

But it's also a moment where Madhubala's second suitor, a rich man played by actor Premnath is sulking on the loss of the girl. So Talat adds,
'Dil ko kitna khoobsurat gham diya, shukriya'
(You have given my heart a beautiful sorrow, thank you...)

Once you hear this song in the context of the plot, you realize Talat's finesse in expressing one person's happiness to another person's sorrow in the same breath.

Behind the scenes, the residual effect of the rumoured taunts that Talat heard about his vibrato was still weighing heavy on his mind. So when he met Anil Biswas to record this song, he gave his first take in strict control of the vibration in his voice. Biswas was angry at him. He said, "I had called Talat Mahmood to sing my song "Shukriya". But who are you? Please ask the real Talat Mahmood to come back to me once he finds his vibrato". With this, Biswas walked out on him.

While taking a stroll on Juhu beach, Talat was in deep thought and discomfort with what just happened. He realized that Biswas was right. Why should his unique God-gifted voice be trolled this way? He went back to record the song with renewed gratitude to the musician and his soul friend. The music composer's daughter, Shikha Biswas recalls, "Talat ji said that when he finally recorded 'Shukriya, aye pyar tera', it was truly heartfelt in gratitude."

The song emerged decades later once again as a reminder of their friendship. The most touching moment of their deep care for each other was witnessed by the entire country on national television in an episode of the superhit reality music show called the Sa Re Ga Ma. It was hosted by a young singer, Sonu Nigam and aired on Zee TV every week. In 1998, Anil Biswas was appointed one of the judges for the reality show. He placed a framed picture of Talat on his table and made an emotional appeal to the country to pray for Talat's health since it had suddenly deteriorated. He cried on the show for Talat's recovery as the world watched. At the end of the episode, he asked for a video of Talat's song to be played. A young Talat was seen on the screens again, shyly singing 'Shukriya aye pyaar tera'. Anil Biswas further said on the show, "Talat sahab was the only singer with the greatest ratio of hits to his credit. He is the only singer whose every song is a classified hit. All the singers from Mukesh to Lata have sung for me but while the other singers had their share of flops, it is only Talat whose every song has become a hit!"

This co-incidental tribute by Talat's most cherished mentor came just before Talat passing away, when he breathed his last in the same year on 9th May 1998. Every singer has one signature hit in his/her career that defines their essence or their landmark moment in the industry. Apart from that signature hit, there comes another song which becomes their epitaph for news channels. For Talat, that epitaph was -

'Meri yaad mein tum na ansoo bahana'
(Shed no tears in memory of me).

In my late teens while my family mourned his passing away, the house was suddenly full of media crews taking our soundbytes and shooting images from our family albums featuring Talat. I remember the news channels flashing his smiling face and playing this particular song on loop when he passed away. This was a song from the film 'Madhosh' (1951) that marked another formidable partnership. The coming together of two legends whose names became synonymous with Ghazals and melancholy, etched in the history of Indian cinema. Ace music director Madan Mohan's delicate notes with Talat Mahmood's silken sheen. And the poignant strings of the sitar played by the great sitarist Ustad Vilayat Khan, who was Madan Mohan's assistant at that time.
The song is lip synced by lesser-known actor Mahnhar Desai and features the actress Meena Kumari playing the part of his heartbroken lover who is married off to someone else. But because of her exceeding fame, it is often referred to as her song. Listen to Talat pour out his soul in lyricist Raja Mehdi Ali Khan's powerful poetry –
'Meri yaad mein tumna aansu bahaana
Na ji ko jalaana, mujhe bhool jaana
Samajhna ki thaa ek sapna suhana
Woh guzra zamaana, mujhe bhool jaana'

(Shed no tears in memory of me
Smoulder not in regret, I am best forgotten
Consider those times just as a glorious dream
With those days gone past, I am best forgotten)

The trio of Dilip Kumar, Talat Mahmood and Anil Biswas came together once again for the film Taraana (1951). Starring the vivacious Madhubala who was paired opposite Dilip Kumar for the first time. This on-screen pair went ahead and gave many more hits together, notwithstanding their own off-screen love which almost became Bollywood folklore on the epitome of burning desire and tragedy. The film features two sad songs by Talat and one upbeat romantic number. Let's get you the happy number first –

'Nain mile nain hue baaware,
Chain kahan morey sajan saaware'

(It was love at first sight when our eyes met
How can we stay calm, my love)

The song is full of young love and mischievous smiles by the lead pair. Talat's low pitch matching the subtle tease by Dilip Kumar and Lata Mangeshkar's lilt lending the sparkle to Madhubala's sparkling eyes. The next duet is a classic for lovers. The song 'Seene mein sulagte hain armaan' has stood the test of time and often features as an immortal duet in blue mood. The opening piece is an operatic orchestra, the signature style of Anil Biswas. The pitch dramatically falls into a smooth transition by a single note of the string instrument. This breathing space sets the ground for Talat's mellow voice to open the song while the on-screen actor Dilip Kumar is shown lying in bed recovering from injury. The music can best be described as the tempest felt by two separated lovers. Legend has it that he composed this song within just 15 minutes of being given the lyrics by Prem Dhawan. Such was the power of the musical genius. Interestingly, this duet has three stanzas, but all three of them are sung in a different tune which makes it a journey worth experiencing.

'Seene mein sulagte hain armaan
Aankhon mein udasi chhayi hai
Yeh aaj teri duniya se hamein
Taqdeer kahan le aayi hai'

(My heart burns for your love
My eyes have been clouded in sorrow
Away from your world today
Where has destiny brought me)

Many years later, when Talat became more frequent with his world tours, he would joke about this song by giving an interesting insight to the audience. "This was actually my solo song composed by Anil da. But Lata liked it so much that she insisted she be given the song too. That's how it became a duet. But in my concerts, I make it a point to sing the entire song solo. So this is my revenge. Hahaha..." And the audience would burst into laughter along with him.

Talat's niece, Romana Zaman, recalls her conversation with Anil Biswas. He told her, "Talat was a very emotional and expressive person. And he never forgot to tell me how much he held me in reverence. He once said, had he been allowed to bow his head in sajda (prayer) to anyone apart from Allah, that person would be me. It was the most touching thing I heard."

This reflects how Talat managed to pour in so much soul into his songs because it came from the artist's personality. While watching the Alia Bhatt starrer Gangubai Kathiawadi (2022), I was taken aback by a lovely surprise. The character was shown to be a huge fan of superstar Dev Anand. And suddenly in the middle of the devastating scene where she learns about being sold to a brothel by her own boyfriend, the filmmaker Sanjay Leela Bhansali chooses a snippet of an old Dev Anand song in Talat's voice to play in the background. The hard blow of the brothel could only be softened by Talat's caress.

'Aa teri tasveer bana loon'

(Come, let me paint a picture of you)

This song is originally from the film Nadaan (1951) starring Dev Anand and Madhubala.

'Aa teri tasveer bana loon
Main apni taqdeer bana loon
Dil ke kore kaaghaz par
Ulfat ki lakeer bana loon'

(Come, let me paint a picture of you
Let my destiny shine with it
On the clean slate of my heart
Let me draw my love-line)

This was the year where almost every music director wanted to use Talat's voice. And they did. S. D. Burman used his voice for the first time. Contrary to popular belief that the two men don't have too many films together, they actually started off with their partnership with four films this year. The film Sazaa (1951) had a duet with Lata Mangeshkar, starring Dev Anand and Nimmi. The song was penned by lyricist Rajender Krishan.

'Aaja aaja tera intezaar hai,
Tujhe dhoond raha mera pyar hai'

(Come to me, as I've been waiting for you
I've been looking for you, my love)

Since 1951 defined many debut partnerships in Talat's career, the one worth mentioning just for its uniqueness and rarity is the one with Kishore Kumar. It's perhaps the one and only time the two men recorded a song together. A forgotten, light-hearted song on the struggles of the middle class. It's from the film Hamaari Shaan (1951) with music director Chitragupta. The song goes as -

'Damri damri paisa paisa
Jod jod mar jaate hain
Arre is duniya me kanjooson ka maal
Aji doctor khaate hain Is liye yaaron
Maze udaalo duniyaa waalon
Duniya aani jaani hai
O duniya aani jaani hai'

(Nickels, coins, money
Adding it up kills us all
The wealth of the misers
Is eaten up by doctors
And that's why folks
Just live your life to the fullest
The world comes and goes)

Music director C. Ramchandra who had later achieved colossal fame with India's most famous and favourite patriotic song 'Aye mere watan ke logon' (O' my countrymen), used to be Anil Biswas' music assistant. Once he started out as an independent composer, he wanted to use Talat's vocals too, just like his mentor Biswas. So he recorded the first song with Talat which was a duet with Lata Mangeshkar in the film Sagaai (1951). Starring the actor Premnath, the song is picturised with him clad in a T-shirt in jail, trying to ace the trendsetting look of Marlon Brando from 'Streetcar Named Desire' (1951). In Indian cinema in those days, the actors usually wore kurtas or formal shirts but not casual T-shirts. Premnath tried to break out of that mould with this song. It was once again in a blue mood but unexpectedly in a fast pace and with no long drawn out violins.

'Mohabbat mein aise zamaaney bhi aaye
Kabhi ro diye hum kabhi muskuraaye'

(I have seen such days of love
Some days I cried, other days I smiled)

SUPERSTAR SHYAM'S FINAL SINGING VOICE

With all the ups so far, came a major jolt for the entire film industry. An ambitious period drama was being shot with marquee names - actor Shyam and actress Naseem Bano. The film 'Shabistan' (1951) was about two kingdoms at war. Superstar Shyam was one of the best looking actors of early Hindi cinema and already an established star at a time when the popular trio of actors Raj Kapoor-Dev Anand-Dilip Kumar were just about beginning to make a mark. His personality shone through in Shabistan, suiting the swashbuckling character of the film, with royal costumes and action scenes. But there was a horse riding scene that turned horribly wrong. As the plot is about two warring kingdoms, there was a requirement to shoot fight sequences on horseback. The action scene required Shyam to be riding a horse. During the shoot, the actor lost control of the reins and fell off. He sustained head injuries and was quickly rushed to the nearest hospital. But it was difficult to survive a fractured skull and the nation's heartthrob succumbed in the prime of his career and life. His few remaining scenes were completed with a body-double and the shots were taken from behind.

His obituary in the Times of India, dated 26th April, 1951 read, "High, wide and handsome Shyam, most popular of the Indian screen's male stars, idol of millions of film-goers throughout India and adored by lakhs in Bombay where he was mobbed at every appearance, went laughing off to work from his Chembur home on Wednesday morning. By afternoon, he was dead." The sudden accidental death sent shockwaves across the film industry and his fans. People thronged the streets, pulled chains to stop trains to catch a glimpse of him and joined the massive procession as the star set off on his last journey.

If you recall the recent biographical film Manto (2018) on the controversial writer, it is shown how both Manto and Shyam were close friends in real life because they both worked together for Bombay Talkies. In fact, Manto was so fond of Shyam that he dedicated a complete chapter to him in his book titled, 'Stars from Another Sky'.

Shabistan (1951) became the last film in which the star could be seen talking, singing, flashing his charming smile and romancing his co-stars. The film features three romantic songs with Shyam lip syncing to Talat's voice. All three were happy duets with Geeta Dutt composed on Western beats and rhythm. My favourite of the three being this -

'Kaho ek baar mujhe tumse pyaar
Mujhe tumse pyaar, tumse pyaar, tumse pyaar'

(Say it once that you love me That you love me, love me, love)
The final moments of Shyam's dashing persona on screen have forever been locked in Talat's voice. His death was a grim reminder of the delicate uncertainty of life. No matter how popular, successful or rich you were, your last breath could be a minute away. We have to live a life with compassion and empathy.

RAISING FUNDS FOR SENIOR COLLEAGUES

(Talat performs in a fund raiser. Seen here with Geeta Dutt)

Talat's compassion was reflected in a campaign by the Playback Singers' Association. It decided to raise funds for singers who had grown old and were out of work. They were in a situation of distress and many needed support for survival. The current singers enacted a comedy skit at the Liberty Cinema in Bombay. The proceeds of this show were shared with the needy singers. Talat was part of this skit, along with Geeta Dutt, Hemant Kumar, Lata Mangeshkar, G M Durrani, Mukesh and Kishore Kumar. Each singer had to sing and act out a funny version of their song. It was a parody show to make it different and entertaining for the audience. When it was Talat's turn, he tied the neck tie on his forehead with the straps of his gallace slipping off his shoulders. Mocking sadness, he hit his forehead, tugged at the tie and sang his chartbusting hit 'Aye dil mujhe aisi jagah le chal jahan koi na ho' (Take my heart to a place of loneliness). While Kishore Kumar jumped all over stage yodelling out loud, Mukesh lit a matchstick and hit his chest, singing 'Dil jalta hai to jalne do' (Let the heart burn if it really has to). It was a hilarious night which ended well for a good cause to help their own former colleagues.

Meanwhile at the work front, the great composer, Khayyam's talent was aptly recognized by Talat for composing soft music and Ghazals. He approached HMV to sing two non-film Ghazals recorded on the 78rpm format and chose Khayyam to make the music for them. In those days, Khayyam used the name of 'Sharma Ji' on records. These Ghazals were -

1. Aa gayeen phir se baharen (Spring has come again)
2. Ro ro beeta jeevan saara (My life has been spent in sorrow)

This non-film record featuring both Ghazals was driven by Talat's brand name and became a huge hit. It brought Khayyam's solo talent to the notice of filmmakers in the industry. Earlier, he used to compose music with his partner in the name of 'Sharma Ji - Varma Ji' up until Partition. It will be fair to say that the success of this record paved the way for Khayyam's solo career and helped provide a stronger foothold in the film industry. It was also the start of the great Talat-Khayyam partnership over and beyond just the film industry. In the non-film category, the two men recorded 22 Ghazals, Geets and Naats (songs in praise of the Prophet Mohammad, PBUH).

GENTLEMAN'S PROMISE OF MARRIAGE

(Newly weds Talat and Nasreen)

Talat was in and out of studios and recordings. A singer's life is much busier behind the scenes than what one gets to see in the public eye. The continuous riyaz (early morning practice of classical music), the song rehearsals, multiple appointments for new recordings, sittings, discussions, etc etc. These initial years in Bombay were a crucial litmus test for Talat. Could he make it big here just as he did in Calcutta? Can Talat Mahmood be as big a name as Tapan Kumar? Creating a new identity for an already established personality was a challenge he had taken up. As one day slipped into another with the daily struggles of tinsel town, Talat wanted to keep focus on his personal life as much as he did on his singing career. He was sad without his lady love. In 1951, when he sang 'Aa gayi phir se baharein' in Khayyam's music, it must have reflected his frame of mind as he was trying to find the right time to get back to his love in Calcutta.

'Aa gayin phir se baharein aa gayin
Dil pe gham ki badaliyaan si chhaa gayin
Hasaraton ke baagh viraan ho gaye
Ham to duniya se pareshan ho gaye
Aap ki yaaden hamein tadapa gayin'

(Spring has come again
My is heart is filled with sorrow
Gardens of desire are left deserted
I feel troubled by this world
Memories of you make me yearn for your love)

Despite Talat's packed year, he made to sure to keep a wedding on the cards. He had to honour his lady love, actress Latika, who was patiently waiting for him in Calcutta. He was now stable with his earnings in Bombay and doing fairly well, actually. He was the highest paid singer in the 1950s with a fees of Rs.500-700/- per song. Talat was choosy and recording an average of at least two songs in a month. This number, of course, doubled in the coming years, at the peak of his success.

As was the case with his choice of career, his choice of a life partner outside the Lucknow social circle was something that his father decided to accept with respect in due course of time. But not immediately. His sister Laila, who was always his most trusted comrade, was asked to break this news to the family. She was somehow the best buffer Talat could have asked for each time his decisions were not in sync with their father. First with his singing career and now with his choice of wife. Undoubtedly he must have missed his aunt, Mahlaqa Begum, the most at this point in his life as she had remained his staunchest supporter till the time that she was alive. As a liberal woman herself, she would have stood by Talat in these lonely days too.

An issue of the popular Urdu language film magazine called 'Shama' printed an exclusive interview which got its readers and Talat fans excited. It spoke with the lady who was said to be Talat Mahmood's wife. It was meant to be a teaser for their readers on what would follow in their next issue. Being a gentleman and true to his promise, once things started looking up in Bombay, Talat decided to marry Latika Mullick , who was a Bengali Christian, and took the name of Nasreen Mahmood after marriage. Talat was a man of conviction and he ensured that he kept his word. 'Nain mile nain hue baaware' (Love at first sight when our eyes met) rang out loud in real life too. Iftikhar, his brother–in-law (Laila's husband and my maternal grandfather) and close friend, was sent from Lucknow on behalf of the family, to meet with Talat's wife in Bombay. Nasreen was a fabulous cook and homemaker. Iftikhar wrote back to Manzoor, saying, "She is an extremely warm person and a fabulous cook. You couldn't have found a better girl for Talat. She takes care of him so well."

In the next issue, the film magazine 'Shama' made a full page announcement with pictures of the newlyweds. The film industry also celebrated Talat's new beginnings in life, living in the ethos of what their films preached about finding true love and keeping it. The Indian Express Ltd group launched the publication of their film magazine called 'Screen' in the same year in 1951. Their launch issue did a similar exclusive with the romantic couple. It was the coming together of two film industries - the Bengali and the Hindi. With this marriage, Talat inadvertently sent out a message of love to his fans in Calcutta. Now he was their daamaad (son-in- law). Tapan Kumar was no longer just an outside Lucknow boy who filled their music with gentle melody but was now part of the extended Bengali family.

The handsome star set a shining example of being the complete man both on the professional as well as the personal front. But he had an ever growing following of female fans who were left broken-hearted with the news of his wedding. He had a fandom not just for his voice but for his charming looks as well.

Popular Ghazal singer, late Pankaj Udhas was one of Talat's biggest admirers. "He was very handsome and girls used to run after him. But in those days, in the 1950s and 60s, Talat sa'ab generated so much euphoria as a singer which was unheard of. I am told of an incident where Madan Mohan, Jaikishen and Talat, who were very good friends, would have a competition for fun. It was about which one of them would give the maximum autographs. They would sit together at a coffee shop in South Bombay and invariably there would be a whole flock of young girls running for Talat sa'ab. Madan Mohan and Jaikishen would just be sitting and looking at each other", chuckles Udhas.[11]

1952

SINGING FOR INDIA'S LAND MOVEMENT

A series of developments in a new nation's democratic structure gave hope to all industries where every citizen became a stakeholder. With the first General Elections concluded this year, the stability of a newly declared Republic and the first Parliamentary sessions of both Lower House and Upper House (Lok Sabha and Rajya Sabha) were promising signs. When Prime Minister Nehru presented India's first ever 'Five Year Plan' (FYP) in Parliament for the national economy, one of the primary focuses was the development of agriculture. This was synchronised with a voluntary land reform movement in India called the The Bhoodan movement (Land Gift movement). It was led by non-violent social activist Vinoba Bhave who persuaded wealthy landowners to voluntarily give a percentage of their land to landless labourers who could cultivate the land for their own
subsistence.

You must be wondering how Talat is related to all of this? The Government of Bombay wanted Talat to sing two theme songs for India's first FYP. In those days, Bombay was a huge State which included parts of present day Maharashtra, Gujarat and Rajasthan. Both songs were in Gujarati language, produced by the Gramophone Company Limited for the Directorate of Publicity in the Govt of Bombay. Below is one of the songs on land donation –

'Avdhoot aayo, alakh jagayo Aayo che upvasi
Deen dalit na dukhda harto, Sant Vinoba tyagi
Bhoomi daan do, bhoomi daan do'

(An ascetic has come, awakening the world
A fasting person has come
Removing sufferings of poor and deprived,
The sacrificing Saint Vinoba,
Donate Land, Donate Land)

GROWING HEFT OF FILM BUSINESS

All-round development of the nation was instrumental in making the market of films stable as well. It was showing signs of a new thrust of confidence. Films in Bombay had broken all previous box office records. The Dilip Kumar starrer Aan (1952) was the biggest blockbuster ever, doing a business of Rs. 1,50,00,000 (1.50 crores). Out of the top 10 grossers of the year, Talat had songs in 5 of those films starring Raj Kapoor, Dilip Kumar, Ashok Kumar, Bharat Bhushan and others. In order of the top 10 box office success that year, these were films that Talat sang for -

4th ranking film - Daag (playback for Dilip Kumar)
5th ranking film - Anhonee (playback for Raj Kapoor)
6th ranking film - Anand Math (playback for Pradeep Kumar)
7th ranking film - Sangdil (playback for Dilip Kumar)
9th ranking film - Bewafaa (playback for Raj Kapoor)

All three Ghazals from the film Daag (1952) were sung for Dilip Kumar who won the first ever Filmfare Award in the Best Actor category for his portrayal of the protagonist, Shankar. Many of us today would find it difficult to have the appetite for a morose storyline of Daag where Shankar is swinging between poverty and debt and drowning in alcohol like a rudderless person, hoping that his lover's family will accept his marriage proposal. But pain and tragedy was the opium of those times in films. Ironically, while the country's market forecast was beginning to look up, the scars of human sufferings through the struggles of Independence and Partition were too deep to be done away with that easily. Dilip Kumar and Talat Mahmood's subtle grief breathed in empathy for these characters on screen. Daag became another landmark film to further the success of the Dilip-Talat team. The film also brought together a new partnership for Talat with the music director duo of Shankar-Jaikishan, adding to his repertoire of Ghazals. These three Ghazals were -

1. Aye mere dil kahin aur chal
   Gham ki duniya se dil bhar gaya
   Dhoond le ab koi ghar nayaa
   (Take me away from here
   My heart is full with this sorrowful world
   I need to find a better place)

2. Koi nahin mera iss duniya mein
   Aashiyan barbaad hai
   Aansoon bhari mujhe qismat mili hai
   Zindagi naashaad hai
   (I have no one left in the world
   My home is destroyed
   I have been given a life of tears
   My life is sorrowful)

3. Hum dard ke maaron ka
   Itna hi fasaana hai
   Peeney ko sharaab-e-gham
   Dil gham ka nishaana hai
   (People who suffer in pain
   Have this tale to tell
   We are intoxicated by sorrow
   The heart is a victim of sorrow)

I sometimes wonder how a single film album could have so many sad numbers drenched in such deep sorrow. But it did, and each of them was a big hit, ruling the airwaves on radio.

The film Anhonee brought in the much needed lift in mood for Talat's list of songs in 1952. Starring the charming blue eyed boy Raj Kapoor with his on-screen flame Nargis, Talat's voice made a smooth transition for Raj Kapoor's impish charm. Playing the prelude on piano at a lavish bungalow dinner party, the suave Kapoor wooes the young maiden, Nargis by singing -

'Main dil hoon ek armaan bhara
Tu aa ke mujhe pehchaan zaara
Ek sagar hoon, tehra, tehra
Tu aa ke mujhe pehchaan zara'

(I am a heart full of desires

Come, recognize me
I am as still as an ocean
Come, recognize me)

In this song, music director Roshan makes prominent use of the piano for his composition throughout the song. The original plan was to have two pianists for the track, but a last minute malfunction

meant that there could be only one piano for the recording. When you hear the track, it doesn't sound like a second piano is missing. In fact, the song makes for a perfect number to do a waltz. I had used this song for one of my Jashn-e-Talat concerts in 2017 with a set of 20 waltz dancers at the atrium of India's largest DLF mall in Noida. The shoppers were left spellbound. Never had they seen vintage music from the Golden Era being showcased this way. Our young dancers were thrilled with the response which had three floors full of a LIVE audience, dropping their shopping bags to watch them dance to a foot tapping Talat Mahmood number!
The other song from Anhonee (1952) is picturised as a phone conversation. In those days, films created a popular genre called 'phone songs'. These were shot as duets over the landline phone instrument. Across the country, the landline used to be an important form of communication, especially for lovers and young couples who couldn't meet often but could at least hear each other's voice over the phone. If dating wasn't allowed by parents, you could always talk over the phone! Hindi cinema was in the forefront of building romances over the phone. While watching these phone songs, one was always amused by how long could the chord really stretch, which benevolently allowed the person to walk across rooms in flirtatious twirls while whispering sweet nothings in rhythm. Talat's duet with Lata for actors Raj Kapoor and Nargis went like this -

Talat - 'Meri dil ki dhadkan kya bole' (What does my heart say?)
Lata - Kya bole? (What does it say?)
Talat - Main jaanu aur tu jaane (That's for both of us to know)
Lata - Mera pyar bhara man kyun dole? (Why do I dance in joy?)
Talat - Kyun dole? (Why does it dance?)
Lata - Main jaanu aur tu jaane (That's for both of us to know)

He maintained the same upbeat mood for another film of Raj Kapoor's this year, Bewafaa (1952). The music for this film was composed by A.R.Qureshi who was better known as the legendary tabla player , Allah Rakha. "He created such grace and pathos in the songs he sang that he entered the hearts of people. When he sang in my films, he moved me too much and I found a good friend in him as well", recalled Allah Rakha.[12]

"Talat saheb (sir) sang with a rare gusto and inspiration. He was flawless in his rendering of songs and always touched the hearts of the people", added Raj Kapoor.[13]

Let's revisit one of the songs from their film Bewafaa (1952). This is where Raj Kapoor is sitting outside the wall while Nargis is busy swimming in the pool inside, looking out and wondering who is singing for her. It's a playful, flirtatious song in Talat's voice.

'Tumko fursat ho
Meri jaan to idhar dekh toh lo
Tumko fursat ho
Chaar aankhen na karo
Ek nazar dekh to lo
Tumko fursat ho'

(Spare some time for me
Look towards me, my love
Find some time for me
Don't wander around your eyes
Give me one glance at least
Spare some time for me)

With a total of 54 songs recorded this year, it's impossible to mention all, of course. But some of these that find mention in this book are either my favourites or landmark renditions. In the film Sangdil (1952), Dilip Kumar plays a rich landowner. A young thakur (landlord) with inherited wealth and not a care in the world. It has a song which shows his character in the most flirtatious mood, crisply dressed in a black bandh-gala (formal coat with high collar closed at the neck) looking out the window at the moon lit sky while supporting actress Shammi teasingly strums at the strings of the sitar.

'Yeh hawa yeh raat yeh chandni
Teri ek ada pe nisar hai
Mujhe kyon na ho teri arzoo
Teri justjoo mein bahaar hai'

(The breeze and this moonlit night
Are admirers of your elegance

Why shouldn't I desire you
There is the joy of spring in finding you)

If you notice the long extensive pieces on the sitar in this song, they are classical compositions believed to be played by one of our Sitar maestros. But the music director, Sajjad Hussain, known to be a perfectionist was not satisfied with the rendition. The recording of the song would be abruptly stopped at the slightest waiver of the sitar notes and the song would then be performed right from the start again. The song underwent 17 retakes !! "Till the day he died, whenever he heard the sitar piece of the song's interlude, he would sigh and say - They didn't play it like I told them to", recalls his son Nasir Ahmed.[14] How did Talat's voice withstand the strain? He sounds perfectly at ease. Talat threw no starry tantrums. He was always a well mannered professional in the studio. It's important to remember that recording of songs in those days could only be possible in one single take. The slightest error or interruption would mean starting all over again. Talat also had once spoken about this perfection and striving for excellence being common in those days. "The standards were then very high - in the lyrics, the composition and orchestration. Perfection was aimed at all times. We spent up to 10 days recording just one single song. Moreover, our own integrity was so high that even after all the initial rehearsals, if we could not do justice to the song in the final recording, we could still ask for a re-take." [15]

(Varied moods of Dilip Kumar and Raj Kapoor on screen sung by Talat Mahmood)

The film was another unforgettable Dilip-Madhubala starrer which had a memorable romantic duet as well. This melodious Talat-Lata duet was -

Lata - 'Dil mein sama gaye sajan
Phool khile chaman chaman
Pyaar bhi muskura diya'
(You live in my heart entirely
Flowers blossom everywhere
How my love smiles at me)

Talat - 'Masti bharee hawa chalee
Hasne lagi kali kali
Tumse mujhe mila diya'
(What pleasure in the blowing wind
Flower buds cheer up in sway
As we are destined to meet)

Sajjad maintained that this was a simple composition with the consistent rhythm of beats throughout the song. But Talat was given some base notes along with Lata which would suddenly swing up to a higher tempo. His compositions, that were usually a challenge for the singers, could be perfected only with skillful and trained voices of that time.

Talat's next hit was with another giant of cinema. The leading actor and director of the times, V.Shantaram had built a legacy of producing ace films under his banner Rajkamal Kalamandir. It was a noted film production company and studio in Mumbai which produced films both in Hindi and Marathi. In 1952, his film 'Parchhain' was cited by critics as that of exceptional merit. Talat Mahmood was chosen to sing for the great star. This helped build a formidable repertoire for Talat where his voice was increasingly being chosen for every leading man in the industry.

'Mohabbat hi na jo samjhe
Wo zalim pyar kya jaane
Nikalti dil ke taaron se
Jo hai jhankar kya jaane'

(One who doesn't understand love

What would that wicked soul understand affection
Emerging from the strings of heart
Those beats cannot be appreciated)

It helped to have C. Ramchandra as the music director, who was already smitten by Talat's unique vocal quality, just as his mentor Anil Biswas. This track was one of the biggest hits in the music director's career. The song is picturised on V. Shantaram who plays a visually-challenged man touched by the poignant notes of the sitar being strung on-screen by actress Jayashree, impeccably played by noted sitarist Ustad Abdul Halim Jaffer Khan.

A duet that is lesser known but which I particularly like in the same film is called 'Dil-dil se keh raha hai' (My heart tells your heart). It's worth mentioning it because this is perhaps the softest song sung by Talat and Lata Mangeshkar. The singers are barely whispering to each other in the setting of a romantic dream, accompanied by sounds of violin, flute and piano. The orchestral lavishness of this track by C. Ramchandra is noteworthy on how to use a multi piece composition and still keep the whispers of the singers rise above the music. Actress Jayashree arrives on a lotus chariot dressed in luminescent white while actor Shantaram is woken up by the brightness of her presence on a full moon night which bathes the whole garden in silver. And then they sing -

'Dil dil se keh raha hai
Jo tum ho, woh hi main hoon
Dono ki ek sada hai
Jo tu hai, woh hi main hoon'

(My heart tells your heart
You are what I am
Both are always the same
You are what I am)

Some of Talat's old friendships from Calcutta provided him some warmth and reassurance in the new city of Bombay. Out of 54 songs recorded in 1952, Talat had many duets with singer Geeta Dutt this year. She, along with singer Hemant Kumar, were some of his close friends from his days at New Theatres in Calcutta. 'Anand Math' was a film that brought all three of them together again in an unlikely song. The film is a historical drama based on the Sanyasi Rebellion

(rebellion by Hindu ascetics) of 1770-77 in Bengal against the British East India Company. The most famous soundtrack from this film is the eternal 'Vande Mataram' sung by Lata Mangeshkar. The Talat-Geeta duet in the film with music composed by Hemant Kumar is a motivational song which cocks a snook at the British and dares them to stop their rebellion! The song also manages to blend in the forbidden love of two characters both caught in the ascetic duty of celibacy and the duty of fighting against the Colonists. The lead roles were played by actors Geeta Bali and Pradeep Kumar. Noticeably, it was Kumar's debut film in the Bombay film industry. How this song transitions from a pro-independence rebellion to the pain of letting go of their love interest is worth experiencing in both their voices.

Geeta - 'Kaise rokoge aise tufan ko
Ye umange ye dil hai jawan ho'
(How will you stop this storm
These are passions and desires of the young)

Talat - 'Jisko chhoo kar ke doobe hazaaron
Dhoondta hai ye dil wo kinara'
(A thousand drowned by its touch
My heart looks for that resting place)

This year Talat sang a devotional song dedicated to Lord Ram - a bhajan - for the film 'Lanka Dahan'. It's the story of Ramayan starting from the point of Sita's abduction and ending with her rescue. Today, as you read through the comments on Youtube for this bhajan, many fans and listeners are astounded at how the King of Ghazals brings new freshness to the emotion of religious devotion. One listener says, "Your voice is peace, it is a manifestation of Bhagwan (God)." Listen to this Bhajan in Talat's consoling voice –
'Basa le man mandir mein Ram, banenge bigde tere kaam
Ram naam jivan ka sahara, Ram bina suna jag sara'

(Surrender yourself to Ram, it will resolve all your problems
His name supports all life, without him the world is lonely)

THE BIRTH OF BINACA GEETMALA

This was also the year that the broadcast of Hindi film music took the biggest hit. The Information and Broadcasting Minister, B.V. Keskar disliked Hindi film music. In his personal opinion, he found it too risque and crass. And therefore, he decided to reduce the playout of film songs at the All India Radio to barely 10 percent of its music programming. It is believed that this drastic decision was taken in an attempt to promote and popularise classical music instead, which was part of India's rich legacy. He also set up a strict list of guidelines for which film songs were "worthy enough" to be played out. This reduced the presence of film songs on AIR to almost naught. The film industry called this a de-facto ban. This is when Radio Ceylon, based in Sri Lanka, came to the rescue. Hindi film producers decided to switch entirely to Radio Ceylon which could be heard across South Asia.

It led to the launch of a show that was set to become the most formidable list of top songs from the Hindi film industry. It was an original, one-of-its- kind weekly show that ended with an annual ranking of the most successful songs. The first ever episode of Binaca Geetmala was broadcast on Radio Ceylon in December 1952, hosted by a young star in the making, 21-year old Ameen Sayani. He would record the show in Bombay and the tapes were then sent to Colombo for broadcast. Before this, there was no such ranking list for the top popular film songs. The only yardstick of a hit song used to be based on how often it played on the radio or how well the film sold at the box office. But the Binaca Geetmala set up a formidable market system which music directors, singers and filmmakers followed with baited breath. The songs were ranked by a combination of the number of records sold in India, views from record store owners and votes posted by the listeners.

This ranking system was introduced in the program only from the next year in 1953. But for its debut in December 1952, the program could not list the top songs of the year. Instead, it just released a list of nine most popular songs of the year with no particular order. Out of these nine songs, Talat had the maximum songs by any singer. A total of five songs. These included -

1. 'Main pagal mera manwa pagal' from the film Ashiana with Raj Kapoor sitting over the piano, caressing his broken heart (music

director Madan Mohan)

2. 'Mohabbat hi na samjhe wo zalim' from the film Parchhain, starring the superstar V. Shantaram giving a persuasive lesson on true love (music director C Ramchandra)
3. 'Main dil hoon ek armaan bhara' with lover boy Raj Kapoor charmingly trying to woo Nagis in the film Anhonee (music director Roshan)
4. 'Ye hawa ye raat ye chandni' from the film Sangdil, starring Dilip Kumar in the role of a stylish rich man flirting with a gushing Shammi (music director Sajjad Hussain)
5. 'Aye mere dil kahin aur chal' starring an anguished Dilip Kumar from the top grossing film Daag (music director Shankar-Jaikishen)

This list provides us with a perspective on how Talat made his position as the most preferred singer. He showcased a wide range while singing in different emotions for different actors, keeping up with the varied styles and challenges of different music directors. It's important to take note of this diversity in Talat's oeuvre since a lot of critics have wrongly tried to box him in a limited category of just Ghazals or just songs in the blue mood. As a true singing icon of the rich Golden Era, Talat switched to multiple styles and genres with poetic ease. His repertoire in Hindi film songs continued to expand but he never forgot about his Bengali fans back in Calcutta. He released a new album of Modern Bengali songs with HMV. The music was composed by an all time admirer of his voice, Robin Chatterjee.

Side A. Alote Chhayate dinguli mor (These days in light and shadow)

Side B. Chander Eto Alo (The moon is here)

These non-film albums were important for HMV as Talat came with a track record of high sales. Despite dropping his nom de plume of Tapan Kumar, his Bengali listeners lapped up his voice each time he offered them a new release.

1953

(Talat's publicity shot from his film 'Dil-e-Nadan')

SINGING STAR OF 'DIL-E-NADAN'

Barely a handful of years into making it big as a singer in Bombay, Talat's meteoric rise could not be contained. Film studios and production houses who had noticed Talat's popularity with female fans because of his good looks were willing to bet their money on Talat as an on-screen actor in the main lead now. If we remember, in the 1940s, the film industry had undergone a sea change with the technology of playback recording, where playback singing was meant only for singers and actors were meant to only act on-screen and lip sync the songs. But in the 1950s, when good looking playback singers were asked to act on screen, it led to the coinage of a new term - 'Singing Star'. It meant an exceptional talent where a singer would be asked to act on screen as the main lead. This was a popular trend not just in India, but a simultaneous one in Hollywood too. The world's biggest and most good looking rockstar Elvis Presely also had his career take a similar turn. While his first film 'Love Me Tender' released in 1956, Talat was ahead of the curve. Other singing stars of the 50s in India included Kishore Kumar and Suraiyya.

Film producer Abdul Rashid Kardar decided to launch Talat's first film in Bombay playing the lead role of a hero. While Talat had already acted in a few films in Calcutta, the Bombay launch introduced him as the 'Singing Star' in all the film publicity material and posters. This debut had to be done with all the right tick boxes. It had to be sensational.. And it had to further spur the interest of his fans. For this, Kardar announced a beauty contest, in partnership with the toothpaste brand Kolynos. This was called the Kardar-Kolynos Talent Contest and it was supposed to find a fresh beautiful face who would not just make her debut opposite the heartthrob Talat but also sign a two- year contract with Kardar Productions for other films. A young and pretty student of medicine at the Ludhiana Medical College, Peace Kanwal, who was studying to be a doctor, was declared the winner of this contest!

The film was called 'Dil-e-Nadan', a love triangle played by two sisters (debutant Peace Kamal and actress Shyama) who fall in love with the same man (played by Talat Mahmood). While the drama of jealousy and rage between the two sisters ensues in seeking attention from their common love interest, the initial plot of the film took

Talat on an uncanny trip of deja vu. Strikingly similar to his own personal life, the character in his film, Mohan, wants to pursue a career in music. For Mohan, music is his raison d'etre but for his father, it is a blot on family prestige because of which Mohan has no choice but to leave home. He moves to Bombay looking for work in music. He ends up meeting a rich man who supports him and helps him become an established music director. This man also turns out to be the father of the two sisters who fall in love with Mohan. Whether or not Talat's life inspired the film's script is unknown but the struggle of taking up films or music in Bombay was a common problem that most of Talat's contemporaries had with their respective families.

Since the film was pegged to be the start of a new innings for Talat, the premiere had to be big as well. It was a star-studded affair where his friends and colleagues showed up in full strength. Right from Dilip Kumar, Raj Kapoor, V.Shantaram, Shammi Kapoor, Nimmi, they were all there to support Talat's premier.

'Dil-e-Nadan' features four songs sung and acted by Talat. For me, this one stands out for its gentle disposition despite the lyrics, penned by Shakeel Badayuni, which are full of rage, almost cursing the Almighty. Music director Ghulam Mohammed chose to treat this rage with docile detachment. Talat's vocals with the prelude of the strumming guitar and flute evoke sympathy towards the character. Like a moment in the twilight zone, Talat sits atop a rock, bemoaning his life while Shyama looks on bewildered. It was #6 at the Binaca Geetmala top songs of the year.

'Zindagi dene wale sun
Teri duniya se dil bhar gaya
Main yahan jite ji mar gaya

Raat katati nahi din guzarta nahi
Zakhm aisa diya hai ke bharta nahi
Aankh viraan hai
Dil pareshaan hai
Gham ka saaman hai
Jaise jaadu koi kar gaya
Zindagi dene wale sun'

(O, Giver of Life, hear me out

I am cloyed with your world
I feel that I am dead

Night and day are painfully slow
My wounds never seem to heal
My eyes wear a deserted look
My heart is troubled
I have a load of sorrow
Like a spell of black magic
O, Giver of Life, hear me out)

(A dapper Talat Mahmood on the film's poster)

(Star studded premier of 'Dil-e-Nadan' with Talat's friends, actors V. Shantaram and Dilip Kumar supporting his on-screen launch)

The songs hit the right chord with his fans but the film didn't do well at the box office. The mega debut didn't send the ticket counters ringing but a potential talent had been established. This was certainly not going to be Talat's last film as an actor. Soft romances was a genre that suitably fit like a glove on Talat's persona. "I filled a necessary void in those days. I was a singing hero and I enjoyed acting," recalls Talat. "And these were soft, romantic roles in films that had a number of songs. The films of this era followed the singing hero concept very closely", added Talat. While acting in films created a conflict in his schedule as a singer, Talat made sure that he never neglected his singing assignments. He recorded 49 songs this year. This was despite the fact that for an actor, the film shoots often extend to late in the night but for a singer, the day starts early in the morning with riyaz (practising and exercising vocal chords). Talat had to demolish rumours that since he was now an actor, he would not continue with playback singing anymore. He clarified, "It's true that playing the leading man in some films did bring in more money than I earned as a playback singer. But then I had made it clear to every single music director who mattered, that I was first a singer, then an actor."[16]

THE FIRST VOICE FOR SHAMMI KAPOOR

This year marked the entry of an unforgettable, inimitable actor in the film industry. Shammi Kapoor. "I remember meeting him at the premiere of his film Dil-e-Nadan. I told him to please save his talent exclusively only as a singer because actors like me will be needing his voice. And that's exactly what happened. He sang for my early films like 'Laila Majnu' and 'Thokar'. It was a dream come true for me."

In his debut year, Shammi Kapoor starred in five films out of which two films - 'Laila Majnu' and 'Thokar' had Talat's playback singing for him. The song from the film Thokar was Shammi Kapoor's biggest hit from his early career. It was written by poet Majaz Lucknawi which became the best remembered nazm (Urdu poem) of his entire career. Testimony to this fact is that when a biopic of Majaz was made in 2017, it was titled - 'Majaz : Ae Gham-e-Dil Kya Karun'. The music was composed with a sense of haunting grief by music director Sardar Malik. It was #4 at the Binaca

Geetmala top songs of the year.

'Ai gham-e-dil kya karoon
Ai vahashat-e-dil kya karoon
Kya karoon, kya karoon
Ai gham-e-dil kya karoon

Yeh rupahali chhaon
Yeh aakaash par taaron ka jaal
Jaiise sufi ka tasavvur
Jaise aashiq ka khayaal
Aah lekin kaun samjhe
Kaun jaane dil ka haal
Ai gham-e-dil kya karoon...'

(O' sorrowful heart what should I do
O' restless heart, what should I do
What should I do? What should I do?
O' sorrowful heart, what should I do

This silver shadow with the cluster of stars in the sky
Like the fancy of a poet
Like the thoughts of a lover
But the sigh, who can understand
Who can know the state of my heart
O' sorrowful heart, what should I do)

He reminisces how Talat was his first voice in films much before the Shammi-Rafi partnership. "I had been listening to him since I was in college. And then he sang some wonderful numbers for me. Like in Laila Majnu -
'Aasmaan wale teri duniya se ji ghabra gaya'
(Lord of the skies,I am flustered by this world of yours)

Then my next movie Thokar was the only hit I had in those early years. And he sang this wonderful number for me - 'Aye gham-e-dil kya karun'. It was my biggest hit of the time."[17]

FAMILY CELEBRATIONS

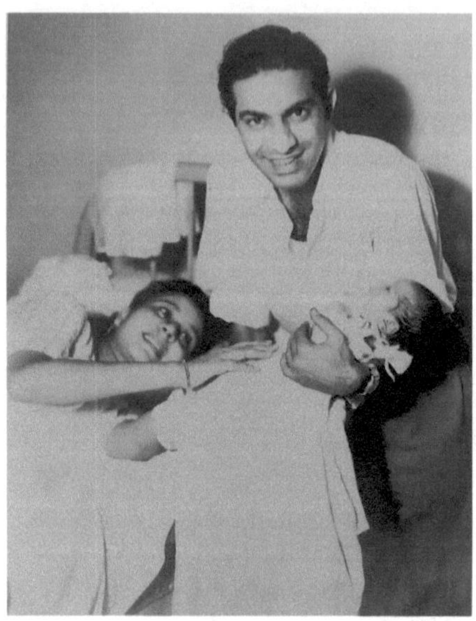

(Talat and wife Nasreen with new born son, Khalid)

This was also the year that lady luck at home shone brightest on him. At the age of twenty nine, Talat and his wife Nasreen were blessed with the start of a family. It was exciting news and film magazines had to be there to report the moment for his fans. Talat was racing up and down in nervous anticipation when he heard the louds yells of the newborn. At the Pratap Nursing Home in Nepean Sea Road, the new born and beaming parents were presented for a quick photo opp.

Reporter asks , "Was the voice like yours?"
Talat quipped in his subtle humour, "It was music to my ears but I shouldn't think anybody else would say so."

New mom Nasreen was beaming with pride after the exhausting labour. "Why not? He looks like his father and must have his voice!" They lovingly called him Guddu at home but he was named Khalid Mahmood by Talat's father who sent an emotional wire from Lucknow at the birth of his grandchild. Khalid's first cousin, my mother Romana Zaman, who was also born in the same year, recalls from cuttings of old film magazines which had announced the birth of Khalid.

(Talat with his son, Khalid and niece, Romana)

"It's rather sweet that Talat uncle's fans wanted to closely follow his personal life with such genuine love. He was at his absolute peak and one of the reigning stars of the film industry at the time. So obviously Khalid's birth was covered by Screen, Filmfare, Shama and many other media houses. It was done so touchingly with multiple congratulatory messages as if a member of their own family was born."

As a new father and for someone who loved children, Talat was happy to lend his voice to the recording of a childrens' play called 'Roopa Rani Ki Kahaani' (The Story of a King and Queen), inspired by the story of Cinderella. This was a 78 rpm disc which had the recording of the whole play with different voices including actors David and Lila Chitnis. Talat sings a few lines for the Prince:
'Mere man ki rani,tumne aane mein kyun der lagaayi
Tum meri zindagi bankar aayi, mere man ki rani'

(The queen of my heart, why did you come to me so late
You are my new lease of life, the queen of my heart)

Charity was always close to his heart and like many film artists who often stood up for a cause, Talat performed in aid of poor students.

A variety show was organised by the Bombay Youths' Circle at prestigious Naaz cinema where Talat sang his latest hits on stage with a LIVE orchestra conducted by composer Ghulam Mohammad. It was headlined as the number one playback singer lending his voice for a noble cause.

This was also the time when commercial advertising with radio jingles was gaining ground. Radio Ceylon was already popular with playing film songs and interviews of Indian film stars and it was the perfect platform for Indian brands to target the middle class consumer. According to the 'Strategic Biz Quiz' listed in the newspaper, Business Standard, the first wholly India- made commercial was for Dalda Vanaspati, the most popular edible oil brand of the time. And guess who sang the radio jingle for it? Talat Mahmood. If one really wants to write a headline about it, one can add that Talat's voice was riding the wave of the beginnings of India's advertisement industry too!

CLOSE FRIEND'S WEDDING

(Talat with close friend, singer Geeta Dutt)

New beginnings on the personal front also came knocking for Talat's friend Geeta Dutt. She got married to actor Guru Dutt after three years of being engaged to him. The wedding was nothing less than a music mehfil. Apart from most of the reigning stars of the day, the top singers were there to liven up the evening. They all decided to sing for the newly wed. Lata Mangeshkar, Hemant Kumar, Kishore Kumar chose to sing only those songs that featured the groom in his films. Talat Mahmood sang a new recording from an upcoming film in which Guru Dutt was making his acting debut apart from directing it.

'Mujhe dekho hasrat ki tasveer hoon main
Jo ban ban ke bigdi woh taqdeer hoon main'

(Look at me as a picture of inspiration
Rising up with each defeat, such is my destiny)

Written by Majrooh Sultanpuri, it was Talat's first song with music composer O.P.Nayyar. It was from the film Baaz (1953). which had a fascinating plot of pirates fighting the Portuguese occupation of the Malabar Coast in the 16th Century. It was perhaps inspired by the real history of the valour of the Malabar Pirates with Guru Dutt and Geeta Bali seen doing action sequences on the ship. Talat's song occurs in the film when Guru Dutt's character gets arrested on land. He sang it with just the right revolutionary fervour.

MAGIC OF 'SHAAM-E-GHAM'

Talat's next song for actor Dilip Kumar and composer Khayyam, is on the top list of hits of all three of their careers - 'Sham-e-gham ki qasam'(I swear by the sadness of this night). It's from the film Footpath (1953). It's also a personal favourite of mine not just for Talat's rendition but it's gentle cinematography with flowing curtains and flickering candles as Dilip Kumar sits through a painful night of waiting for his lover. The actor is crisply dressed in a suit and tie in anticipation of meeting his love interest, played by Meena Kumari. The mood was set for a candle night dinner which never happened. It's perhaps the most dignified song on being stood up on a date by someone. Who would've thought of such eloquence after hopelessly waiting through the night! It was #2 at the Binaca Geetmala top songs of the year.

'Shaam-e-gham ki qasam, aaj ghamgeen hain hum
Aa bhi ja, aa bhi jaa aaj mere sanam
Dil pareshan hai, raat veeran hai
Dekh ja kis tarah aaj tanha hain hum'

(I swear by the sadness of this night I am inconsolable today
Come over, come over my love
My heart is worried, the night is deserted
Come and see how lonely I am)

"Iss gaane ne dhoom macha di thi (The song was a sensational hit), even though it was an experiment for us. I decided not to keep any percussion instruments. There was no tabla, no dholak, no duff. It was a completely new kind of orchestration", explained Khayyam. "And his voice, so sweet and soulful. What style."[18]

Talat often spoke about how this song was his own personal favourite too. Right from the start, a gentle ambience of the night is created with a prelude of violins. On screen, the flowing curtains under a moonlit night are perfectly in sync with the symphony. The flickering flame of the candle struggles like a storm in the heart. Suddenly, a high pitched cry by Talat's gentle voice marks the start of the stanza. The helplessness of a man's waiting heart could not have sounded more urgent –

'Chayn kaisa jo pehlu mein tu hi nahin
Maar daale na dard-e-judai kahin
Rut haseen hai to kya, chaandni hai to kya
Chaandni zulm hai aur judaai sitam'

(How can there be any peace with your absence
This pain of separation can leave me dead
So what if there's a gentle breeze under the moonlight
It is but a painful reminder of your absence)

From Talat's exemplary list of hits, there was another song with which he mostly chose to start his LIVE concerts with. And it was especially because of the poetry in the song. In 1820 , the great English romantic poet Percy Bysshe Shelley wrote these lines in his poem 'To a Skylark' –

Our sweetest songs are those
That tell of saddest thoughts
Not to shed a tear
I know not how thy joy we ever should come near

Exactly 133 years later, our film lyricist and Urdu/Hindi poet Shailendra was inspired by this classic work of poetry to pen down these lines –

'Hain sabse madhur woh geet jinhen
Hum dard ke sur mein gaatey hain
Jab had se guzar jaati hai khushi
Aansoo bhi chalaktey aatey hain'

It's from the film Patita (1953), starring Dev Anand and Usha Kiran in the main lead. As many Golden Era films which boldly spoke on social consciousness, this one tried to open up the debate on accepting rape survivors in society instead of victim-shaming them. Talat captures the poignant moment when the protagonist Dev Anand sits with his on-screen wife played by Usha Kiran and tries to heal her from the crime committed upon her - the irreparable offence of rape, the resulting child birth, and the social boycott that can haunt a survivor all her life. The song is the soul of the film that Talat captures in his empathetic voice. Even when you hear this out of context of the film's plot, it is the most melodious motivational piece hitting the centre of your consciousness.

On the national level, the Government of India released the crime data report of 1953 which declared the lowest ever reported crime cases in the country but shockingly, rape was not acknowledged as a category of reported crime at that time. Undoubtedly, the film Patita was making a statement on the rehabilitation of rape survivors much, much ahead of its times.

Noticeably, the film's supporting actor Agha had his career's best remembered songs from Patita. Usually, the trend in the film industry is that the singer for the main lead does not sing for the supporting actor, especially someone who plays light-hearted comic roles. But Talat decided to keep the spirit of his close friendship with Agha. Talat reasoned that this was a good role for Agha to play and these two songs were perfect for him –

1. Andhe jahan ke andhe raaste (Dark paths of a blind world)
2. Tujhe apne paas bulati hai teri duniya (Your world calls for you)

From these two songs, the first one had a strong recall value. While growing up in the 1990s, I remember it being a favourite on the popular TV show called 'Chitrageet', which played old film songs from the Golden Era in a loop on the national channel Doordarshan. It used to be a great joy watching the show every week at 10pm to inevitably find some or the other song of Talat listed for playout.

1954

(Talat was a voracious reader of Urdu and English literature)

OBVIOUS CHOICE FOR MIRZA GHALIB

Who understands Urdu poetry best amongst the main male singers of 1954? Who can express the nuances of Urdu poetry with just the right pronunciation? And whose voice brings alive the ethos of Ghazals? All these would have been the elementary questions reasoned by the filmmaker and music director of the film Mirza Ghalib (1954). The one and only obvious answer for this was Talat Mahmood. The iconic film features some of the best duets of Talat with the diva Suraiyya whose success and market value surpassed many of her male co-stars. She was considered the first female superstar of Indian cinema, and what's more, she was a singing star with strong vocals and a wide octave range. As always, Suraiyya only sang for herself on-screen. In this film, she plays the role of Moti Begum (poet Mirza Ghalib's courtesan lover) and the poet is played by actor Bharat Bhushan.

Talat has extensively sung Ghalib throughout his career. Right from his early days in All India Radio as a young teenage star to his film career and his non-film Ghazal albums as well. The film won the National Film Award for Best Feature Film. The inaugural category in the National Film Awards for Best Music Direction was given to composer Ghulam Mohammed. It sealed the unbreakable bond of Talat's voice with Ghalib's poetry. It is impossible to serenade Ghalib without being reminded of Talat's voice.

Talat - 'Dil-e-nadan tujhe hua kya hai
Aakhir is dard ki davaa kya hai'
(What has happened to my naive heart
What is the medicine to cure my pain)

Suraiyya - 'Hum hain mushtaaq aur vo bezaar
Ya ilahi, ye majraa kya hai'
(I am interested but he seems indifferent
Lord, what kind of a love story is this)

Ghalib's poetry was highly Persianized. He believed that the language of poetry should not be the same as the spoken language of the common man. Yet, despite that the filmmaker went ahead with his original couplets for the film's songs. He did not try to modernise it to an easily understandable form of Hindustani language. The challenge for Talat was to make this hummable and relatable to the listeners. So when you hear Talat being at complete ease with Ghalib's verses, it becomes easier to listen. This is abundantly displayed in the next song –

'Phir mujhe deeda-e-tar yaad aaya
Dil jigar tishna-e-fariyaad aaya
Dam liya tha na qayaamat ne hanoz
Phir tera waqt-e-safar yaad aaya'

(Those tearful eyes came to my mind again
My heart and body is thirsty with all the crying
The calamity had barely paused for a moment
Our times spent together came to my mind)

"I was singing for such divergent heroes as Dilip Kumar, Raj Kapoor and Dev Anand, on one hand; and Bharat Bhushan, Shammi Kapoor and Ajit, on the other. I always insisted on a certain standard of poetry, no matter what the budget of the film. It was to give nuanced expression to such poetry that music directors sought me out. During 'Mirza Ghalib' by Sohrab Modi, it went without saying that I was going to sing for the film", expressed Talat.[19]

The film was the first popular cinematic/theatrical adaptation of Ghalib's life. It was written by yet another great writer, Sadat Hasan Manto. Talat was known to be deeply fond of Urdu poetry and literature to the extent of being known as a connoisseur of the language in the film industry. That was Talat for his professional work. On a personal note, he was equally interested in English literature as well. His niece Romana recalls, "My mother Laila (Talat's sister) and him were both voracious readers and used to exchange a lot of books from their personal collection. Apart from Urdu, he used to read a lot of English classics by Shakespeare, Daphne du Maurier, Rafael Sabatini, Charles Dickens, etc." Some of the books that Romana still has from Talat's collection with his signature dated early 1950s are King in Prussia (by Rafael Sabatini), The King's General (by Daphne du Maurrier) to name a few. These were bought in Bombay as they carry the stamp of the bookstore in Ritz Hotel at Churchgate Reclamation, right behind Eros Cinema.

BEGINNING OF FILM AWARDS

This year was abuzz with the start of a new phenomenon - the film awards. It was the debut year for the National Film Awards by the Govt of India. Awarded by the President of India in the Vigyan Bhavan in New Delhi, it started with only three award categories for films made across India in all languages. In a much more starry affair, the same year was also witness to the launch of the most formidable private film awards. The first ever Filmfare Awards by the Times Group were held at the Metro Cinema in Bombay. This also started with only three award categories but the evening was marked with multiple stage performances.

On the debut Filmfare awards night, Talat sang a medley of his songs. Starting with 'Zindagi dene wale sun' from the film Dil-e-Nadan. After a thunderous applause followed an insistent encore which made him sing 'Ae dil mujhe aisi jagah' from the film Arzoo. The other performers included actress Vijayanthimala and Nalini Jaywant, singer Mohammand Rafi, dancers Suryakumari and Satyavati. Hollywood star Gregory Peck was invited as the special guest for the ceremony. He was delayed by his flight from Colombo but attended the after party and mingled with many of our stars eagerly awaiting his presence. It was a night that perhaps for the first time marked the coming together of so many artists performing LIVE on stage. Even though premiere nights of films were well established with the red carpet walk of stars, but this was an amalgamation like no other.

Talking about premiere nights, Navketan's memorable film Taxi Driver's red carpet turned out to be a rare sight. Since the film was dedicated to the taxi drivers of Bombay, members of the drivers' union had been invited to park their cabs at the entrance of Minerva theatre before stepping in. It was a strong statement made by the filmmaker Chetan Anand for the film's protagonist played by actor Dev Anand. But the overwhelming response meant that the crowd management went a bit out of hand. Both Talat and Dev Anand arrived together and saw the massive crowd headed towards them. Dev held Talat's hand and said, "Aao Talat, yahan se nikalna padega (Come Talat, we will need to get away from here)."

The movie pulled the Navketan banner out of a financial crisis and became the third highest grossing movie of the year. Talat sang only one song for the entire album but it became the most famous song which defined the plight of the protagonist. With Dev Anand sitting alone on the moonlit Juhu beach watching the waves crash like the sound of his broken heart who just lost his lover, played by co-star Kalpana Kartik.

'Jaayen to jaayen kahaan
Samjhe ga kaun yahaan
Dard bhari dil ki zubaan'

(Where does one go
Who is there to understand
This heart filled with anguish)

In his signature style, Talat brings out the abject grief of the film's character with subtle sighs and gasps in tune with the melancholic melody of SD Burman's composition. The song had two versions in the film. One sung by Lata Mangeshkar and the other sung by Talat. The male version of the song ranked #1 in the Binaca Geetmala show. In those days, the Filmfare Awards did not carry the category of Best Singer but SD Burman won the Best Music Director award for Talat's version of the song. The winning song was performed LIVE on stage for the Filmfare Awards night next year (1955) with SD Burman conducting his full orchestra and Talat singing to his magical baton.

ACTOR WITH CHARM AND ROMANCE

(Still from the film 'Dak Babu'. Talat stars with actress Nadira)

Talat's calendar was getting busier by the year. With 65 film songs recorded this year, acting also became a regular part of his schedule. He had two movie releases in 1954 as the main lead - 'Dak Babu' and 'Waris'. If the soft, velvety caress was his signature style as a singer, romantic charm became his style as an actor. In Dak Babu (1954), he was cast opposite actresses Nadira and Kuldeep Kaur. There is very little known about the film and I still haven't been able to find a copy of it. But the film's songs are easily available today. The solo song by Talat created magic and became one of music composer Dhaniram's better remembered songs of his short career.

'Ghir ghir aaye bidarwa kare
Rang bhare ras bhare pyare pyare
Chalee nashe mein choor hawayen
Mastee se bharpur hawayen
Machal machal kar bijli chamke
Do naina matware'

(Covered by the dark clouds
Full of rainbow colours and sweet rains
Winds drunk on joy begin to blow
Winds of abandon
Exciting flashes of lightning

Enthralling the eyes)

This song has also been a favourite with Kathak dancers on my Jashn-e- Talat platform today. That's because it's a classical composition. Prominent dancers like Vidhal Lal, Raghav and Mandala Bhatt recreated the choreography of this song that allowed them the space for footwork and twirls on stage. Through the book, my frequent recollections of Jashn-e- Talat is also to help you understand how some of Talat's songs got a chance to be seen in a new light with today's contemporary performers and were watched by a young audience.

The second film that Talat acted in in 1954 was Waris. It was much awaited since it brought together two of the biggest singing stars of the time in a romantic role - Talat Mahmood and Suraiya. After the success of their duets in Mirza Ghalib, it was time to see them act together on screen. Their first scene together had cinema-goers on the front row flipping their coins at the big screen. That scene was soon by the sound of the chugging train which used to be a rhythm in music, much in-vogue those days. Talat can be seen sitting by the window in the train, looking out and feeling the cool breeze. His mesmerising face burst into his charming smile with the peppy notes of the song. Composer Anil Biswas exploits the best of Talat's lilt in his voice in this happy number.

'Rahi matwale,
Tu chhed ek baar, man ka sitaar
Jaane kab chori-chori aayi hai bahaar
Chhed man ka sitaar'

(O' excited traveller
Tug at my heartstrings
Could this mean the coming of spring
Tug at my heartstrings)

While the entire album has been sung mostly by Talat and Suraiya, this film interestingly doesn't have any sad number by Talat, which many fans considered to be his core competency. They're all happy, optimistic songs. This duet is particularly cute where Talat - the actor, has shed his hesitancy and shyness on camera to emote romance on screen.
Suraiya - 'Ghar tera apna ghar laage

Jaye kahaan man iske aage, jaye kahaan
Mili man ki dagar se teri gali'
(Your house feels like my home
Where do I go beyond this
This is where our hearts meet)

Talat - 'Jaise musafir paaye watan mein
Chain hai waisa tere nayan mein'
(Just as a wanderer finds his destination
There is so much peace in your eyes)

(Talat and Suraiya in the film 'Waris')

Talat's screen presence is visibly more relaxed and he manages to show a better range of emotions in this film. 'Waris' was a social family drama of a rich man's son who rejects the luxuries of life to marry his innocent lady love living alone and homeless in a big city, followed by a case of mistaken identity after the leading man signs up for World War II and is reported dead. Working with director Nitin Bose added to the repertoire of Talat's acting career. Under his able hands, Talat flourished as an actor in Waris. Bose had also started his career in Calcutta from New Theatres, just like Talat. Bose later went on to win the prestigious Dada Saheb Phalke award.

While filmmakers and directors were becoming more serious about Talat as an actor, he himself was very clear in his head that he was not here to compete with Dilip Kumar or Ashok Kumar. Soft, romantic films were appreciated in those days and a singing hero like him fit the bill just right.

DISCOVERING LATA'S YOUNGER VERSION

Talat was a giving person and his generosity reflected in how he promoted new talent apart from just helping colleagues. He spotted a young student of the JJ School of Art while she was singing at her college function. It was Suman Kalyanpur. He was impressed by her strong vocals and control in pitch. He introduced her to a recording company and she was immediately offered her debut duet with Talat for the film Darwaza (1954).

'Ek dil do hain talabgar, badi mushkil hai
Kashmakash mein hai mera pyar, badi mushkil hai'

(A single love summoned by two, it is troublesome
The dilemma of my love, it is troublesome)

The industry was amazed to hear a voice which sounded so similar to Lata Mangeshkar. Most listeners thought it was Lata's duet with Talat. The young Suman Kalyanpur was hardly trained in music nor interested in playback singing as a career. It was a hobby for her. But soon enough, offers started to pour in and she managed to make a mark despite the dominance of the Golden Era legends.

Moving away from romance, there is an unlikely duet that Talat sang with Asha Bhosle this year. It was for the film Boot Polish (1954) under the Raj Kapoor banner. It was about two street children orphaned by fate and struggling to earn a living by polishing the boots of pedestrians. A poignant and heart breaking tale of ruthless street life. Talat's song features celebrated lyricist Shailendra playing the role of one of the beggars while Asha Bhosle sings for child actor Baby Naaz. The song is about a place of love and comfort that the street urchins dream of. It's a strange mix of hopefulness, saddened by the difficulty of life and yet a gentle conversation with a child. Both singers aced it with Shankar Jaikishan's music and Shailendra's lyrics.

Talat - 'Chali kaun se desh Gujariya tu saj dhaj ke'
(Where do you want to go Like a dancer, all dressed up)

Asha - 'Jaun piya ke desh O' rasiya main saj dhaj ke'

(To where I find my love, to my suitor, all dressed up)

Talat's following continued to soar and the public's interest in his non-film Ghazals remained as strong. He was very loyal to the cause of independent Ghazals away from the packaging and presentation in films. Music composer Khayyam worked with him for two Ghazals written by poet Jan Nisar Akhtar. The insatiable appetite for Talat's voice made this a top selling album in 78rpm. They're both of similar mood and rhythm with a strong use of the violin. Even today, you will find a huge number of online hits for these two Ghazals.
SIDE A - 'Kaun kehta hai tujhe maine bhula rakha hai'
(Who says that I have forgotten you)
SIDE B - 'Tujhme jo baat hai gulshan ke nazaaron mein nahin' (The sight of rose gardens don't match your beauty)

When one looks at Talat's career in hindsight, his passion for the Ghazals kept him afloat during the sunset years of his film career. His popularity had a wider audience beyond the boundaries of Bollywood and often, during his LIVE concerts, the demand for singing his non-film ghazals would be at par with his film songs.

1955

(Talat with actress Nadira for the cover shoot of a popular magazine)

SPECIAL SHOOT FOR A COVER ISSUE

The cover issue of a top film magazine splashed pictures of Talat and actress Nadira spending a sunny day on Juhu beach. Talat was dressed in a royal blue suit with a loose necktie and the coat casually thrown over his shoulder. Nadira was looking every bit the diva, sitting on the rocks with Talat, wearing a chiffon blouse and trousers. The readers were being given an exclusive sneak peek into the on-screen pairing of the two actors for their upcoming film 'Raftaar'. Nadira speaks about her leading man in the film, calling him an exceptional co-star, "I love working with Talat. He is one of the few real gentlemen we have in the industry. Talat is courteous, considerate, patient and co- operative." [20]

While the film was a mish-mash of an emotional family drama which didn't do well, the critics were kind to Talat's on-screen presence. His performance was visibly noteworthy with the maturity required for playing the role of the family's reformed younger brother and a lover in the main lead. Talat took these professional reviews seriously, as much as he did his fan mail. With a global following, he would get letters from East Africa, Singapore, Middle East, Malaysia, etc. He was very particular about reading each letter. Once they saw him on-screen, many expressed their fear had he chosen to leave playback singing. But that was never Talat's plan. "I never do more than one or two films at a time", he would need to keep reiterating. In his replies to their letters, many of the fans had to be gently pacified with an assurance that he would never give up singing. "They're my only contact with the real world", he would often say. As he was beginning to enjoy the process of shooting, he also noticed how differently the film sets in Bombay functioned from Calcutta. "Unlike the more artistic city of Calcutta where movies were made at a slow pace, Bombay was commercial. Life was hectic. Everyone was in his own world and was, of course, very professional."[21]

PERSONAL LOSS , FATHER'S LEGACY

This was also the year when his favourite sister, his comrade in crisis, Laila moved closer to him in Pune. Her husband, Iftekhar, was a senior Civil Defence Officer in the Indian Army. He was much loved by Talat as a close friend, cousin and now, brother-in-law. Pune is a few hours away by road from Bombay and Talat would often drive down to meet them. His visits always had to be kept a secret but once, the word got out and his car got stuck in a sea of people. It took him almost an hour getting past many hysterical fans to finally enjoy a peaceful lunch with Laila.

(Talat sings with his younger sister Laila on stage)

During one of these trips, Talat performed at the heritage Poona Club for an Army function. Laila was popular amongst her friends within the army circle for singing well. So the audience requested Talat to call his sister up on stage to sing along with him. Talat called her out, saying "Aap meherbani se besuri mat ho jayega kahin." (I request you to please don't go off key). The crowd was in splits as he teased his younger sister but they were soon cheering and clapping for them when they sang the duet 'Seene mein sulagte hain armaan'.

The same year, the siblings got news that their father, Manzoor, was suffering from a prolonged illness. In his final years, the father and son managed to mend hearts after their earlier differences which had led Talat to leave home in pursuit of his music career. It was a rush of memories of what both men had been through together. It was a moment for Talat to reflect and understand what made Manzoor the father that he was.

(Talat's father, Manzoor Mahmood, served in the India Medical Mission)

After all, Manzoor was protective towards his son and was used to taking decisions in the right interest of the family over anything else. He was a man of the world who had seen the worst of human suffering in his bachelor days, when he served as a member of the Indian Medical Mission to Ottoman Turkey in 1912-1913. The Mission took an arduous month-long journey to reach the war-ravaged Ottoman Turkey, travelling by ship from the Arabian sea to the Mediterranean Sea. Manzoor had a melodious and strong voice with a great throw (unlike Talat's soft vibrato) who kept the mission entertained and motivated with his singing during their difficult times there. The onslaught on the Ottoman Empire during the Balkan War 1, resulted in huge casualties. The Ottomans reported as many as 125,000 dead. The 25 members of Indian Medical Mission including Manzoor set an example of humanitarianism in serving the wounded Ottoman soldiers in the peak of the long and difficult winter that year. He also met the revolutionary leader Mustafa Kemal Ataturk who was the Commander of the Ottoman forces at that time.

This entire experience had left an impact on Manzoor which instilled in him the fighting spirit to protest and participate against the British in India's freedom movement. The British were aware that the pro-Turkish stand taken by the Indian Muslim intelligentsia was also a way of giving vent to their dissatisfaction against the British Rule in India. It drew them closer to the independence movement under the Congress fold and Manzoor Mahmood was one of them. He would often be asked to sing motivational songs during public meetings. He would sing songs by the poet Alaama Iqbal like Qaumi Tarana or the Tarana-e-Hind (better known as Saare Jahaan Se Achcha Hindustan Hamara). At one such meeting of the independence movement, Iqbal was also present. It was a huge gathering where the lights suddenly went off and the microphone stopped functioning. But Manzoor sang on, nevertheless. His sharp voice reached right up to the last person, as if an echo in the mountains. The crowd was so moved by his rendition that they picked him up on their shoulders and celebrated his presence.

But in case of Talat's strong artistic leaning, Manzoor realized that it came less from him and more from his beloved sister, Mahlaqa Begum. She was a firebrand feminist who outraged many people with her liberal views. But she was also strikingly beautiful and her presence attracted much attention. Sometimes, it was unwarranted attention which became problematic. Like in the case of Nawab Hamid Ali Khan of Rampur. He helped establish Rampur as the seat of cultural renaissance after the fall of Awadh. But he was also known as a notorious womaniser interested in every beautiful woman in town. Mahlaqa Begum was the wife of the Nawab's Treasurer (Safdar Ali Kidvai) while her brother Manzoor had become the Nawab's aide-de-camp (ADC) after his return from Istanbul. Once the Nawab heard about the beauty of Mahlaqa, he asked his Treasurer to send his wife to the palace to 'meet up' with his other begums (wives). The Treasurer obviously understood what this meant and snapped back at the Nawab, "There is no need for my wife to visit your palace." The Nawab was outraged at such defiance. This caused the Treasurer, his wife Mahlaqa and her brother Manzoor to leave Rampur and settle down in Lucknow. They also left behind all the wealth and property which had been gifted to them by the Nawab. The family took a principled stand and started afresh in Lucknow.

It was with this baggage of the past that Manzoor had made Talat promise that he would never perform in Rampur. Talat respected this and kept the promise all his life. The next Nawab of Rampur, Raza Ali Khan would often invite Talat to his lavish and sprawling Khas Bagh palace to sing, but Talat never went. The Nawab also casually assured Talat that all his ancestral wealth left behind in Rampur will be settled and handed back but Talat chose not to ever reopen a chapter that had been firmly shut by his father.

When Manzoor passed away in 1955, Talat and his five siblings came together and met at their father's home in the Aminabad locality after years. Manzoor's belongings and his store of electric curios and antiques had to be sold off and divided amongst the siblings. Running on thin time, a lot of it was hurriedly done. The store was full of antique lamps, crystal decanter sets for liquor, English dinner sets of the Royal Tudor ware, Czechoslovakian sweet bowls with gold paint, etc. Some of these pieces Talat carried back home to Bombay. His most prized possession from his father's store was an artisanal hand blown glass lamp from Italy, in the shape of a tree where every flower and bird lit up from inside. This was often featured in film magazine shoots of Talat that were done at home.

When Manzoor was buried in the family burial ground in the city of Amethi (134 kms from Lucknow), it was also the time of reckoning for Talat to take on another role from his father. He was made the titular head or the 'Sajjada Nashin' of a dargah (shrine) in Amethi dedicated to the Muslim saint Makhdoom Bahaul Haq. This was the position of a spiritual head that Talat inherited as caretaker of the shrine where devotees come and pray at the tomb of the saint to put forth a prayer or a plea to Allah. Talat's family were the direct descendants of saint Makhdoom Bahaul Haq who was extremely revered by the Mughal Emperor Akbar.

"It was a very sad moment. After Manzoor uncle's death, Talat bhai (brother) took his youngest sister and mother to Bombay to help them settle there. Our whole courtyard and the lane ahead got filled up by people to catch a glimpse of him. My family was helping them with their luggage and was there to see them off", recalls their neighbour Akbar Khan.

SORROW DURING 'DEVDAS'

After Talat returned to Bombay, he was in a sentimental frame of mind. But the world of showbiz doesn't wait. Grieving or not, recording slots were piling up and he didn't want to delay them any further. He locked himself up in a room alone to sing the most evocative and tragic song he ever performed in his career. The song was raw grief. It demanded his naked voice to do the talking with almost no background music. Composer S.D. Burman was clear in his mind that only Talat's voice could do justice to the torment of Devdas!

In the minds of film lovers, the voice of Devdas was epitomised by Talat's idol, the iconic K.L.Saigal. His film Devdas had released in 1936 with a box office record which made him a household rage. The film was based on author Sharat Chandra Chattopadhyay's novella with the same name. In 1955, filmmaker Bimal Roy wanted to remake this film with the Tragedy King, actor Dilip Kumar. It was a challenging proposition. A remake of a blockbuster after barely 20 years was no mean task. But somehow, Bimal Roy's Devdas also became an equal classic and did fairly well at the box office too.

The signature song from this film was 'Mitwa'. It features a lonely Dilip Kumar sitting by the river under the mango orchards. An extreme close up of his face on the big screen tells the haunting tale of a man who thinks he has lost everything in life. In sync with the silence of his swelled up eyes is the faint voice of Talat.

'Mitwaaa, laagi re yeh kaisi anbujh aag
Mitwa, Mitwa Mitwa nahin aaye
Laagi re yeh kaisi…'

(O' my beloved, the burning of this inextinguishable fire of passion
O' my beloved, you haven't come
The burning of this...)

Composer S.D. Burman used minimal instruments to highlight the mood of the song. Perhaps just the sitar and sarangi. Lyricist Sahir Ludhianvi also decided to keep the song understated. Unlike his other songs in which he used heavy poetry and messaging, Mitwa had disjointed and repetitive words, almost reduced to just gasps of breath and sobbing. Along with Burman and Ludhinavi's brilliance, the song largely rested on Talat's bare voice to do the magic.

"The greatest compliment I was ever paid was that people thought it was Dilip sa'ab himself singing", recalled Talat while speaking to his sister, Laila, who was a huge fan of the actor, whom she called Yusuf bhai (his real name) and was friends with his sisters. The other Talat solo in the film, 'Kisko khabar thi', saw Talat render Dilip's drunken lament on screen so well, that it is impossible to separate the actor from his playback voice.

ANOTHER 'TASVEER' HIT

This year, Talat was given another popular song with the word 'tasveer'. It was a word which had given him two hits in the past. The song from the film 'Baradari' (1955) became a big hit too. It is inevitably found in all of Talat's top 10 playlists. It's called 'Tasveer banata hoon'. Featured on character actor Chandrashekhar, it is once again a lovelorn song where the man is unable to find the girl he loves. So he sings -

'Tasveer banaata hoon, tasveer nahin banti,
Ek khwaab sa dekha hai, taabeer nahin banti'

(I wish to make a portrait but I'm unable to paint it
I've seen it in a dream but I'm unable to interpret it)

It's a melancholic song in the film but it took on an amusing role during my Jashn-e-Talat stage shows. Now, for an artist it can be a nightmare if you are unable to complete a portrait that you are working on. But most of the portrait artists who came for my show to paint Talat's portrait were happy to paint it in the echo of this song. This added a visual element to the concerts where professional portrait artists would paint Talat's mug shots LIVE on stage as the evening progressed.

Let's get you another song from 1955 which became popular with the millennials at Jashn-e-Talat. This is from the film Yasmeen (1955). Believe it or not, today's dancers decided to do a Bollywood Salsa and Bachata on Talat's foot tapping number.

'Bechain nazar betaab jigar
Yeh dil hai kisi ka deewaana hai deewaana
Kab shaam ho aur woh shammaa jale
Kab udh kar pahunche parvaana hay parvaana'

(My restless eyes, eager soul
My heart is crazy after someone
I wait for the evening lamp to light up
As the moth rushes towards it like a lover)

The song was composed by C.Ramchandra and written by poet Jan Nisar Akhtar, the latter's first song in films. The film's plot is based in 18th century Persia, so the song features a heavy use of string and percussion instruments sounding similar to the *tambour* and *tombak*. The rhythm and beats of the song make it one of his most popular numbers.

SWAMI VIVEKANAND'S ICONIC BHAJAN

Talat recorded a total of 51 film songs this year. This includes a timeless bhajan which is believed to have been originally sung by Swami Vivekandanda for his Guru, Ramakrishna Paramahansa. Swami Vivekananda was an iconic Hindu monk, philosopher, and religious teacher who played the most pivotal role in introducing Vedanta and Yoga to the Western world. He is fondly called the Father of modern Indian nationalism.

The film Swami Vivekananda (1955) is a biopic on his life. It is believed that when he met his guru Ramakrishna for the first time, he was asked to sing. He sang a bhajan (spiritual song). One of the most popular versions of this Bhajan can be heard in Talat's voice.

'Man chalo nij niketan mein ae ae
Pardes hai jag, pardesi hai tu
Bhoolaa kyun apnaapan re ae ae
Man chalo nij niketan mein ae'

(O' heart, let's return to the real abode
Here in this foreign land, in a stranger's guise
Why wander aimlessly
O' heart, let's return to the real abode)

The music for this film was composed by R.C. Boral. He used the soft persuasiveness in Talat's voice to highlight the moment where a young Vivekananda had had a profound effect on Ramakrishna. The wisdom and vulnerability in the bhajan regarding the truth of life is reflected in Talat's vibrato. The words of the song worked as a catalyst to awaken within the state for a person who is already in a very high spiritual station.

His non-film Ghazals also continued without a pause and steadily built up to almost 40% of his singing career. But surprisingly, his approach to Ghazals was not traditionalist. While he was very vehement about not diluting the original structure and essence of Urdu poetry in Ghazals, he was happy to experiment with the form of music. This year, he composed the music for one Ghazal. The 78rpm record proudly reads 'Singer and Composer - Talat Mahmood'. It had two versions. One in 1955 and the second in the late 1960s. The second version opens with a prelude on the Hawaiian guitar played by Van Shipley. The orchestra of violins play along with his voice with an almost inaudible percussion. It shows Talat's open mindedness as an artist. For someone who grew up in the company of an extremely traditional form of Ghazal, this was a leap of faith in this genre of music.

'Tum ne ye kya sitam kiya Zabt se kaam le liya
Tark-e-vafã ke baad bhi Mera salam le liya'
(How hurtful are your actions How you seized the moment Amidst our arguments of loyalty You accepted my advances)

Written by Shakeel Badayuni, the Ghazal is melodious and hummable. Guitarist Van Shipley was a music legend in his own right. He was Talat's friend from his Lucknow days and became an important companion in his career .

1956

(Talat has a good laugh with the Maasai tribe in East Africa)

THE ORIGINAL WORLD TOUR

This was a time when most of East Africa was under British rule and several enterprising Indians moved to Tanzania, Kenya, Uganda, etc for better opportunities. There's a misconception that all Indians who were working in Africa were sent as migrant labourers. A big part of the Indians working there were actually a class of rich entrepreneurs playing an important role in the construction, agricultural and industrial sector, local media business and money-lending firms. And thus, involved in building the economy of these countries. But working in a country away from home created a vacuum of longing for the motherland, but frequent trips to India were not possible. This vacuum was filled by films! Indian cinema, particularly Hindi films from Bombay were an important connection to the language, traditions, festivities and culture back home. It played an integral role in the social lives of Indians who were flourishing in East African countries. With their deep pockets, they helped set up cinema halls and distribution of Hindi films. The Globe Cinema, Odeon and the Shan Cinema were part of uptown Indian movie goers every weekend in Nairobi where the Indian community connected over films that set the trends for the latest fashion and music in their lives. Uganda's capital city Kampala was practically owned by local Indians who made sure to remain connected to their value system, language and tradition. Not surprisingly, they turned to Hindi films to teach them their language and traditions. Cinema-going on the weekends always led to massive traffic jams there. In Zanzibar, there was an active trans-local film marketing network established between Western India and the East African coast which ensured a steady flow of the latest Hindi films to be screened at the popular Empire Cinema and the Sultana Cinema in the island city.

The popularity and demand of Indian cinema in the East African nations was at its peak from the 1950's to 1960s. The films were not just being watched by the rich Indians settled there but also the East Africans, with the dialogues dubbed in Swahili. Despite the presence of the Hollywood imports, Hindi films appealed to the local crowd much more for their melodramatic form, which reaffirmed the importance of family and morality over individuality.

In the context of all this, it will be easier to understand Talat's first ever music world tour. Adventurous as ever, he was the first Indian playback singer from India to kick start a multi-nation world tour. As he made the debut for this, he helped start the trend of concert tours for singers from the Hindi film industry in Bombay. This was a multi-nation tour across the East African nations. The original bookings for this tour were only for six shows. But the response and sales of these concerts was so overwhelming that Talat ended up performing in about 30 concerts.

(Debut team for first ever world tour. Talat (left) arrives for his East Africa tour with Enoch Daniels, C.H. Atma and Van Shipley)

But who was Talat's team for this tour? It was a carefully curated group of talent that Talat put together and they remained with him for most of his tours in the coming decade. Musician and guitarist Van Shipley's claim to fame are the films that he did for Raj Kapoor. The man with the golden touch on the strings who played for Raj Kapoor in the film Barsaat (1949). But Van and Talat's association did not start from films. It goes back to their early Lucknow days when both were close friends and struggling to make a start in music. While Van was studying in university, Talat had already made a name for himself in the All India Radio station of Lucknow in the early 1940s. He took Van to the radio and introduced him to professional recordings where Van could use his music training in classical music to good benefit. Soon both of them had their own journey into films but had promised to stick together whenever one needed the other. Taking Van on board for the world tour opened up new vistas for both their careers.

The second musician that Talat selected on Van's recommendation was the accordion player Enoch Daniels who went on to become an icon in background music in films later. The success of the East Africa tour with Talat helped put the spotlight on Enoch's talent to the extent that Columbia Records signed him up as solo artiste the next year! Talat also took along fellow Ghazal singer C.H.Atma for the tour. His style was similar to K L Saigal and was known for his soulful non-film hit 'Pritam aan milo' (Come and meet me, my love). "Talat ji was extremely busy those days, since he had taken up acting assignments as well. But he was the star of the group and the main crowd puller, he had to be rushed in with a flight from Bombay. The rest of us had more time at hand, so the organiser put us on a ship from Bombay to Mombasa, the main port of Kenya. It took us 7-8 days to reach", recalled Daniels when I met him at his home in Pune.

"There was so much demand for our music. The hall was always packed, waiting for us. And the people knew all of Talat ji's latest hits. I also realised how humble he was. Very well trained and ever ready for rehearsals. He never skipped or avoided these crucial rehearsals. And people found it very easy to approach him", added Daniels.

Since it was the first ever tour, they carried a maximum of just six to seven musicians and did not take any female artist with them. It was an all guys team and together, they experienced mass hysteria in a far away land where people knew their songs and films. There were traffic jams where they performed. Most of their shows happened at the popular cinema halls which I had mentioned earlier, including Shan and Sultana. The tour organiser Nandi Duggal was making his debut as well. Struggling to make ends meet in Bombay with two jobs as assistant cameraman and as taxi driver, Talat came to his life as the golden goose. "There was a time when I didn't know where my next meal would come from."

"I've never met anyone so incredible. Talat sa'ab was such a great and stately personality. I was a novice, a young man struggling in the industry. I had organised some concerts within India but I had this dream to try out a world tour. My brother-in-law used to work at the HMV recording studio. So he suggested that I meet Talat when he comes to the studio. I met him and that was it. Talat agreed. It meant no problems, no hiccups. When we decided for East Africa, some big film distributors from there came to Bombay and met Talat, enquiring about his fees for the shows. They wanted to poach him, saying that members of our tour are too young and unknown but as the star attraction, Talat should partner with bigger brands. But Talat was so decent. He declined their offer and sent them straight to me if they wanted to enquire more about his fees. I was so touched about this faith he placed in me."

When Talat landed in East Africa, he was originally booked for only six shows but he ended up doing about 30 shows across three countries because of public demand. It became very hectic but no one had reason to complain. Ticket sales were not an issue. As the organisers announced and lined up more nights, the shows ran to full capacity. Even though this tour was mid- career for Talat, he had more than enough hits to sing in multiple shows. This included his film songs as well as his non-film Ghazals. The tour took Duggal about ten months to fully organise before they set sail, tying up with sponsors, handling passports and coordinating with local partners.

"Everyone was starry-eyed about Talat but he was very unassuming and practical. It was an experience to watch him. We did an average of 3-4 shows in a week. Once the curtains failed on stage. So he just went and pulled the curtains himself! This happened at one of our shows in Dar-Es- Salaam", recalls the delighted nonagenarian, Duggal. I could sense the excitement in his voice when he was asked to recollect those memories.

The long tour also gave them time to experience some exotic adventures in East Africa. Wildlife safari in 1956 was a completely new concept for tourists from India. It was a global tourism trend barely 50 years in existence but mostly catered to visits by the British Monarchy, American politicians and Hollywood stars. It was set up by the British to form an important part of their tourism sector. For many people throughout the world, an African safari was synonymous with the unattainable leisure activities meant only for the ultra-rich. Popular interest in safari excursions were largely driven by celebrity visits and Talat was an important member of that global celebrityhood. It took another 20 years for safari tourism to be introduced in India in the 1970s. While touring East Africa, Talat and his team were in for a very original experience in Kenya. They lived in mud houses with thatched roofs and went into the jungle with their cameras. They also met with the friendly Masai Mara tribe with one of the tribesmen choosing to share his walking stick with Talat.

"Our guide told us to be absolutely silent when the elephants are nearby because if they heard us or smelt us by the direction of wind, they could come charging directly at us", chuckled Talat. He said unlike the Indian elephants, the African ones are bigger in size and tend to be more ferocious.

After wrapping up their shows in Kenya and Uganda, the team got on to the train headed to Dar-es-Salam (Tanzania). But before reaching their final destination, the train stopped over at the Mwanza station, a beautiful port city on the shore of Lake Victoria. It was around 12 noon and 30 to 40 people entered Talat's compartment. Duggal recalls the entire incident with much excitement as he speaks to me. It happened more than 65 years ago but it's crystal clear in his mind. "Those people knew we were headed to Dar-es-Salam for our next show, they knew our train and our compartment number, and came with the intention of stopping us from going ahead. It took me a while to realize that they meant no harm. All that they wanted was a show to happen in their town as well. They were such huge fans of Talat and were very upset as to why our itinerary didn't include Mwanza ", gushes Duggal.

Talat was touched and decided to oblige. They were treated to lunch and soon after Duggal got down to ground work. This impromptu performance was to happen the same night in their local cinema hall. When he went to inspect the place, he was surprised to see about 100 men, women and children already there, cleaning up, setting the stage and putting up curtains. There was a long list of things to add - lights, microphone, audio system, extra chairs, etc. Duggal had no idea how they would manage all this in a matter of a few hours! "I was in tears because I had never seen such love for any artist. And Talat was so sweet, he decided to waive off his fees for this show", adds Duggal.

The cinema hall had 400 seats despite which several extra chairs needed to be added. Many people just carried chairs from their home. The team performed by 8pm and not surprisingly, the place was packed. After a night's rest and a heavy breakfast, Talat and his team were sent off in luxury cars to drop them all in Dar-es-Salam.

Duggal reiterates, "I must add that I've done about 1000 tours across 35 countries with different singers including Kishore Kumar, Lata Mangeshkar, etc. But I have never ever seen this kind of love and hysteria that Talat would get. They loved his voice, they loved his face. He was such a charming star."

(Talat celebrated his birthday in the middle of his tour in Dar-es-Salaam, Tanzania)

The tour took a long time away from home as well as the recording studio. Talat ended up celebrating his birthday in Dar-e-Salam with all his fans and followers. Daniels explains, "After 30 shows, Talat rushed back because of his shooting and recording commitments." After Talat's return to Bombay, his concert tour was the talk of the town. Colleagues in the industry heard about their experience and craved to go themselves. For Nandi Duggal, receiving Talat's support was the biggest boost to the start of his new career as a tour organizer for Indian playback singers. This debut tour tapped a new and hungry international market.

PERFORMING FOR ZHOU ENLAI

Talat sealed the year on yet another high with a performance for the visiting Chinese Premier Chou En Lai in December 1956. It was the peak of Sino- Indian friendship when Prime Minister Pt. Nehru tried to instil good faith in the strong partnership of the two giant countries of Asia. He was received on the streets with slogans of 'Chou En Lai ki jai', 'Hindi Chini bhai bhai' (Hail Chou En Lai, Indians and Chinese are brothers). All this bonhomie was before the Dalai Lama's escape to India offering him shelter in exile and the deceitful attack by China in the 1962 war. This was a joyous trip where a lot of cultural shows were put up for the visiting Premier. The Hindi film industry in Bombay led from the front in arranging a special night of music for him. Talat Mahmood and Geeta Dutt were the star performers of the night along with actress Waheeda Rehman, dancer Sitara Devi.

Talat realized that unlike East Africa, Hindi films had a limited reach in China. A lot of the duets that he was performing with Geeta Dutt on stage were not familiar with the Chinese Premier. But suddenly Chou En Lai surprised everyone when he had a special request for Raj Kapoor's song 'Awaara hoon' (I'm a vagabond). It was the only Hindi song he knew. Both Geeta and Talat didn't know the complete song since Mukesh had sung the original soundtrack. And it wasn't part of the orchestra's rehearsal either. But everyone decided to improvise on the spot. Talat knew the opening lines and the hook of the song. He sang the hook with one of his own songs which went something like that,

"Main dil hoon ek armaan bhara. .. Awaara hoon"

That was enough for Zhou Enlai to bob his head and enjoy the performance.

UNFORGETTABLE DUETS

Assessing his career in this adventurous year, it is clear that Talat had recorded 20 percent fewer songs compared to the previous years. But he still gave some memorable duets which were chart toppers. Musician Madan Mohan took two of his favourite singers , Talat and Lata for a soft, romantic duet in the film Pocket Maar (1956) starring Dev Anand and Geeta Bali -

Lata - 'Ye nayi nayi preet hai, tu hi to mera meet hai
Naa jaane koi saajna, ye teri meri daastaan'
(This is our new love, you are my only companion
No one else should know, this is our love story)

Talat - 'Samaa hai ye pyaar kaa, naye iqraar ka
Na ho koi jahaan, bana lein wahi aashiyan'
(This is our moment of love, of new promises
Away from the prying eyes, let's build our love nest)

In another film, Shammi Kapoor was in his element of being the vivacious and impish lover in a romantic comedy with Meena Kumari in the film Mem Sahib (1956). Once again, it was Madan Mohan's music with a very peppy Talat-Asha Bhosle duet –

Talat - 'Kehata hai dil tum ho mere liye, mere liye, jii mere liye'
(My heart says, you are for me, just for me)

Asha - 'Haan dilruba hum hain tere liye, tere liye, jii tere liye'
(Yes sweetheart, I am for you, just for you)

Another melodious hit with Asha Bhosle worth mentioning is from the film Insaaf (1956) with lead actors Nalini Jaywant and Ajit . It's the sweetest, softest romantic number composed by music director Chitragupt.

Talat - 'Do dil dhadak rahe hain, aur aawaaz ek hai'
(It's the beating of two hearts, in sync with a single rhythm)

Asha - 'Naghme juda juda hain, magar saaz ek hai'
(The music is different, but the melody is the same)

(Talat Mahmood with Asha Bhosle)

These were the early struggling years (1951-59) for Asha Bhosle when she was trying to establish herself away from the shadow of her sister, Lata Mangeshkar. Talat stood by her as a pillar of support and was always happy to encourage more voices to record with. They had about 50 duets together in this brief period.

BLENDING TO SOUTHERN STARS

In his large repertoire of hits, Talat added all the big stars to his playback list. This was not just restricted to Hindi films. He sang two songs for two of the biggest stars from South Indian cinema as well. They were the superstars Gemini Ganeshan and M.G.R. While Talat has sung some songs in Malayalam, Tamil and Kannada in his career of regional cinema, but both these particular songs were in Hindi.

The song for Gemini Ganeshan was a duet with Lata from the film Devta (1956). It was a happy romantic number composed by C. Ramchandra and written by Rajendra Krishan -

Lata - 'Kisi se pyar hai humko magar hum na batayenge'
(I am in love but I won't tell you with whom)

Talat - Tumhaari in jhuki aankhon se hum to jaan jayenge'
(I will find out from the shyness of your eyes)

The song for M.G.R. was from the cult hit Tamil film Gul-E-Bakavali (1955). It grossed around one crore rupees with a share of 50 lakh rupees in Tamil cinema. Its dubbed version in Hindi, in 1956, grossed around 25 lakh rupees with a share of 10 lakh rupees. Collectively, its total gross amount for both versions was around 1.25 crore rupees with a share of around 60 lakhs rupees. These figures were unheard of in those days. The film was a costume period drama based on the story of Arabic folklore, One Thousand and One Nights. It's about a young prince who sets out to the kingdom of Bakavali to find a mysterious flower which is believed to have the power to restore his father's eyesight. M.G.R.'s well orchestrated fight sequences were much talked about, particularly one with a ferocious tiger. Talat sang for M.G.R. in a romantic duet with the prominent female singer of the South Indian film industry, Jikki.

'Mera kahan hai man mera woh to ek hi pal mein tera hua, na jaane kya hua'
(I seem to have lost my heart, in an instant, it now belongs to you, I don't know how)

THE MISSING 'DIWALI....'

After a hectic multi-nation tour and some 30 film song recordings this year, the unstoppable Talat packed in a film to act in as well. The film was Diwali Ki Raat (1956) in which he was paired opposite Shashikala and Roop Mala. But it's an unreleased film of which nothing else is known apart from one official film poster and a few songs on YouTube.

(Talat in a promotional shot from his film 'Diwali Ki Raat' (Courtesy: NFAI))

Remembering one of his ghazals in the film, 'Zindagi kis mod pe laayi mujhe'', lyricist Naqsh Lyallpuri said in an interview to journalist Avijit Ghosh that the producer liked Talat's rendition during the rehearsals so much that he told music director Snehal Bhatkar to use only three instruments (harmonium, violin and tabla) during the final take to highlight the soulfulness of his voice.

'Zindagi kis mod pe laayi mujhe
Har khushi roti nazar aayi mujhe'

(What crossroads has my life brought me to
I can see all my happiness reduced to sorrow)

During my research, I was very lucky to unearth some more information while visiting the National Film Archives of India (NFAI) in Pune. Their visual library has some studio images from the film saved in their archives. One image shows him dressed in a uniform holding a cap. The second image shows him dancing in a song, dressed in harem pants and holding a banjo in one hand.

The recording label HMV would often re-release a lot of Talat's old songs on popular demand. This year they released an album with 12 old songs. The name of the album was 'Talat Mahmood - Ghazals to Remember'. The back cover of the album stated - "Handsome, debonair and soft spoken, Talat Mahmood is one of India's foremost singing artistes in the popular category." Since his association with HMV went back to 1941, this album featured a range of Ghazals that were recorded in a span of 15 years. He had few equals in the country in the genre of non-film Ghazals, so HMV gladly kept the sales running with his old recordings too. One of them features Ghalib's poetry with Khayyam's composition.

'Koi din gar zindagaani aur hai
Apne ji mein humne thaani aur hai
Aatish-e-dozakh mein ye garmi kahan
Soz-e-gham haaye nihani aur hai

(Destiny decides which turn life takes
Plans are different of what the mind makes
The fires of hell are not as hot
As the burning sensation of grief)

Talat moved ahead with connecting different generations to his music. As a final offering this year, he released one album in Modern Bangla music. Recorded in the Dum Dum studios in Calcutta for HMV, the music was composed by Shyamal Mitra who was among the most notable musicians of the golden era of the Bengali music industry.
SIDE A - Tomar Akash Bhore Alor Madhuri (Your sky is filled with sweetness of light)
SIDE B - Je Mala Shukay, Je Khela Phuray (Once the garland dries, it's game over)
He juggled different styles of music with contrasting sensibilities from different parts of the country with absolute elan.

1957

(Talat with his cousin, Major General Enaith Habibuallh, the first Commandant of the National Defence Academy (N.D.A.))

THE FIRST SINGER AT THE N.D.A.

The NDA - National Defence Academy had recently launched and it was the first tri-service academy in the world with a joint defence service training institute of the Indian Armed Forces. The cadets of the three services i.e. the Indian Army, the Indian Navy and the Indian Air Force train together before they move on to their respective service academies for further training. Early years of the National Defence Academy (NDA) embodied the hope of a new nation preparing for their next generation of the armed forces . It was a pioneering institution that imparted joint training to officer cadets, situated in Khadakwasla, Pune.

The first Commandant of NDA in charge of taking Prime Minister Nehru's vision forward for the academy, was Talat's cousin and family friend from Lucknow, Major General Enaith Habibullah. This year, the cadets were provided a brand-new space for entertainment and relaxation. The newly- constructed Habibullah Hall at the cost of Rs. 1, 25,000/- with a magnificent double balcony auditorium was built as the venue for central functions and LIVE performances. It was named in honour of Major General Habibullah.

One of the first performers to be invited there was the reigning singing star Talat Mahmood. The performance was to honour the visit of the Army Chief General Thimiyya. Notably, it was the first entertaining night with a LIVE performance for the cadets at the brand new venue. Once again, Talat made history by being the first member of the film industry to perform at the Habibullah Hall. He was the unsung hero who took these pioneering steps and humbly continued to open up new vistas for singers without making any noise about it.

"I remember the excitement in the air. I must have barely been 10-11 years old but to have Talat uncle come and stay with us was such a thrill", recalls Wajahat Habibullah, the son of Major General Habibullah. "His romantic image was so appealing and it was great to have a celebrity uncle. But personally, he had no celebrity-like hang ups. He was very affectionate with us. My father was very fond of his polite disposition and always made sure that Talat uncle felt comfortable at home," adds Wajahat.

As the evening progressed, Talat sang some of his best known hits including 'Shaam-e-gham ki kasam', 'Jaayen to jaayen kahaan' and 'Hain sabse madhur wo geet'.

As a special treat, he sang some new songs which were slated to be released later that year. This included the peppy number called 'Jhoome re'. It was from his upcoming film 'Ek Gaon Ki Kahani' (1957) in which he was the on-screen actor paired opposite his good friend and actress Mala Sinha.

'Jhoome re, neela ambar jhoome, dharti ko choome re
Tujhko yaad karke, mera dil bhi jhoome, mera dil bhi jhoome'

(Look at the clear blue sky, sweetly kissing the ground
When I remember you, my heart dances with joy too)

In his inimitable humour, Talat quipped, "Since I play the role of a doctor in this film, I treat my patients by singing songs. My tip to real life doctors is to try out this happy and hopeful song for their patients."

FAVOURITE CO-STAR MALA SINHA

Talat's film with co-star Mala Sinha, 'Ek Gaon Ki Kahani (1957) was a social family drama and it did fairly well at the box office. Given the fact that this was the same year when iconic films like Mother India, Pyaasa, Naya Daur and Do Aankhen Barah Haath were made, the debut director Dulal Guha and actor Talat left a mark with their film being a moderate hit. Guha used to be filmmaker Satyen Bose's assistant who was visiting the Berlin Film Festival for the screening of his hit film Bandish (1955). The next film he decided to make was Ek Gaon Ki Kahani (1957). All the dates with the studio, actors and technicians had already been booked. But suddenly, Bose had to be away in Berlin. That's when he decided to give the film to his assistant Guha who then marked his debut as the film's director.

The pertinent issue raised in Ek Gaon Ki Kahani (1957) is something that concerns the lives of people in India even today - fake doctors and quacks who jeopardize the lives of villagers. Talat plays the role of a qualified doctor who comes to a village to serve the sick and counter the fakery of someone who is just a compounder but sells medicines to the sick without any qualification. Things get complicated when Talat's character falls in love with the compounder's daughter, played by actress Mala Sinha. The two can be seen romancing in the village fields with this foot-tapping romantic duet sung by Talat and Lata Mangeshkar, in a delightful music composition of Salil Chowdhary-

Lata - 'Hai koi dekh lega
Mere sang piya, ghabraye mora jiya re
Hai koi dekh lega'
(Someone might see us
Should I be worried meeting you, my love
Someone might see us)

Talat - 'Koi kya dekh lega
Preet ki ye dori, duniya se nahin chori re
Koi kya dekh lega'
(It's okay if someone see us
Loving you is not a crime in this world
It's okay if someone see us)

Talat and Mala Sinha were good family friends off screen and she would often drop in at his home, sharing recipes with Talat's wife Nasreen. The two women got along very well and often hung out together. Mala Sinha's father would often join in on these family dinners as he was a huge admirer of Talat's voice. Once Talat drove the families to Bandstand in Bandra for some snacks. It was great weather with a cool breeze and Mala grabbed Talat's hand to sing something together. Talat got worried and said it would get difficult to get out if a crowd spotted them. "Koi dekh lega, bheedh jama ho jayegi. Mushkil hogi, Mala" (It will be a problem if people spot us, Mala, we'll get surrounded by the crowd), said a worried Talat. She giggled and replied, "Yehi to hamara gana hai - koi dekh lega" (Isn't that our song, that someone will see us).

"He loved fish and we'd tease him that he married a Bengali only beccause he loves fish so much. He would chat with me in Bengali and surpise me. His Urdu was superb but his Bengali was good too. Though he was both an actor and a singer, he was a better singer. His voice compared to today's voices was like *asli ghee* (clarified butter) compared to cheap oil", she once told Laila.

Their film's soundtrack was a success and no album of Talat is complete without a song in the blue mood. But composer Salil Chowdhary always chose to step away from the trend to give Talat some upbeat melodies. Even in the sad song, he made a fast-paced composition. A very popular rhythm of those times was the sound that came from the running of the horse while pulling a passenger cart. That rhythm was the opening piece of this song blending with the flute. The scene shows Talat sitting in a horse cart and riding away from the village of his lady love after a misunderstanding.

'Raat ne kya kya khwaab dikhaaye
Rang bhare sau jaal bichhaaye
Aankhen khuli to sapne toote
Reh gaye gham ke kaale saaye
Raat ne kya kya khwab dikhaaye'

(The night fooled me with lovely dreams
Trapping me with a hundred webs of deceit
The dreams were broken as I awoke
And left behind the darkness of sorrow
The night fooled me with lovely dreams)

Late ghazal singer Pankaj Udhas fondly remembers this song, "I am hugely influenced by his (Talat's) music and style; by his tone of singing and his soft voice. His songs and Ghazals were so sweet. You can hear his voice for hours together, it feels like a sweet nectar being poured inside your ears."

PART OF FILMDOM'S YOUNGEST STARS

Talat acted in an average of one film per year and that made him the most visible singer of his times. Top stars of the year were invited by film magazines. This year, Talat was invited for a shoot by the Powai Lake in Bombay. The shoot included jubilee star Rajinder Kumar, actress Waheeda Rahman and Mala Sinha as well. They were all shown spending a day at the hills surrounded by the lake.

(Talat (centre) claps and sings while Mala Sinha (right of Talat), Rajender Kumar (extreme left) have a laugh)

The article said, "Join filmdom's youngest and brightest stars on a jaunt". The magazine showed the young guns having fun with a boat ride at the lake, enjoying a picnic at the green expanse of the hills and then driving back to the main city after a full day of enjoyment. In those days, Powai was only a place for breezy picnics and weekend getaways but by next year, it would become home to the prestigious IIT Bombay, an institute teaching world class technology that still holds the top spot for India's 'tech-edu' and start-up sectors.

One of Talat's songs this year which was not a big hit at the time of it's release but it has found a new lease of life for a very special purpose. It's from the film 'Captain Kishore' (1957), composed by Chitragupta to the words of veteran lyricist Tanvir Naqvi.

'Badal jaaye duniya, na badlenge hum, tumhaari qasam
Tumhaare hain jab tak ke dum mein hai dum, tumhaari qasam'

(The world may change but I won't change, I promise you
I will remain yours till the last breath, I Promise you)

Now, when I keep talking about the soulful quality of Talat's voice, this example is a strong testimony to it. This song in his soft rendition has been chosen by the Brahma Kumaris to be part of their meditation schedule. The Brahma Kumari or BK is a spiritual movement that originated in Hyderabad, Sindh (presently in Pakistan), during the 1930s and has spread across 100 countries today. Women play a prominent role in this movement where their collective mediation focuses on soul consciousness. Remarkably, Talat's soul lifting voice finds place in their meditation centres, emphasizing their prayers to the supreme soul.

JAGJIT SINGH'S GREATEST INSPIRATION

Talat's voice was heartbreaking for another song of penance and regret. One that can burn you up for orchestrating a sinister plot against the one who truly loves you. It was for a top grossing film that year, Ek Saal (1957), starring Madhubala and Ashok Kumar. The song encapsulates the deep anguish of the protagonist played by Ashok Kumar for cheating on an innocent patient of brain tumour, played by Madhubala; for faking his love for her with the motive of looting her wealth. Lyricist Prem Dhawan writes the song of deep regret threaded into Talat's voice of a realization of lost morality. It was the first time Talat sang for the then newcomer music composer Ravi, who built a contemplative mood for this song, resulting in a career-defining hit.

'Sab kuchh luta ke hosh mein aaye to kya kiya
Din mein agar chiragh jalaaye to kya kiya
Sab kuchh luta ke hosh mein aaye to kya kiya

Hum badnaseeb pyaar ki rusvaai ban gaye
Khud hi lagaa ke aag tamaashai ban gaye
Tamaashaai ban gaye
Daaman se ab ye sholay bujhaaye to kya kiya'

(What is the point in waking up after all is lost
What is the point in lighting up lamps in daytime
What is the point in waking up after all is lost

I am notorious to be unlucky with love
I became a mere spectacle after lighting the fire myself
What is the point in dousing the flames now)

This song was one of the favourites for another legendary Ghazal singer, Jagjit Singh. He would often talk about how he would always sing songs by Talat for his school and college competitions and then later, in his own concerts as well. He explained that since he was a big Talat fan, his songs would always be at his fingertips. "When I go for my performances, if I sing some song by Talat on stage, it is an instant hit. I know that everybody in my audience has gone through that stage when Talat was on the top. Because of his popularity, every contemporary hero, every person in the industry was his fan", explained Singh.[22]

In 2020, when the whole world was hit by a global lockdown because of the Covid-19 pandemic, my phone was suddenly flooded with one particular song by Talat Mahmood. It was a classic combination of the Madan Mohan- Talat Mahmood team from the film Dekh Kabira Roya (1957). The lyrics of the song were written by Rajendra Krishan which suddenly found new meaning during social distancing.

'Humse aaya na gaya
Tumse bulaaya na gaya
Faasla pyaar me dono se
Mitaaya na gaya'

(I was unable to come
You were unable to call me
This distance of our love
Could not be erased by either)

The song is now considered one of the most definitive Ghazals from films. Once again, Rajendra Krishan scored an ace with these heartwarming words. The experience of multiple lockdowns during Covid19 pandemic had inspired me to write an article on listening to Talat's songs during this time of isolation. His voice provided a soothing touch to our frazzled nerves during.

(The author promoted listening to Talat Mahmood during the Covid-19 lockdown. Seen here with her collection of Talat portraits)

Coming back to 1957, Talat came together with his favourite composer Anil Biswas for an unreleased film Jasoos (1957). This film has a song inspired by Doris Day's 'Que Sera Sera' (Whatever will be, will be) which was a huge international hit the previous year. Anil Biswas used a solo pianist for his signature style of a counter melody. This was very popular in Western music but Anil Biswas was the first to introduce it to Indian film music. While Talat's sweet voice takes you through the primary melody, the piano plays a secondary melody in counterpoint to the primary melody. Enjoy this song with the motivational lyrics of Indeevar -

'Jeevan hai madhuban
Tu is mein phool khila
Kaanton se na bhar daaman
Ab maan bhi jaa
Jeevan hai madhuban'

(Life is like a sweet abode
Let flowers blossom in it
Don't crowd it up with thorns
Let's agree to this
Life is like a sweet abode)

In the case of this song, the essence of 'whatever will be, will be' had to be accepted with cheerful fatalism since the film never saw the light of day.

Nonetheless, the song enjoyed popularity on the Binana Geetmala countdown show that year, and regularly featured on compilations of Anil Biswas songs released by HMV. Acutely aware of Talat's equally effective impact in the world of non-film numbers, Anil Biswas also composed two *geets* in Talat's voice which have stood the test of time, both written by the actor Sajjan –

1. Sitaaron tum gawah rehna (Bear witness dear stars)
2. Phir pyar kiya phir roya (Embraced love and tears again)

Talat's long-time admirer and frequent collaborator Khayyam continued weaving magic through the singer's voice, showcasing his versatility in not only conveying the pathos of the ghazal, but also other forms of music such as *geets* and *naats* (devotional songs dedicated to the Prophet Mohammad (P.B.U.H.). The year saw the release of two popular *geets*, with poetry by Madhukar Rajasthani –

1. Chupke se kabhi jab yaad meri (If you remember me silently)
2. Jeeven mein tujhe khoya (Have lost you in my life)

Khayyam recalls, "Apart from our hit songs in films, whenever he sang my non-film Ghazals, I felt that he has the cultured delicacy of Lucknow. Sweetness and melody are under his command. By listening to his songs, one can feel that a well- educated gentleman is singing with a soulful voice. He never cared for commercial gimmicks." [23]

There was another important development this year which meant that a lot of these songs that were missing from the big screen could still reach the ears of the listeners. That's because the Government of India finally relented on film music. The Information and Broadcasting Minister, B.V. Keskar had to bow to public demand and the Vividh Bharati service of All India Radio (AIR) was introduced. This was launched specifically to cater to popular tastes in music. Film music finally made a comeback to the national broadcaster. Indian listeners would no longer need to depend on just Radio Ceylon for their favourite songs but could now catch them on Vividh Bharati as well.

THE UGLY TREND OF VERSION SONGS

At the same time, there was also the new trend of 'Version Song', created as a new business concept by HMV. In Talat's case, let's first explain what this 'version song' meant. During the 1950's, HMV would officially create another version of their own original song. They asked Talat Mahmood to sing the first version of the song 'Chal udh ja re panchhi' (Fly away, O'bird) for the film Bhabhi (1957). But in the final copy of the film, the song was sung by Mohammad Rafi instead. The singers were unaware of this double recording but it was profitable for the recording label. The 'version song' by Talat was sold as a separate 78rpm record. And Mohammad Rafi's version was sold as part of the film album. Talat's version was equally popular as it often played on the radio. Today, it can be heard on YouTube. Composed by Chitragupta and written by Rajendra Krishan, the song is a metaphorical reference to getting uprooted from your home.

'Chal udh ja re panchi
Ki ab ye des hua begaana
Khatm hue din uss daali ke
Jis par tera basera tha'

(Fly away, O'bird
This is no longer your home
Gone are the days of that branch
On which you would roost)

Incidentally, this happened with other singers as well where they suddenly found another voice in the songs that they had recorded. It wasn't met well by the singers, prompting the recording label to bring an end to it. While the sale of version songs in the music stores stopped but the practice of recording version songs still continues inside the film industry. It has only gotten uglier with time, with today's singers still complaining about this deceitful practice.

1958

A FRIEND IN NEED FOR MUKESH

('Madhumati', the film album that Talat generously handed over to his friend, Mukesh)

The biggest hit of this year was the film Madhumati (1958). An eternal romance across the seven lives of birth (the concept of "saat janam" in Hindu mythology), starring Dilip Kumar and Vyjayanthimala. Considered one of Bimal Roy's best films, it held the record for the longest time to win a total of nine Filmfare awards. The film was meant to have Talat Mahmood sing for Dilip Kumar. But Talat shocked everyone with his decision. Rarely had the film industry seen such empathy and generosity of placing friendships above work. That too, in a Dilip Kumar-Bimal Roy film!

Talat's friend and fellow playback singer Mukesh was going through an extremely difficult time financially. Few years back Mukesh had put all his energy and resources into acting. He played the lead role in the film Mashooqa (1953) which flopped miserably. He then decided to produce his own film and put several singing assignments on hold. This film was Anurag (1956) which Mukesh produced himself, acted in it as main lead, composed music for it and sang for it as well. But the entire exercise cost him a fortune.
Unfortunately, the film was unreleased and Mukesh found himself in financial distress. Running the home became a challenge. Talat

knew about this and reasoned with Bimal Roy, Dilip Kumar and composer Salil Chowdhury to consider giving all his songs of Madhumati to singer Mukesh.

This was something I had often heard about in my family. It was talked about at home with pride as an exemplary show of support and help in the cut throat world of showbiz. Of course, Talat was not the kind to publicize his personal help to a friend. But more recently, while celebrating 50 years of this blockbuster film, Madhumati, the exemplary act of generosity by Talat got publicly verified by filmmaker Bimal Roy's daughter.

SUPERHIT YEAR WITH NUTAN, SURAIYA AND SHYAMA

(Talat with Nutan in their film 'Sone Ki Chidiya')

It was a busy year for Talat on-screen. He had three films as singer-actor: Sone Ki Chidiya, Lala Rukh and Maalik. The title of the film Sone Ki Chidiya (1958) translates into 'golden bird' which is metaphorically used for a rich person who is exploited as a highly valued prize. The film was written and jointly-produced by the grand doyenne of Urdu literature and the biggest feminist of her times, Ismat Chughtai, and her director husband, Shahid Lateef, under their Film India Corporation banner. The protagonist of the film is portrayed by leading actress Nutan who plays the role of an impoverished orphan, exploited by her extended family after she becomes a successful actress. Nutan's co-stars were Talat Mahmood and Balraj Sahini.

"Nutan was very helpful to me. In one song, I couldn't understand the dance steps. So, she just held my hand and started dancing together", laughed Talat.[24]

Talat plays the role of her love interest, who seeks her wealth by deceiving her into an affair and disappearing on the promise of marriage. Desperately looking for care and love, she bumps into a poor poet played by actor Balraj Sahini who teaches her the importance of using art as a tool for improving lives, in contrast to movies which he felt objectified women and represented only hollow entertainment. The film was a hit and the message that it carried of socialism, pay parity and equality was well received by the audience. Ironically, Chughtai's message used the medium of an entertaining movie to hit out against the film industry.

Talat's role of a scheming lover in a negative role was a surprising departure from his chocolate boy image. It was one of his best performances with two unforgettable romantic songs from the album composed by O.P. Nayyar. My favourite is the one where the boat gently glides over the Powai lake just like Talat's voice gently taps the notes of Nayyar's minimalist composition and singer Asha Bhosle gives the opening notes for Nutan.

'Pyaar par bas to nahin hai mera lekin phir bhi
Tu bata de ki tujhe pyaar karun ya na karun

Mere khwaabon ke jharokon ko sajane wali
Tere khwaabon mein kahin mera guzar hai ke nahi
Puchh kar apni nigahon se bata de mujhko
Meri raaton ke muqaddar mein seher hai ke nahin'

(Can't help falling in love with you but
You can still tell me if I could love you or not

You occupy my dreams with your presence
Do I even pass by your dreams?
The answer is in your eyes, if you ask
Will there be an awakening of dawn after my dull nights)

O.P. Nayyar was once asked by a film magazine to list the top 10 favourite songs of his own compositions, to which he placed 'Pyar par bas to nahin' as the No.1 in his list. The minimalist orchestral use in his composition was in sync with Talat's soft vocals. But you will be surprised to learn that Nayyar wanted Mohammad Rafi to playback for Talat. Nayyar boldly suggested to Talat that since Rafi was singing for Balraj, he could sing for Talat as well! Of course, this was a non-starter!

As an actor, Talat had made his position clear that he will be the only voice to playback for himself. There was to be no compromise on this or else he would leave the film. The producer and director were not ready to lose Talat at the behest of an unreasonable demand being made by the music composer. Talat stayed on for the film which became one of his best performances as an actor.

The lyrics of this song are written by revolutionary writer and poet Sahir Ludhianvi who dedicated his personal love to fellow poetess Amrita Pritam in this song. These lines have been taken from his longer writings of a nazm (Urdu poem) called 'Mata-e-ghair'. It is fascinating to listen to Talat's voice mix the pain and desire of unattained love of two different couples in two different worlds. One being the on-screen love of Talat and Nutan in the reel world, the other being the burning passion of Sahir and Amrita in the real world.

The biggest impact of Talat's voice has always been that it conveys the essence of any poetry that he has sung; in understanding the style of the poetry, the use of vocabulary and the intent of Urdu. Talat's voice can best be described akin to the language itself. Urdu is known to be sophisticated, gentle and steeped in the rich heritage of culture, irrespective of the mood of the message. Whether its anger, passion, agitation or love, Urdu maintains an equilibrium of grace and dignity. Such is the voice of Talat too.

The next song from another film written by revolutionary poet Kaifi Azmi, is a stern command to stand up for love and respect its power; to defy all norms and bondages.

'Udaas udaas fizaaon mein noor chhalkaao
Bujhe bujhe hue taaron ko hans ke chamkaao
Ghurur-e-husn salamat na raah dikhlaao
Rabaab doob gaya khoon mein, ab to aa jao
(Opening slow lines of the song)
(Shine a light on these sad surroundings
Illuminate the dull stars with your smile

Lead the way shunning arrogance of your beauty
My rabaab (string instrument) is swimming in blood, will you still not come?)

The opening four lines of the song are in a slow pace that Talat has sung in the lowest note, almost unrecognizable to his voice. The main part of the song starts from the lines 'aana hi padega' where Talat's voice suddenly shoots up to a high pitch. Music composer Khayyam skillfully uses Talat's voice range to the hilt.

Aana hi padega
Sar ishq ke kadmon pe jhukaana hi padega
Aana hi padega

(You will have to come
Bow your head to the power of love
You will have to come)

This song is from the film 'Lala Rookh' (1958) which means 'tulip cheeked', a term of endearment in Persian. Talat is the main lead opposite actress Shyama. It's a period drama set in an imaginary kingdom where Talat plays the young King of Noorabad named Shah Murad and Shyama plays the title role. She is the Princess named Lala Rookh of another kingdom called Malikabad. The two have been set to marry in a political alliance but have never met. Talat plans to disguise himself as a poor poet/singer to go meet her at her durbar so that he can catch a glimpse of her without the trappings of a king. She falls in love with him thinking he is a poor artist. Talat's character teases her while lying about her soon-to-be-husband King being ugly, undesirable and dishonest who spends all his time at his harem with 200 women. Eventually she realizes the joke was on her and the film ends with a happy royal wedding.

Actress Shyama has often spoken about how bedazzled she had been by Talat. She was quoted in a film magazine about how she had a crush on him just like any other fan. And he didn't disappoint her when she got to meet him and work with him because he was a genuinely charming man. Lala Rookh was the second film that she co-starred with him. "But my heart would still miss a beat whenever we acted together! He was my heart-throb for as long as I can remember and I made it a point never to miss a song of his on the radio. One thing about Talat was that he was almost perfect, hardly troubling his directors with retakes."

It's interesting to note that this became Talat Mahmood's second film to be jointly-produced by Ismat Chughtai and Shahid Lateef. Lala Rookh (1958) was inspired by an English poem of the same name written by British poet Thomas Moore in 1817.

Music composer Khayyam gave one of his most experimental compositions for this film keeping in mind the period drama. Sadly, it fails to find a prominent mention in his repertoire of work. But sample his melody and the rich poetry of Kaifi Azmi in this romantic and cheeky duet by Talat and Asha Bhosle -

Talat - 'Pyaas kuchh aur bhi bhadka di jhalak dikhla ke
Tujhko pardaa rukh- e-roshan se hatana hoga'
(Glimpses of you leave me thirsty for more
Remove the veil from your illuminant face)

Asha - Itni gustakh na ho ishq ki awaara nazar
Husn ka paas nigaahon ko sikhaana hoga
(How insolent are your wandering eyes
They must learn to respect beauty)

(Talat and co-star Shyama from the film 'Lala Rookh')

Talat's wife Nasreen believed that his look in this film was his personal favourite. Dressed royally sporting a moustache and turban, he found himself the handsomest in the costume and would secretly enjoy admiring himself whenever the film played on television. Shyama and Talat made a wonderful on-screen pair with loads of chemistry.

While a lot of people enjoyed watching Talat in a light hearted rom-com film, he was clearly done with the job of acting. It was his last film and he decided that it was becoming too exhausting for him. "I was feeling tired very often and it was beginning to affect me as a singer. After a full day's shoot, I would feel like cancelling my song recordings. Acting did not interest me as much. It just so happened by chance with one film after another." [25]

Interestingly, one gets to see glimpses of Talat's real persona in this film. Not the soulful singer that you hear in his songs. But the jovial and mischievous person that he actually was in real life. In fact, Talat is at his flamboyant best while doing some comedy scenes in the film. "Vivacious and full of laughter", recalls his niece Romana Zaman. "I remember him always being in a jovial mood. He would take us out for ice cream treats and end up eating from our bowls too. But that is if he managed to finally get us our bowls. He once got out of his car to buy us some ice cream. But it took him so long. By the time he got back to the car, the ice cream was all melted. I asked him like a spoiled brat on what took him so long. He said he was suddenly surrounded by people. I told him that I had seen him signing bits of paper for everyone outside the ice cream parlour. Why would he waste time signing pieces of paper for people? He would just laugh it off. I realised many years later that he was a star who would be busy signing autographs on those bits of paper."

(Talat felt he looked best in the period drama 'Lala Rookh')

At work, Talat got along with most of his colleagues with the exception of very few. Much has been written about a rumoured tiff between music director Naushad Ali and Talat Mahmood. After their brilliant success together in Babul (1950), it was expected that this composer-singer pair would go a long way. They were two Lucknow boys who made it big in Bombay. It has truly been a loss to music that they didn't work together as often as expected. Undoubtedly there was a difference in temperament that kept them apart. Talat was a talented multi-tasking film singer in which he added global tours, non-film Ghazal albums, regional cinema songs and acting assignments to his list. He was too much of an independent, free spirited man to agree with Naushad's straight jacketed expectations of what a playback singer's trajectory should be. While Naushad settled with the absolute preference to Mohammed Rafi's voice in most of his films, the two legends agreed to disagree with their outlook. Somehow they still held immense respect for each other. This was to the extent that Naushad, in his brief stint as film producer, decided to cast Talat in his next film. Naushad had already produced films like Babul (1950) and Uran Khatola (1955) in the past. Naushad's next film as producer was Maalik (1958). Naushad decided to cast the two singing stars Talat and Suraiya. They were paired to romance on-screen once again. After their success in Waris (1954), there were high expectations from Maalik (1958). But shockingly, the film tanked. The only reminder of the film today is a song that frequently features on hits from the Golden Era.

Talat - 'Man dheere dheere gaaye re, maloom nahin kyun
Bin gaaye rahaa na jaaye re, maloom nahin kyun'
(The heart hums a gentle tune, I wonder why
I can't stop humming this tune, I wonder why)

Suraiya - 'Ek baat zubaan par aaye re, maloom nahin kyun
Kehte huye dil sharmaaye re, maloom nahin kyun'
(There's something on my mind, I wonder why
I am shy to express it, I wonder why)

This is a romantic duet sung by Talat and Suraiya while they can be seen leisurely walking across the garden and sitting on swings on-screen. Naushad didn't compose the music for his own film but instead chose his one-time assistant Ghulam Mohammad for it.

Suraiya was one of Talat's favourite colleague. He recalls a funny incident from the sets when teased her. "We had to shoot the wedding scene. So I told Suraiya 'Be careful, after seven rounds around the fire, I can claim you'. She started laughing and replied, 'Well, I hope that happens. At least you said it otherwise you are always so shy that you hardly speak.' She was lovely", laughed out Talat. [26]

(Talat and Suraiya's film poster, Maalik)

Being romantically linked or the talk of rumoured affairs with your co-stars is inevitable in the film industry, especially for those who are popular and play the main lead in front of the camera. So how did Talat deal with this? Were there any affairs? For a person known as the perfect gentleman in showbiz, this question was boldly put forth to him by his own nephew and senior journalist, Rishad Mahmood. "Well, there were a few projected flings more out of the film's publicity, than anything else. But certainly not any affairs", clarified the charming singing star.

CONTINUING WITH MODERN BENGALI MUSIC

Talat was steadfast in contributing to the genre of Modern Bengali music. This year, he recorded a timeless hit composed by Sudhin Dasgupta.

'Ei rimijhim jhim barosha
Haoya him him him parosha
Tumi ele aaj mone sahasa
Path chalite je taai bharosa'

(Listen to the pitter patter of the rain
And whistling of the wind
Have the courage to come over today
That's how we can build trust together)

He became an important part of Durga Puja celebrations, the biggest annual festival in Bengal which marks the triumph of Goddess Durga over evil. Each year, special songs would be recorded in the build up to the festival. This year, HMV released a record called 'Jetha Ramdhanu Othe Heshe: The Smiling Rainbow of Talat Mahmood'.

'Jetha ramdhanu othe heshe
Aar phul phote bhalobese
Balo tumi jaabe ki go saathe
Ei path gaechhe se deshe
Jetha Ramdhanu othe heshe'

(Where the rainbow rises and smiles
And flowers bloom in love
Tell me, will you come with me
On this road that leads to the place
Where the rainbow rises and smiles)

When his songs blared out on loudspeakers amidst the festivities, the softness of his voice balanced out the surrounding noise. It evoked peace and calm that only Talat could bring out.

1959

THE IMMORTALITY OF 'JALTE HAIN JISKE LIYE'

The country was taken by storm with the release of a new song in Talat's voice. It was famously shot over the phone. The message in this romantic song had layers of context which was impeccably handled by the tempestuous musical notes of S.D. Burman and the delicate lyrics of Majrooh Sultanpuri.

The film was about inter caste love between an untouchable woman and an upper caste Brahmin man. It was filmmaker Bimal Roy's lyrical direction in tactfully handling this bold subject. He was once again set to write history for the industry. The film was called 'Sujata' (meaning well-bred'), named after the female protagonist in the script, who is a lower caste girl adopted by an upper caste family. Throughout her life, she is unable to forget her lineage. The film is inspired by the Bengali short story of the same name written by award-winning writer Subodh Ghosh. It starred actress Nutan playing the titular role of Sujata in one of her most powerful performances. It is a case study in cinema on how to put out an act of restraint and emotional outpouring in the same frame! Actor Sunil Dutt plays the young suitor named Adheer who falls in love with her and remains steadfast in his desire to marry her irrespective of societal outrage.

Talat's song 'Jalte Hain Jiske Liye' is the *pièce de résistance* of the film. It has often ranked as one of the best romantic solos in Indian cinema, appearing in the top most personal favourite list of songs for both Talat and S.D. Burman. It also became the highlight of Talat's entire career, which won him a Filmfare Award nomination and his most popular song. The song deserves a separate chapter and which is exactly what I will do right now as you read ahead. In the film's plot, the composition of the poetry is building in Adheer's mind when he starts humming to Sujata by the lakeside. He promises her he will sing it out to her once he has the words for it. It was one of the happiest evenings in Sujata's life when she felt loved and accepted. When she returns home, she is shattered to learn that Adheer is meant to marry her upper-caste sister instead. As an untouchable herself, Sujata should never dream of marrying Adheer. The tragic silence felt in her room is broken by the ringing of the phone. It is Adheer calling her up to sing her the song he just completed. He is happy and full of excitement, expressing his feelings unabashedly, unaware of the torment in Sujata's mind. He starts with a sweet humming, which can only be possible in Talat's voice, caressing her tormented heart over the phone's receiver. While she stands in her bedroom's corridor clutching the phone, he sings to her, sitting at his home's library with the street's neon light blinking in the background, adding to his sparkle.

'Jalte hain jiske liye teri aankhon ke diye
Dhundh laayaa hun wohi geet main tere liye
Jalte hain jiske liye'

(Whom do they burn for, the light of your eyes
I have found you the desired song
Whom do they burn for)

Talat's voice effortlessly changes from happiness to poignancy with the realization of what Adheer feels on the purity of his love, while Sujata listens on, helplessly trying to hold back her tears instead of celebrating along with him.

'Dard banke jo mere dil mein raha, dhal na saka
Jaadu banke teri aankhon mein ruka, chal na saka
Aaj laya hoon wahi geet main tere liye
Jalte hain jiske liye'

(The heartache that I nurtured within, would not abate
Magically, it reflected in your eyes and stayed there
Today I bring you the same song
Whom do they burn for)

S.D. Burman's orchestra gently lifts up to a crescendo, wanting to empathize with Sujata's plight. She is beholden to her upper-caste family who adopted her for a better life but she dare not dream to enjoy the privilege and love received from an upper-caste suitor. Talat's tremolo lifts the anxiety with gentle restraint. Adheer continues to sing with a nirvanic smile but Sujata begins to muffle her tears. A conflicting state of two hearts which Talat and S.D. Burman have to tactfully handle with the right balance.

'Dil me rakh lena ise haathon se ye chhute na kahi
Geet nazuk hai mera sheeshe se bhi tute na kahi

Gun gunaoonga yahi geet main tere liye
Jalte hain jiske liye'

(Hold the song close to your heart, let it not slip away
A melody more fragile than the shattering glass
I will keep humming for you this song
Whom do they burn for)

Bimal Roy had asked Nutan to hold the emotion through the song and allow the flood gates to open at the end. By the third stanza, the character Sujata was profusely crying while coming to terms with her misfortune. S.D. raised the pitch of the orchestra to the highest note but gave just the required few seconds of breathing space to drop the notes before they touched Talat's mellow serenade. By this time, Adheer was enjoying her silence as acceptance and added a flirtatious smile to his face. You can feel that subtle change in mood in Talat's teasing voice.

'Jab talak na ye tere ras ke bhare honton se mile
Yun hi aawara phiregaa ye teri zulfon ke tale
Gaaye jaoonga yahi geet main tere liye
Jalte hain jiske liye'

(Till the time it meets your lips
It will wander around like a vagabond
I will keep singing you these sounds of music
Whom do they burn for)

After the song's recording was over in the studio, the lyricist Majrooh Sultanpuri said, "Wah Talat kya gaya hai (What great singing, Talat)", to which Talat responded, "Kya likha hai, janab! (What great writing, sir)."

The whole team felt with certainty that this was a song which will go down in history as one of the greatest ever. And they weren't wrong about it. The lasting memory of this song is undoubtedly created by the vulnerability of Talat's voice with his signature combination of dignified charm, gentleness and poignancy.

The process of selecting the right singer has also been a story in itself. From what I've heard at home, the idea was to choose a singing voice that can sound pleasant over the phone as well. It is rumoured but unconfirmed that the top singers of that time were asked to sing over the phone to see how their voice reverberates over the receiver. Talat's vibrato gave it the edge over the phone. With filmmaker Bimal Roy certain about how the song is to be picturized, it's the element of a phone- serenade that played the winning role for Talat!

He received the Cinegoers' Association of India and the Film Journalists' Association of Bombay award for this song. Apart from the National Film Award and the Filmfare awards that were won at home, Sujata (1959) was also nominated and screened at the 13th Cannes Film Festival the next year at the 'Feature Films Competition' for the Palme d'Or. It was the same time when Hollywood films like Ben-Hur and La Dolce Vita were screened at Cannes for the global audience. There was pin drop silence when Talat's voice pierced through the dark cinema hall like an arrow through a cloud, drenching the audience in a shower of delicate mist and balsamic aroma. The silence that was broken only by the sniffles of the audience. An audience that was primarily European and Western who hardly understood what he sang. But hasn't that always been Talat's forte which became a testimony to his global fandom in the following decades of conducting back-to-back world tours!

While the success of this single song became a defining moment for his career, at the personal front, things couldn't have been better. Talat's family was complete with the birth of a baby girl. Sabina Mahmood was born, much to the excitement of the local press, which was once again part of the celebrations with the birth of Talat's second child. There were family pictures taken at the hospital bed soon after her birth. It was the mark of a complete family with both parents holding their new born baby and elder brother Khalid looking on in wonderment.

PERFECTION IN TELUGU

He wrapped up the final year of this golden decade with another feather in his cap. He sang for another regional film, this time in Telugu. The film's name was Manorama (1959). He sang three songs with music composed by Ramesh Naidu. This is Talat's solo song in the film -

'Andala seema sudha nilayam
Ee lokame divya prema mayam
Valape modalayaka telavaru bratukela
Tolinati kalyayikalu phalamiana, kalayaina
Mayani gayamai migilina adi nayam

Andala velugulo alararu aanandam
Alarinchu sogasule anandamuna tele'

(This beautiful sweet abode
The world is filled with divine love
Life blooms with the start of romance
Was it just a dream that we met, did it bear fruit?
Like a wound that won't heal, better that way

Radiating happiness in the beauty of love
The delightful wonders that float with joy)

The music composer Ramesh Naidu knew Talat from his Calcutta days and he wanted all songs of the main lead sung by Talat. He was called to Chennai and rehearsals of all the songs would happen at the Taj Connemara Hotel where Talat was staying. It is often said that out of all the languages of South India, Telugu is the hardest. Despite Talat not knowing the language at all, Naidu was confident of his ability to sing comfortably in it. After all, he had witnessed how Talat had completely blended as a native speaker while singing in Bengali.

"His pronunciation was perfect. There was no hint of any non-native accent. It is especially difficult to do a 'murki' (inverted mordent in music) on the right word to evoke the right feeling, when you don't understand the language. But he sang his 'murki' just at the apt moment", adds his co- singer, P. Susheela. She is known as one of the tallest singing legends of the country, with a career spanning six decades across South Indian cinema. She has sung one duet with Talat in this film. I fortunately had the chance to speak with her, despite her frail condition but the mention of Talat brought in a rush of fond memories about him. "His ability to sing on key was amazing. His voice never wavered in 'shruti' (musical pitches). When he hit the note on his harmonium, it was difficult to differentiate his voice from the harmonium key because his voice was in perfect alignment."

Talat - 'Marachi poyevemo mayani bhasalu, mankideyo sakhi' (Did you forget our promises, hard to get over o' dear)

Susheela - 'Marachi poradoyi cheysina vhaasalu, aashalu masina' (Should not forget the promises made, even if hopes dwindle)

Talat - 'Beyligeynu ni kuluke na kannudoyi
Beyligeynu na madilo ni cheylimihaayi
Beylugondu aa taar lona mayani bhasalu, mankideyo sakhi'
(Your lingering quirks light up my eyes
Your comforting friendship warms my heart
Like the star that shines, the promises light up o' dear)

She further adds, "His control over emotions was remarkable. It would never overflow. You never felt he was overtly weeping or wailing because if emotions overflow, the listeners lose touch with song. My favourite song of his has been 'Jaayen to jaayen kahaan' which he sang in absolute perfection."

Talat's personality had the gift of making personal connections and fond friendships with colleagues very soon. People would feel the warmth of his affection and genuine care. Another great singer of that time from the South Indian music industry was P. B. Sreenivas, popularly known as PBS. He had once gone to visit Talat at his home in Bandra. Susheela recalls how PBS would often talk about that evening spent with Talat who sat with his harmonium and sang Ghazals for at least half an hour in honour of his visiting guest. PBS was mesmerized by his voice and touched by the gesture. He believed that there was no greater crooner than Talat, he was a natural in this genre and never required to scream out any emotions. Subtlety was his forte.

This 50s was the most successful and significant decade in Talat's career. The 50's made him a superstar singer and a filmstar to the outside world and a complete family man at home. But there was never any time to take a breath and rest on some laurels. Talat didn't believe in that. He was looking forward to the 1960s with more gusto and fervour.

CHAPTER 6 - THE SWINGING 60S

(Could Talat manage with the loud influence of Rock music?)

LET'S GET LOUD

The swinging 60's weren't called swinging for nothing! Hindi film music was also showing signs of accepting newer sounds with faster rhythms and louder music, influenced by the growing popularity of Elvis and the Beatles worldwide. It meant that singers and musicians in India had to adapt to the changing tastes of their listeners. Remnants of the pathos of the previous decade reflected in the early years of the swinging 60s. While 1960 was a year that barely had eight songs sung by Talat for Hindi films, his partnership with composer Madan Mohan stood out for a song that became hugely popular in Talat's concert circuit. This was from the film Bahaana (1960), a lesser known Meena Kumari - Sajjan starrer. The film is largely forgotten but Talat's song keeps alive the mere mention of it. This was the truest blue mood example of the Talat - Madan Mohan partnership which couldn't get deeper than this! With the opening notes of the weeping violin, Talat declares a taunt to the Almighty residing in the skies above.

'Beraham aasmaan, meri manzil bata hai kahaan
Beraham aasmaan

Jo na socha tha wo ho gaya
Kyu nasiba mera so gaya
Gham ki aisi ghata chha gayi
Chain dil ka kahi kho gaya
Ye bata kis liye, le raha hai mera imtihaan
Beraham asmaan

(O 'merciless sky, what has been destined for me
O' Merciless sky

The unforeseen has happened
Why has my luck slipped to a slumber
Surrounded by a storm of unhappiness
I have lost all peace of mind
Tell me why am I being tested by you
O' merciless sky)

It can be a very intense song to listen to for a LIVE audience. In one of his shows, Talat had to lighten up the mood. He jokingly said,

"When there's no one else to blame for our mistakes, it's always God who becomes our punching bag." The hall broke into light chuckles and laughs.

The early 60's became a defining year for the Talat-Sunil Dutt partnership. But unlike their earlier hit filled with pathos (in the song 'Jalte hain jiske liye'), the duo teamed up for numbers that were fast paced and louder in this decade. The first duet featuring Sunil Dutt opposite Waheeda Rehman is from the film 'Ek Phool Char Kaante' (1960). Talat along with Lata Mangeshkar make this a memorable duet for young lovers who can hum along the light, romantic number while out on a date. The duet was shot at the breezy beach with waves crashing on the rocks.

Talat - 'Dil ae dil, baharon se mil, sitaron se aankhein mila
Ye sama, ye rangeen sama, ye mausam bhi hai pyar ka'
(My dear heart, let's enjoy the spring and the stars
This joyous moment is an ambience for love)

Lata - Yahi hai mere tere khwaabon ki duniya'
(This is the world of our dreams)

Composed by the musician duo Shankar-Jaikishen and written by Shailendra, this was a melody in their signature style which began to define the advent of candy-floss romance in the film industry combined with the growing influence of the sounds of rock music in Hindi films.

There's another peppy number with a hugely challenging composition with a play of classical notes that swings like a pendulum in two extremes. It had the characteristic complexity of most compositions by Salil Choudhury. He would often tested the skill of the singers in holding, dropping and scaling up notes in quick succession. Talat's duet with Lata Mangeshkar from the film 'Usne Kaha Tha' (1960) stars Sunil Dutt and Nanda. Very often, radio playlists celebrate the onset of monsoons with this endearing number written by Shailendra -

Talat & Lata - 'Aaha rim jhim ke ye pyaare pyaare geet liye
Aai raat suhaani dekho preet liye
Meet mere suno zara hawa kahe kya aa
Suno toh zara jhingar bole chikimiki chikimiki'

(Listen to the sweet pitter patter of the rain
It brings in a lovely night along with my love
Can you hear the whistling of the wind
Can you hear the ringing of crickets)

Their next film Chhaaya (1961) offered another immortal song for both the careers of Talat and Sunil Dutt. And this came to be known as the song which displayed Talat's strength away from the blue mood. Whenever there is an argument to reduce Talat's oeuvre to a limited basket of only sad songs, this peppy duet with Lata is used in his defense. And why not?

Talat - 'Itna na mujhse tu pyaar badha
Ke main ek baadal aawaara
Kaise kisi ka sahaara banoon
Ke main khud beghar bechaara'
(Don't waste your love on me
I am but like a mere wandering cloud
Unable to support your love
I am but a mere rudderless soul)

Lata - 'Isliye tujhse main pyaar karoon
Ke tu ek baadal awara
Janam janam se hoon saath tere
Hai naam mera jal ki dhaara'
(This is the reason I love you
Charmed by a wandering cloud
We've been together through ages
I am the rainwater that is always within you)

The Rajendra Krishan-written duet is still so popular that even Mozart would not have complained perhaps! The master composer Salil Choudhury managed to Indianize the Great G Minor Symphony No. 40 to the extent that some people in this part of the world hardly realized that this was a composition made 173 years earlier by an Austrian child prodigy.

"If you notice, there was another version of the same song in the film. It was the slower version. Talat sa'ab of course excelled in sad songs because that was his forte but in this particular song, I think he excelled in its sad version, which has some amazing twists and turns in the composition", observes Ghazal singer, late Pankaj Udhas. [27] This version of the song was a solo performance by Talat.

He came back with one of his favourite stars, Dev Anand, this year to repeat their magic. The film 'Roop Ki Rani Choron Ka Raja' (1961) received a lukewarm response at the box office but it gave the duo a hummable hit composed by Shankar-Jaikishan with sounds of soft rock.

'Tum to dil ke taar chhed kar
Ho gaye bekhabar
Chaand ke tale jalenge hum
Aye sanam raat bhar'

(When you tug at my heartstrings
How blissfully unaware are you
We will bask under the moonlight
All night through, my love)

His other commercial hits this year included two films with actor Manoj Kumar , namely 'Suhaag Sindoor (1961) and 'Reshmi Roomal (1961). This was their debut partnership. The latter film had a lovely ghazal composed by Babul and written by the inimitable Raja Mehdi Ali Khan. The blue mood perfectly suited the brooding style of Manoj Kumar in this song -

'Jab chhaaye kabhi saawan ki ghata
Ro ro ke na karna yaad mujhe
Ae jaan-e-tamanna gham tera
Kar dena kahin barbaad mujhe'

(When the sky is cast with rain clouds
Don't weep in my memory
To see your misery, the love of my life
Will leave me shattered)

The young actor was elated to have Talat's voice. He had entered the industry idolizing Dilip Kumar as an actor. To have Dilip Kumar's on- screen voice, Talat, playback for him was a special moment for Manoj Kumar.

For his non-film album (1960), Talat chose to do some special *geet* with V. Balsara, the legendary music composer who was a wizard with instrumental orchestration. They knew each other from Talat's Calcutta days and had a few film songs together in the past, most famously the Shankar-Jaikishan and Shailendra song from Daag (1952), Aye mere dil kahin aur chal, where V Balsara masterfully played the harmonium. But their latest non-film album with HMV featured –
SIDE A - Mera pyaar mujhe lauta do
SIDE B - Birhan baithi aas lagae

'Birhan baithi aas lagae' (Sitting without hope, in wait for her lover) had the sounds and rhythm of a folk song with an extended opening piece of the melodica. A melodica is a pump organ attached to a small keyboard. It brings a poignant mood to its sound and Balsara was a master with it. But the other song on this 78RPM record has become hugely popular on karaoke platforms today, once again with a prominent use of the melodica. The lyrics by Sajjan epitomize the shattering of a broken heart, despite the anger of losing in love. Talat's voice engages with an emotion which is drowned in angst. Would you like to sing along too -

'Mera pyaar mujhe lauta do
Main jeewan mein ulajh gaya hoon
Tum jeena sikhla do
Mera pyaar mujhe lauta do
Thukraane se pehle mujh ko
Lauta do woh preet ki baaten
Meri hansi mastiyaan meri
Lauta do woh chandni raatein
Mere sapnon ko lauta do
Mera toota dil lauta do
Mera pyaar mujhe lauta do'

(Give my love back to me
My life is in a confused state
Teach me how to live again
Give my love back to me
Before rejecting my love
Give me back my sweet nothings
My laughter, my joy
Give me back those nights of love

Give me back my dreams
Give me back my broken heart
Give my love back to me)

Talat's music repertoire extended beyond India because of his Bengali, Punjabi and Urdu songs. He continued to remain popular in East Pakistan (present day Bangladesh). Rajdhanir Buke (1960) is a Bengali-language Bangladeshi film that was released in Dhaka. The music was composed by his friend from his early days at New Theatres, Robin Ghosh. Talat sang two songs -

1. 'Tomare Legechhe Eto Je Bhalo' (How much you are admired)
2. 'Amar Se Gan Hariye Gechhe' (I've lost my senses)

Meanwhile, his popularity in Pakistan was not only because of his film songs and Ghazals but also for a few Punjabi songs. The Punjabi film Sassi Punnho (1960) had three songs sung by him, including this duet with singer Nirmala Sapru -

Nirmala - 'Pardesi naal preet lavi hun lakh suney kya haowey' (Heard a million times, what happens when you love a stranger)

Talat - 'Ek galo pardesi changa ek yaad karey ek roweyho pardesi' (The stranger is well-meaning, who weeps in remembrance)

The film is based on a Punjabi folktale by the same name. It is a tragic love story of Sassi and Punnho who were forcefully separated by their families and ended up getting swallowed in a mountain valley. The belief in this folktale is so strong that their alleged graves are marked as tombs in the Baluchistan province of Pakistan.

THE PAKISTAN TOUR

Soon after the success of Sassi Punnho, 1961 was a good time to think of another concert tour. But more than that, Talat was aching to meet and catch up with his elder brother, Kamal, in Pakistan. Since Partition, their lives changed and each got busy in their own careers. Talat also had to come to terms with the losses it caused. While each family member was doing very well with their respective nation of choice, it was the forced decision of a sudden separation that needed some healing. This was an emotional trip of meeting some of his siblings who had ended up at the other side of the border. Talat decided to pair his next concert tour with family visits as well. The complicated and emotionally-charged relationship between the two countries was witnessing a bonhomie during this time. Talat enjoyed a huge following in Pakistan. Had he decided not to perform there, it would have hugely upset his fans. He made his stop in Karachi where he stayed with his elder brother, Kamal Mahmood. The two buddies had an emotional reunion and each evening, they would end up having endless conversations about school, music and cricket. Kamal's son Rishad Mahmood, who is now a senior journalist and news editor in Karachi, recalls his father talking about Talat's memorable and landmark trip. "It was his first tour to Pakistan and Talat uncle stayed with us for his entire trip which was almost 20-25 days. All his dates ended up getting blocked for functions, concerts and meeting with fans. The entertainment industry in Lahore and Karachi was abuzz with excitement. This was also the Golden Era of the Pakistani film industry and they wanted him to sing for our films too."

Talat was surprised to see a thriving music industry there and was asked to sing for two Pakistani movies. The first Pakistani film he recorded for was 'Charagh Jalta Raha' which was released a year later in 1962. This happened to be the debut film of Pakistan's superstar actor Muhammad Ali whom his fans would fondly refer to as the 'King of Emotions'. The songs were written by Karachi's top most poet of all time, Fazal Ahmad Karim Fazli.

While the new music trend in Hindi films in Bombay was rushing towards sounds of rock at breakneck pace, Pakistan's music was yet to face the onslaught of loud Western sounds. The traditional compositions in the film 'Charagh Jalta Raha' (1962) were really appreciated by Talat. The second Pakistani film he recorded for was 'Ghanghor Ghata'. Talat and Mubarak Begum were the only two singers from the Golden Era in India who sang a handful of songs in Pakistani cinema. Such crossover recordings of Indian singers for Pakistani films did not happen again until the late 1990s, and only for special collaborations.

WITH FAIZ AHMED FAIZ

Talat enjoyed exceptional popularity in Pakistan to the extent that he also recorded seven non-film songs there. This list included two of the biggest hits penned by the legendary poet Faiz Ahmed Faiz.

Well known art critic Prof Salima Hashmi, who is the daughter of Faiz, was a young college student when Talat had visited Karachi. She informs me how Talat and her father were unable to meet since the singing star didn't get to travel to Lahore. "Talat sa'ab could not meet my father Faiz during his Karachi tour since we were in Lahore. But he was very fond of his poetry and had recorded two ghazals which were very popular. I remember the 78rpm was later sent to our house as a gift. We would hear those ghazals on repeat, 3 minutes on each side."

Hashmi further adds, throwing light on the two poems that Talat chose to sing from Faiz's collection. "It was my father's early romantic poetry with which he had first made his name and gained attention at Mushairas (Urdu poetry gatherings) in pre-partition India. Both poems are from his first collection called Naqsh-e-Faryadi."

Talat both composed and sang 'Khuda woh waqt na laae' and 'Dono jahaan teri mohabbat mein'. These were both recorded for the Gramophone Company of Pakistan (later called the EMI records). Out of these two, 'Dono jahan teri mohabbat mein' has been one of his most popular Ghazals. Interestingly, this poem of Faiz has been a favourite of all Ghazal singers and has been sung by Begum Akhtar, Noorjahan, Mehdi Hassan and Farida Khanum as well.

'Dono jahaan teri muhabbat main haar ke
Voh jaa rahaa hai koi shab-e-gham guzaar ke
Veeran hai maykada, khum-o-saaghar udaas hai
Tum kyaa gaye ke rooth gaye din bahaar ke'

(Having forfeited both worlds for love's sake
There goes a sad soul with a sad night in his wake
The tavern is barren, the chalice and wine is bereft
When you turned away from me, is when cheer from my life left)
His deep love for literature and poetry allowed him to create a

unique musical legacy that transcends time. His profound connection to literature enriched his performances and left an indelible impact on the world of art. For many poets, it was Talat's voice that carried the soul of their Urdu poetry, weaving magic through his melodies.

SILVER DISC BY EMI RECORDS

The 78rpm of the Talat-Faiz duo was a runaway success. The other non- film songs recorded by EMI were composed by ace music director Sohail Rana. The record label made an exception to specially honour Talat Mahmood with a Silver Disc. This meant that Talat entered another list of firsts! He was the first ever singer of the Indian Subcontinent to be presented with an EMI Silver Disc.

Rashid Latif, who was then the Managing Director of EMI records in Pakistan was excited to share the details with me. He currently lives a retired life in Canada but I was fortunate to speak to another nonagenarian whose memory is still as sharp. "Talat was always my favourite singer. While growing up in the Meerut city of Uttar Pradesh in pre-Partition India, there used to be a cinema hall called Nishad Talkies. Every evening before the movie show began, they would play songs on the loudspeaker to attract ticket sales. It seems that the owner of Nishat Talkies was a huge fan of Talat Mahmood because he only played his songs every evening. That's when I first heard his voice and it has captivated me ever since."

When Talat was visiting Karachi in 1961, Rashid Latif had a chance to meet him for the first time. "My job at EMI records was to manufacture music discs and record songs. Doing music concerts was not part of our brief. But for Talat, we went out of our way to lay out the red carpet. I have done this for only two people in my entire career: Begum Akhtar and Talat Mahmood. At our EMI factory, at least a few hundred people were invited to listen to Talat sing LIVE in concert", adds Rashid Latif. In addition to that, Latif had given a full page advertisement in The Dawn newspaper, informing readers that Talat Mahmood will be at the EMI office to sign autographs on his records from 2pm-5pm. This of course meant that sales of these EMI records shot up and each visitor got to own a personally autographed music disc. But not just regular readers, even Pakistani celebrities such as famous actress Shamim Ara also came. "All our records with Talat were a complete sell out. The sales were brilliant", he gushed.

The most striking memory of this trip was Talat's performance at the open grounds of the Gymkhana Club. There were about 15,000 people out of which many had gate-crashed. Those with tickets were getting squeezed and those without tickets pushed through the barricades. This was beyond the seating capacity and the police had no choice but to cool down the crowd and let everyone inside. Rashid Latif still remembers the incident as if it was yesterday. "I was helping my guests at the venue when I got a tap on my shoulder. It was the young and upcoming Ghazal maestro Mehdi Hassan standing along with our established singer of those times, Ahmed Rushdi, holding their VIP tickets, asking me to help them get in!! The emcee for the show, Zafar Ahmed described Talat's style of singing as 'wahdahu la sharika lahu'. It's a quote from the Quran in praise of Allah to say that He is incomparable with no equals. Many people were taken aback with this description that can't be used for a human being but such was the level of craze and idolization that Talat enjoyed."

Apart from this unprecedented public concert, he also did a special performance at the Indian High Commission in Karachi. Rishad Mahmood recounts, "The Indian High Commission's car was parked outside our house to pick up Talat uncle for the function. The car must've been waiting for about half an hour. But after Talat uncle was picked up, a Pakistan Army official came home to question Papa. That's because Papa was a serving Captain in the Army. He had to explain that his brother is visiting from India. He mentioned that his brother is Talat Mahmood and the car was sent to pick him up for a function at the Indian High Commission. The Army official suddenly broke into a wide smile and demanded that the singing legend should perform for them as well. That's how Talat uncle ended up giving a performance at the Fleet Club which was a posh club for the Armed Forces here." Indeed, it's the purity of good music and art that has always transcended boundaries and political differences.

NOOR JEHAN'S OFFER

His Karachi diary was chock-a-block and there was a huge line of artists wanting to meet him. One of them was Pakistani actor Santosh Kumar. He had done about 13 films in pre-partition India and played Dilip Kumar's father in a few. The meeting with Santosh Kumar turned out to be unexpectedly different. He offered Talat to stay back in Pakistan! It sounded like an outrageous thought for Talat but it turned out that many members of the music industry there wanted the same. Including none other than the 'Malika-e-Tarannum' (Queen of Melody), Noor Jehan. She called him up from Lahore.

Rishad Mahmood admits that a conversation between two of the greatest legends that took place in his father's living room has to be the most unique memory. "Our phone rang with a call from Lahore. It was Noor Jehan over the phone who wanted to speak with Talat uncle. She asked him to record film songs in Pakistan with a formal contract."

So this is what Noor Jehan expressed across the phone line from Lahore, "Talat sa'ab, I am requesting you to stay back here. I will ask music director Khalil Ahmed to fly to Karachi to give you a formal offer for a contract of nine movies. I will not ask you what your fee is. Khalil will carry a blank cheque and you can fill any amount that you want."

Talat was absolutely stumped but also touched with such generosity. One must realize that a contract for a chunk of nine movies with an asking price of the artist is an unheard offer in the film industry. As promised by Noor Jehan, Khalil Ahmed arrived in Karachi with the offer letter and a two-page contract. Undoubtedly Talat was a cult figure in Pakistan but he was committed to India. He politely and firmly turned down the offer and flew back to India.

FINDING A FAN IN BAL THACKERAY

Meanwhile back home in Bombay, two patriotic songs that Talat sang for the film Matlabi Duniya (1961) reflected his frame of mind. Once again in life, when he was confronted with the question of choice between the two countries, he emphatically dedicated himself to India. These two songs were, 'Mere Baapu se ye kahna' (Go tell my Bapu - Gandhi ji) and 'Jai Jai Bhaarat'(Hail India).

'Jai-jai Bhaarat desh hamara, jai-jai Bhaarat desh
Aaj shanti ka duniya ko deta hai sandesh
Huye yahaan par baalak neta
Luv-Kush jaise veer vijayta'

(Hail India, our dear country, hail India
It spreads the message of peace across the world
We've had many young leaders
Including the daring and victorious Luv and Kush)

Living in Bombay meant that he contributed to the regional Marathi cinema of Maharashtra as well. Talat could easily call himself a multi-linguist with so many songs of different regional languages under his belt. In 1961, for the first time ever, he sang in Marathi. These were two songs for the film 'Putra Vhava Aisa', composed by Vasant Prabhu and written by P. Sanvalram. One of them was -

'Yash he amrut zaale, sukh swargiche aale
Digvijayachya manorathavar nakshtranche zulate ambar
Mage pudhati raajpathavar laksh deep lagale'

(Success is like nectar, bringing heavenly happiness
The biggest triumph of the heart is cluster of constellations
Back and forth, lighting up the path of success)

Scoring hits had become a habit with Talat but this time he won an award too. Imagine, it was his debut Marathi song that won him the most prestigious award! This song became one of the biggest hits of the year in Marathi cinema. Happy and fast-paced, Talat's voice lifted the mood on- screen which showed the actor basking in his success and achievement, driving around the city in a big car with his wife.

The State Government of Maharashtra awarded Talat as the Best Marathi Singer of the Year. At the award distribution ceremony of the state festival of Marathi films, he received the award at the hands of the Union Minister for Information and Broadcasting, Mr. B. Gopala Reddy. This was a unique feather in Talat's cap because not only did he add a new dimension to his singing but he also established his popularity and acceptance in a language that many thought he could not do justice to.

A few years later, Talat partnered with superstar Ramesh Deo for another romantic song in Marathi, this time, in a duet with Asha Bhosle, composed by Vasant Desai and written by G. D. Madgulkar. A playful romantic number 'Hasale aadhi kuni' from the film Molkarin (1963).

Talat - Hasale adhi kuṇi? Tu ka mi?
Asha - Tu ka mi?
Asha - Sahaja tula mi re sakhya pahile
Talat - Tu baghata mi ga tula pahile
Asha - Tya pahaṇyace vada lagata
Talat - Tya veḍaca tu artha sangata hasale
Asha - Hasale

(Talat - Who laughed first? You or me?
Asha - You or me?
Asha - I saw you
Talat - I saw you when you saw me
Asha - What a crazy sight
Talat - You explain the meaning of this madness
Asha - Who laughed first?)

Talat has barely recorded a total of six Marathi songs in his career. This includes three soulful numbers released in 1965 which were part of a non- film album called 'Manoos Tujhe Naav' (Your are human). And yet, these handful of songs were enough to catch the attention of one of the most revered politicians in the state of Maharashtra, Bala Saheb Thackeray, founder of the political party Shiv Sena. He was a huge admirer of his voice and had once invited Talat for a private evening tea at his home.

"I found out about this thanks to a bunch of beautiful yellow roses. I had just come back from school and found these roses at Talat uncle's home. I felt like taking them so I asked my uncle where he got them from. That's when he explained that these roses were handpicked by Mr. Thackeray from his garden especially for Talat uncle", recalls Talat's niece, Romana Zaman.

Bal Thackeray had expressed that it was the first time that he had heard such heartfelt emotions in Marathi songs when Talat sang them. "He didn't have to put it there. He was born with it. What we call 'dard' (pain). It is rare to find".

GHALIB SE GULZAR TAK

Talat had covered a huge range of poets in his illustrious singing career. I created a tagline for one of the shows at Jashn-e-Talat in this context. The tagline was 'Ghalib Se Gulzar Tak' (From Ghalib to Gulzar). In the film Prem Patra (1962), Talat sang songs for one of poet Gulzar's early films as lyricist. It also brought him together with the remarkable filmmaker Bimal Roy again. The music for Prem Patra (1962) was composed by Salil Chowdhury which meant that the songs were expected to be a challenge with his signature pendulum swings in pitches and notes. Especially the song 'Saawan ki raaton mein', which is a duet with Lata Mangeshkar. As you notice, the singer touches the highest notes in their vocal range only to drop down like a waterfall to the lowest note in the next line. Starring Shashi Kapoor and Sadhna, this stormy romantic number was an instant hit.

'Sawan ki raaton mein, aisa bhi hota hai
Sawan ki raaton mei
Raahi koi bhoola hua, toofanon mein khoya hua
Raah pe aa jaata hai'

(In the nights of monsoon, this happens too
In the nights of monsoon
A wandering soul, lost in the storm
Finds a path to follow)

While Talat was continuing to belt out more hits, his songs from the past decade of the 1950s kept coming up with a resurgence in demand. In 1962, the Angel Records label under the Universal Music Group released a special album compiling 12 of Talat's best songs from the 50's. It was called 'Ghazals from films (Love Songs of Talat Mahmood)'.

A fact that I found shocking from 1963 is that Talat recorded only three Hindi film songs this year. And all three were hits. This is perhaps what had prompted his favourite composer Anil Biswas to once say, "Talat is the only singer in the industry who holds the record for the greatest ratio of hits to his credit."

One of the hits includes the fascinating song called 'Mazandaran' from the superhit period drama 'Rustom Sohrab' (1963). It's a story from the 10th- century Persian epic Shahnameh which features Prithviraj Kapoor and Suraiya in the main lead. Talat's song 'Mazandaran' is the name of a province in Persia which is difficult to conquer, literally translating to the 'valley of giants'. The music by Sajjad Hussain generously makes use of percussion and string instruments to create sounds of Persian and build the mood for an Orientalist period drama. Lyricist Jan Nisar Akhtar excels in bringing alive the glory of this dream land. Taking Talat for this song was an interesting pick for the composer because this is neither a romantic number nor in the blue mood. It's a patriotic and aspirational song praising the glorious land. Talat's voice sounds unique in the base notes while saluting the province; softly praising it and trying to evoke pathos for it.

'Mazandaraan Mazandaraan
Mere watan mere jahaan, aye gulsitaan jannat nishaan
Har phul tera ik chaman, har shakh hai naazuk dulhan
Aye jaaneman, Sadqe tere yeh jism-o-jaan
Mazandaraan Mazandaraan

(Mazandaran Mazandaran
My country, my love, O' land of flowers, beauty of heaven
Each flower like a garden, each tree branch like a delicate bride
O' my love, I am beholden to you
Mazandaran Mazandaran)

As I continue to list multiple songs of Talat from regional cinema for this book, I find it unfortunate that his legacy in this aspect is largely forgotten. Maybe because his Hindi film songs and non-film Ghazals have a towering presence. I must admit that I also had been largely unaware of this until I started organizing shows for Jashn-e-Talat, which truly put me on a path to rediscover his music.

I remember while giving an interview to All India Radio in 2018 to promote an upcoming Jashn-e-Talat tribute concert, the producer Vineeta Thakur left me completely surprised when she said that the next song on their playlist is Talat's song in Bhojpuri language. It was a naughty duet for the film 'Laagi Naahin Chhute Ram' (1963). Now you may wonder how a sophisticated Talat sounds naughty in a Bhojpuri song? Listen to it to believe it!

Talat - 'Laal laal hothwa se barse laliya ho ki ras chuwela

Jaise amwa ke monjra se ras chuwela'
(Your red lips are exuding with desire
Like a ripe mango oozing with juice)

Lata - 'Laage vaali batiya na bolo more raja ho kareja chhuela
Tori miithi mithi boliyaa karejaa chhuelaa ho kareja chhuela
(Your love talk touches my soul
Your sweet nothings touch my soul)

SINGING FOR THE DIVINE

During this time, Talat wanted to sing more devotional songs. This genre in the category of non-films music was niche but it also brought the devout closer to his voice. His voice which was often defined as serene and calm could not be off the mark for spiritual music. It went well with the ethos of devotional songs.

'Bhajan' are songs that are sung in praise and dedication to different Hindu gods. Talat has sung these in various languages of Hindi, Awadhi, Marwarhi, etc. in honour of Lord Ram, Ganpati, Krishna, Goddess Lakshmi, Saraswati, etc. Two bhajans in the Marwari language were written by Madhukar Rajasthani and set to music by Jamal Sen. One of them is -

'Bhakti ko devlo asha ki maala
Charana mein tharey bheynt chadhawa
Bala ji ko raakhi jago mein
Tala sardi jaay manaawa'

(In the light of devotion, prayers of hope
Sacrificing our life at your feet
Keeping awake all night for Bala ji (Lord Hanuman)
Chanting and celebrating your name)

'Naat' are Islamic songs sung in praise of Prophet Mohammad (P.B.U.H.). Talat has sung many Naat in Urdu in his career, one of them was composed by Taj Ahmed and written by Firoz Jalandhari-

'Sar-e-hashra ya Mohammad, hamein dijiye sahaara
Jo khuda ke dil ko bhaaya, wo hai martaba tumhaara
Meri aarzoo ka markaz , meri justajoo ka haasil
Woh hai kaali kamli waala, mujhe do jahaan se pyaara'

(Help us O' Mohammad on the day of resurrection
One who is close to the heart of God, that is your status
The centre of my wishes, the achievement of my pursuit
The one draped in black cloak, is dearest to me from both worlds)

THE CHITTAGONG ADVENTURE

In the early '60s, Talat was invited for a show in Chittagong, the port city of East Pakistan (now Bangladesh). This was a great time for him to meet up with his eldest brother, Hayat, as well as other friends from his days at New Theatre, who had settled in this country after Partition. His concert happened smoothly without incident. Thc ones who really had an adventure were his extended family who had decided to take a boat ride on the ferocious Sitalakhya river. Hayat, his wife and children, along with Talat's wife Nasreen and her children were enjoying the cool breeze on the boat while cruising on the river. The adults were busy clapping their hands and singing songs. "Suddenly there was water seeping into the boat. Our ride was cut short in the nick of time. By the time the boat was tied back to the tier, it was quickly sinking before our eyes. We would have all been drowning in water had the boatman not acted fast", dramatically recounts Hayat's son, Shahzad Mahmood.

Talat was shocked to hear about it when he came back from his show but grateful that all were safe. Always up with the spirits and looking forward to meeting more people, the next day, he went for a family dinner to Dhaka at his friend, music composer Robin Ghosh's house along with his wife, the film star Shabnam. The evening spent at their home, 20, Lavleen Street, was full of remembering the sweet days of the past and how music tastes in popular film music were beginning to witness a rapid change. He would love to travel to catch up with old friends and family along with good music. One of his favourite annual destinations would be the prestigious Dover Lane Music Festival in Calcutta.

"I was a young boy then but I remember being with him for this festival which would have the best performers in Indian classical music. We stayed at the Grand Hotel. It was always fun being with him. He wanted to show me the Calcutta Zoo. Something got into my head and I wanted to be formally dressed for the zoo. I insisted on wearing a tie and shirt. Talat uncle was the only one who gave into my tantrum and sweetly knotted me a bow-tie. We were barely 15 minutes into the zoo when he got mobbed and we all had to rush back to the hotel. Later that evening, we were celebrating Christmas night at the hotel. It was full of big names in music who were letting their hair down. I remember Talat uncle dancing with his friend, the legendary sitarist, Ustad Vilayat Ali Khan in the banquet hall. The next day we went to hear the greatest of all, Ustad Bade Ghulam Ali Khan perform for three hours. He was magnificent. It started raining but no one moved. Everyone stayed on till the end, despite getting wet", recalls Shahzad fondly.

PERFORMING FOR THE ARMY IN LADAKH

The popular practice of Hollywood stars going to army base camps to entertain troops was considered an important service to the nation by keeping their morale up and providing them with a much-required break from their rigorous duties. Everyone down the generations since the 1940's with Marylin Monroe, Bing Crosby, Jay Leno, Robin Williams to Jeniffer Lopez and Katy Perry today, have all performed for the troops.

In India, to entertain Indian army troops in a similar manner was first started by the star couple Nargis and Sunil Dutt in the early 1960s. They formed the Ajanta Arts Cultural Troupe which took actors and singers to remote frontiers. This troupe created history by taking film artists to Ladakh for the first time ever! India was fighting a deadly war with the conditions on the Himalayan Indo-China border being treacherous and cruel. In 1962, the roof of the world became the battleground between the most populous nations on earth. There was little or no comfort with thin air and cold wind cutting through the bones. The feeling of warmth and love was far away as their families waited for the guardians of our nation to return home soon. All they had were family pictures to patiently look at till the war was over and they could be reunited with them soon. But for now, they had the comfort of a caressing voice. Talat Mahmood was singing for the soldiers, in person.

'Tasveer teri dil mera behla na sakegi'
(Your photograph will be unable to console me)

The soldiers were touched. Their hearts were filled with emotions as Talat carried on to sing one soul-stirring hit after another.

'Mera pyar mujhe lauta do' (Give me back my love)

"Singing was an ordeal. The air was too thin for breathing but in a gasping manner, I managed. The oxygen content was just not enough. I had to perform with such thick gloves that playing the harmonium was a new experience", recalled Talat. He travelled with the film troupe which included Nargis, Sunil Dutt, Madhumati and others. They had landed at the highest airfield in the world at that time, in Ladakh, where soldiers were waiting with mixed feelings of love and wonder. This was the first time in the country that a film troupe was taken to Ladakh to entertain and comfort the troops. And Talat was part of this debut endeavour. "They loved us for we sang of their sorrows, hopes and fear. But they also wondered as to how these 'softies' of the film world could climb up the Himalayas simply to entertain them. But they didn't know that we also loved them for their bravery and marveled at their courage. They had left their home, friends and family to go up the treacherous terrains of our frontiers simply so that we could live in peace", expressed a grateful Talat.

After their performance, their departure got delayed because of bad weather. So, they ended up spending three full days with the troops in Ladakh, in the biting cold. They finally managed to take off on a special plane. Since the Prime Minister, Pandit Nehru had been very worried about them, they went to meet him soon after their return. "From the airport, we were driven straight to the Prime Minister's residence. Pandit ji received us with such love and enthusiasm that we forgot what we had gone through. There he was, embracing each one of us and making anxious, affectionate enquiries. It was a home-coming of the most tender kind", Talat added.

Soon, the Prime Minister ordered the photographer to take pictures with them. He posed merrily with each member of the film troupe. "Later on, the clumsy cameraman told us that there was no film in the camera. Can you beat that? His explanation was weirder than his deed. He got nervous with Pandit ji's sudden demand and did not have the courage to ask him to wait till he loaded his camera!!" Talat was distraught about it but his long-standing dream of having a picture taken with Pandit Nehru was fulfilled at another occasion in life. Irrespective of that, the memories of performing in Ladakh for the Indian Army and being received by the Prime Minister at his home remained an unparalleled experience etched in his mind forever.[28]

SINGING FOR REPUBLIC DAY AND HIS LONGEST LIVING FAN

(Talat with Prime Minister Nehru)

In 1963, a special cultural programme was organized in New Delhi to honour the martyrdom of our Indian soldiers from the 1962 Sino-Indian war. This became a defining occasion one day after the country's Republic Day. On 27th January, 1963, three of the top most singers of the time were chosen to perform on stage at Ramlila Grounds in the presence of Prime Minister Nehru. These singers were Lata Mangeshkar, Talat Mahmood and Mohammad Rafi. There was a loud applause by the spectators as Prime Minister Nehru appeared on stage. But this was a difficult time for the leader. India had just faced a debilitating defeat in the Sino-Indian War two months ago. Not only was this a blow to our Armed Forces but believed to be an emotional blow to Nehru as well. A special tribute song was prepared to mark the loss of our soldiers. Kavi Pradeep wrote the lyrics and composer C. Ramchandra gave music to this song which has now become an iconic tribute to the nation's soldiers. It was for the first time ever that the country heard Lata Mangeshkar sing the legendary song 'Aye mere watan ke logon' (O' dear countrymen). Since then and henceforth, this has become the song which embodies the pathos for our Armed Forces. As is famously known, Nehru was in tears after hearing Lata's rendition and he told her, "Tumne aaj mujhe rula diya (You brought me to tears today)".

I was aware that Talat Mahmood had also performed on stage that day. We have an autograph book at home carrying Pandit Nehru's signature from that date. Talat had taken his autograph and sent it to his sister Laila. But we didn't know which song he sang or what was the crowd's response to it. As luck would have it, in the course of my research, I came across the story of a 90-year old lady, Reena Verma Chhibber. She was in the news in August 2022 when the country was marking 75 years of India's Independence. Being a nonagenarian, she took a remarkable trip back to her ancestral house in Rawalpindi (in Pakistan) for the first time ever, after Partition. She was interviewed by various media houses for this trip. I stumbled upon her interview that mentioned Talat Mahmood. He was her favourite singer and she was a spectator in the crowd when Talat sang in the presence of PM Nehru at the National Stadium in 1963! What a remarkable coincidence! I simply had to meet her.
Born in 1932, she was in her 30s when she heard Talat sing at the National Stadium. She was now in her 90th year in life. When I mat her at her house, her living room was a photo gallery of singers she admired. And a black and white portrait of a young, handsome Talat Mahmood hung right in the centre of that galaxy of stars. She was delighted to talk to me about that experience of 1963. "Delhi was always the cultural capital, so there used to be a lot of music shows and performances. But they were all held in the evening. For a young woman like me who was single at the time, I would find it difficult to attend them, even though I am a keen follower of music. But this cultural celebration for Republic Day was happening during the daytime. So there was no way that I would miss it."

The open air show had a circular arrangement of chairs around the stage and she happened to be seated very close to the stage. "I was absolutely delighted when I saw my favourite singer Talat Mahmood come up on stage. He sang a non-film Ghazal from 1960 called Hangaama-e-gham se tang," recalls Reena Varma. This ghazal was written by Shakeel Badayuni with a more than usual classical composition by Taj Ahmed for this genre of music –

'Hangaama-e-gham se tang aa kar
Izhaar-e-masarrat kar baithhe
Mashoor thi apni zinda dili
Daanistah sharaarat kar baithhe
Koshish to bahut ki hamne magar
Paaya na gham-e-hasti se mafarr
Veeraani ye dil jab hadh se badhi
Ghabraa ke mohabbat kar baithhe'

(Frustrated by the weight of grief
I expressed some happiness
I was famous for my liveliness
My mischief was deliberate
Despite my best of efforts
I could find no respite
When loneliness became unbearable
My trembling heart fell in love)

(Talat's oldest living fan, 90 year old Reena Verma Chhibber, at her Pune home. The largest portrait on her living room wall is that of Talat)

"The crowd gave an amazing response to Talat after which he sang a second song. But I'm afraid I can't recall which one", adds Reena.

After this Reena continued being a lifelong fan of Talat. She shared with me her second experience which shows the humility of the singing star. This was an incident that touched her the most. "It was much later in life, decades after I had heard him on stage. In 1988 when I was living in Bangalore, I somehow got hold of his number and called him up with a request to meet him. Even though I was warned that he doesn't entertain fans at home anymore, I tried my luck. It was only for Talat that I wanted to go all the way. His wife picked up the phone who sounded very cheerful. She handed over the receiver to him and I was amazed when Talat said I could come over. I took the journey from Bangalore to Mumbai like a crazy fan."

Talat and Nasreen warmly welcomed Reena. It was a happy atmosphere at home since their son Khalid Mahmood had just released his debut album of pop-Ghazals and returned after the launch party. Reena loved the auspicious timing of her meeting. "I was, of course, talking to Talat sa'ab about his songs and music. But he was surprised when I informed him about how far back I had been listening to him. This was since the time he was singing on AIR Lucknow station in the 1940's during his college days. It was much before his first recording 'Sab din ek samaan nahin tha'. I was a little girl of barely 10-11 years old and Talat's teenage voice connected to me like magic. He was delighted to hear about this fact."

Recalling this episode added to some good cheer for the evening and Talat agreed to oblige for two of Reena's special requests that day. The first one was to sing a few lines of his favourite song. Believe it or not, without music and without his voice being in its prime, the legend sang some lines of 'Hain sabse madhur woh geet jinhe'. Her second request was to pen down a list of 10 of his personal favourite songs and autograph that list for her! "Talat laughed but he still agreed. He was the epitome of Lucknowi tehzeeb (genteel manners of Lucknow)", gushes Reena.

Today, fans like Reena keep alive the digital space buzzing in memory of Talat. She follows multiple fan pages of the singer on Facebook where they share his songs and reminisce about the rarity of his voice. These online fan pages sometimes transform to physical events as well. Reena informs me that just before the Covid19 lockdown in 2020, she and her friends organised a birthday party in celebration of the charming filmstar, with each of them singing one song each for the evening.

On a final note, she adds, "You know that famous couplet,
'Hain aur bhee duniyaa mein sukhan-var bahut achhe
Kahte hain ki ghalib ka hai andaaz-e-bayaan aur'
(There are many others with eloquence of excellence
It is said that Ghalib has a unique style)

I would like to replace that with - 'Kehte hain Talat ka hai andaz-e-bayan aur' (It is said that Talat has a unique style). That's because his throw of Urdu words, deep understanding of the language and poetry remains unmatched to this day. Which is also why I have often preferred his non- film Ghazals to his film songs."

Reena's statement was an original insight on how Talat maintained a separate and dedicated following of his non-film Ghazals parallel to his film songs. His independent Ghazals always kept him in the airwaves and on people's gramophones at home. This was irrespective of the number of film recordings he did in each given year.

WHAT IS 'HUM-RADEEF'?

As an artist, Talat always chose to look ahead with new challenges. He pushed the envelope on making the concept of Hum-Radeef ghazals attractive to both the masses as well as the recording labels. This was an ultra-niche category within the genre of ghazals. 'Hum' means something similar and 'radeef' refers to the last few words in the second line of a couplet. So, in a Hum-Radeef ghazal, there are two different poems written by two different poets which are especially brought together and sung in one single ghazal. The key formula for this being that both these poems should have a common radeef.

"It's not easy to sing Hum-Radeef ghazal keeping in mind the same emotions and feelings of both poets", explains today's well known Ghazal singer and composer Sudeep Banerji. He himself has sung a Hum-Radeef of two poets, Momin and Nazir Banarasi who were 150 years apart. He further adds, "This is mostly possible with classical poets. It is always a challenge because the poetry chosen is often written by two poets who are a century apart".

Talat sang the Hum-Radeef ghazals with his friends Mukesh and C.H. Atma. The first was sung with C. H. Atma in 1962 and the others with Mukesh in 1964. There are a total of four HMV recordings of Hum-Radeef by Talat. One of them was with the poetry of Mirza Ghalib and Daagh Dehlvi, sung by Talat and Mukesh respectively. Ghalib wrote these lines in the mid 19th Century while Daagh wrote his lines in the early 20th Century.

Talat (Ghalib) - 'Kisi ko de ke dil, koi nava-sanj-e-fughan kyun ho,
Na ho jab dil hee seene mein, to phir munh mein zuban kyun ho
(Why must you lament after giving your heart to someone,
When you have already lost your heart, then why complain)

Mukesh (Daagh) - 'Jo dil qaaboo mein ho to koi ruswa-e-jahan kyun ho,
Khalish kyun ho tapish kyun ho qalaq kyun ho fughan kyun ho
(If the heart is in control, then why should there be disgrace, Why this unease, agitation, regret, why this lament)

I'm unaware of the commercial viability of the Hum-Radeef since it demanded a deeper understanding of Urdu poetry but these are very popular on YouTube. Several listeners have admired how the singers made it sound like a seamless piece as if it were a single poem.

While this was a very niche project within the genre of Ghazals, in the same year, he sang a duet with Asha Bhosle in classical music. This song was based on Raag Mishra Nat and is a very popular thumri (a form of Hindustani classical music). Stalwarts like Pandit Channulal Mishra and Ustad Nazakat Ali Khan often sing this in their shows. The song 'Laage tose nain' was a classical composition from the film Chandi Ki Deewar (1964). Sahir Ludhianvi's lyrics set to tune by N Dutta and picturized on Nutan and Bharat Bhushan.

Talat & Asha - Laage tose nain, laage, laage
Daras bina, paaoon na chain
Jagoon sari rain, laage tose nain, laage laage

(I see love in your eyes)
Without a glimpse of you, I have no calm
I am sleepless all night, I see love in your eyes)

TIMELESS CLASSIC 'PHIR WOHI SHAAM'

The ambitious period drama based on the life of Mughal Princess Jahanara Begum was a much-awaited film with lavish sets and rich costumes. The film Jahan Ara (1964) was based on the historical romantic story of Jahan Ara (played by Mala Sinha) with poet Mirza Yusuf Changezi (played by Bharat Bhushan).

The film has a timeless song which has stood the test of time, and is a tribute to Madan Mohan's belief in Talat and Talat's own unparalleled position of being the best blue-mood, Ghazal singer in the film industry. I'm talking about 'Phir wohi shaam', which withstood the box-office disaster of the film and became one Talat's biggest hits of all time. The film director wanted all songs of the album given to a single singer whereas musician Madan Mohan had composed each song keeping in mind different voices, each song suited to a certain kind of voice. For instance, he explained that there are three songs in the film which were suited to only Talat's voice. No one else could do justice to them. These were –

1. Phir wohi shaam
2. Teri aankh ke aansoo
3. Mein teri nazar ka suroor

Madan Mohan was so adamant that he chose to give up the film in support of Talat. He also volunteered to record the songs in Talat's voice at his own expense. It was the producer, Om Prakash, who let the music composer eventually have his way. This film was very special for another member in the music team. The legendary flautist par excellence, Pandit Hariprasad Chaurasia. He had already met him once before during Talat's recording of a song in Odia language at AIR Cuttack radio station in the early 1960s. That's when Talat had noticed the exemplary talent of a young flautist who played the flute for his duet with singer Meena Kapoor-
'Nirola ae , rate Gaaye ke madhure'
(In the silence of the night, I hear a beautiful song)

The song is now a rare classic from the radio archives and attains its legendary status since every person of that generation in Odisha has grown up listening to it. It is the one and only song by Talat sung in Odia language. When I told Pandit Chaurasia about this biography, he was ecstatic and was completely lost in his first memories of Bombay city. "Talat sa'ab (sir) was the first singer I worked with in Bombay. I used to work at the radio in Orissa (Odisha) but soon after I shifted to Bombay, I got a call from Madan Mohan ji who was rehearsing at the Famous Recording Studio located in Tardeo. At that time, one would get 160 rupees per recording which was a great fee", explains Pt. Chaurasia.

He further adds his most favourite moment when he reached the studio. "I saw Talat sa'ab standing at the mic. We had one rehearsal for 'Phir wohi shaam' and then recorded the song", fondly recalls the legendary flautist. The song is written by lyricist Rajendra Krishan and is one of the most popular songs of Talat. Today, many tribute concerts are incomplete without the performance of this song. Each time that I have conducted a Jashn-e- Talat show, every singer on board insists on surely singing this song.

'Phir wohi shaam
Wohi gham wohi tanhaai hai
Dil ko samjhane
Teri yaad chali ayi hai

Phir tasavvur tere pahlu mein bithaa jaaegaa
Phir gayaa waqt ghadee bhar ko palat aayega
Dil bahal jaayega
Aakhir ko to saudaayi hai
Phir wohi shaam...'

(It's that evening, again
With the same sorrow and loneliness
My heart is consoled
With memories of you

An image of you is by my side, again
Reminding me of our time together, again
The heart will be swayed
After all it's insane
It's that evening, again...)

It was a song that became a lasting memory for Pt. Chaurasia as he throws light on how Talat was as a person . "My studio dreams came true. His behaviour was so silent and soft, lost in his thoughts. I wondered how I could strike a longer conversation with him. When he asked me where I was staying, I replied I was at Evergreen Hotel. To my surprise, he offered to drop me back to my hotel after the recording." In those days, Talat's house was at the top floor of a building on Linking Road. And Pt. Chaurasia would often drop by during the time Jahan Ara songs were being recorded. "His wife Nasreen ji would give me evening tea and delicious snacks. They were such a loving couple, I thought they would never quarrel. And as a young man, I would wish for a sweet and loving wife like her."

Those were his observations on his personal life. As a professional, he was equally bowled over by Talat's disposition. "These were times when artists would give space and time to reflect on their music. I felt that he was a very reserved person and whenever he spoke, he only spoke on music. With his behaviour and diction, he seemed like a Maharaja (Great King). He used to talk to me about Lucknow. I felt close to him, like a family member of his", recalls a delighted Pt. Chaurasia, calling him Ustad Talat Mahmood.

This song is an all-time favourite of today's popular Ghazal singer Talat Aziz. He is a legend in his own right and is often asked to sing 'Phir wohi shaam..' in many of his concerts as well. Even though it's not his song, he explains it remains a cult hit. "I get many requests to sing it. My voice is completely different from his. But his voice….you can't put a finger on exactly what it was. He had a very, very soft, rounded voice, yet he had a tremolo on that. On each note. If he stood on one note, you could hear the tremolo on that one note. It's very difficult. You can't do it unless it's a natural tremolo", explains an excited Aziz.[29]

Incidentally, the other songs recorded by Talat Mahmood for Jahan Ara had other musicians who went on to become great artists in their own right. There was Ustad Raees Khan on the sitar and Pt. Shiv Kumar Sharma on the santoor. Pt. Sharma played the santoor for 'Main teri nazar ka suroor'. Sitarist Ustad Raees Khan's work can be heard in an unreleased song from the film. The name of the song is 'Tum juda hokar'. This unheard gem is now available to listen to on Talat Mahmood's official YouTube channel which was handled by his late son Khalid.

By the mid '60s, the North-Eastern state of Assam had begun to make films on a regular basis. Their most promising filmmaker and musician, Bhupen Hazarika invited Talat to sing a duet with him in his film Pratidhwani (1964). The plot is based on a Khasi tribal story which is about the age-old burning issue of relations between the hill people and those living in the plains. The film was awarded the President's Silver Medal for Best Feature Film in Assamese language. This was Talat's first Assamese song.

Talat and Bhupen - 'Liyeng Makao Kaun
Pahare hi khara te, baat saayi sa
Huraar pooja kiya udang rakhi
Aakaal haarey mayin kimaan kaandim
Taane ak maaney bhaavisa'

(Liyeng Makao Who is it?
Which mountain top are you waiting at?
Why should I keep my house of music empty?
How long should I weep alone?
I am always wondering about this thought)

PM NEHRU'S DEATH & INDIA' FIRST WAR FILM

For the country, 1964 was marked with the passing away of our first Prime Minister , Jawaharlal Nehru. The nation was gripped by shock and sadness. For 17 years, he was India's longest serving Prime Minister since independence. His time in office as Prime Minister plus his leading role in India's freedom struggle had brought stability and direction for a young nation which had established itself as Asia's new centre, leading in the space of research in science, medicine and technology. There was a scientific temper and secular ideology that Nehru brought to institutions in that era. Suddenly, the country felt rudderless without him. Spontaneous shutdowns were reported across different cities. Such was the personal loss that people felt on the streets that shopkeepers voluntarily downed their shutters, buses stopped plying and roads became deserted. People chose to sit at home and mark this as a loss to their own family. Millions stood for hours to get a chance to pay their last respects at his home and cremation ground. Pangs of sorrow engulfed the entire country and each person seemed to have a personal memory of the leader to cherish.

The film industry also paid a tribute to his leadership. A landmark war-film Haqeeqat (1964) was dedicated to the emotive subject of the Sino-India war of 1962. The film's plot highlights the bravery of Major Shaitan Singh who led the Charlie Company of 120 soldiers from the Kumaon Regiment's 13th Battalion. They were up against a thousand Chinese soldiers who suffered India a loss of 114 soldiers from the Charlie Company. The film is a fictionalized version of what the soldiers went through, trapped at an altitude of over 18,000 feet, fighting the enemy and braving the harsh weather of minus 24 degrees Celsius in Ladakh. For the first time, a war film touched upon the human suffering of soldiers. It built an emotional character sketch of the soldiers and what they felt in their heart and minds while they were mid battle. Filmmaker Chetan Anand dedicated the film to Nehru and the real soldiers and martyrs of Charlie Company.

This new perspective in the film brought in a new style of patriotic songs as well. It was not just about the soldier holding a gun to the enemy, marching to the fronts, glorifying aggression at the battlefield and braving martyrdom. This time, it was also about the unspeakable emotional challenge of being away from home. Away from family. Away from your wife. Or away from your lover. This scenario gave birth to the heartbreaking song 'Hokey majboor mujhe' which stared into the abysmal possibility of dying in the cold at the hands of the enemy. It dealt with a deep-hearted concern of how your lover back home would deal with the devastating news of death.

Once again, music composer Madan Mohan strikes gold with this song written by the brilliant poet Kaifi Azmi. It was for the first time ever, and perhaps the last time too, that all four singing greats - Talat Mahmood, Mohammad Rafi, Manna Dey and debutant Bhupinder Singh - all came together to record this seven minutes. The emotional and personal touch from the soldiers' life became a popular trend for war-songs in the coming decades, including from the film Border (1997) with its superhit song 'Sandese aatey hain'. But 'Hoke majboor' is the OG in this genre!

All singers: Hoke majboor mujhe usne bhulaaya hogaa
Zahar chupke se dawaa jaan ke khaaya hogaa
Hoke majboor mujhe........

(Her helplessness must've urged her to forget me
Silently taking poison in the hope that it's a cure
Her helplessness....)

Talat: Chhed ki baat pe armaan machal aaye honge
Gham dikhaawe ki hansee me ubal aaye honge
Naam par mere jab aansoo nikal aaye honge
Sar naa kaandhe se saheli ke uthaaya hogaa

(The thought of our love must have stirred up her desires
She must have laughed while suppressing her sorrow
Teared up at the mention of my name
Not have lifted her head from a friend's shoulder)

All singers: 'Hoke majboor mujhe usne bhulaaya hogaa'
(Her helplessness must've urged her to forget me)

Talat was very dedicated to giving his time for entertaining troops of the Indian army. The mid '60s provided him with one such opportunity in Sikkim. There were some skirmishes between the Indian and Chinese armies in 1965. Army veteran Col V N Thapar who was the Company Commander for 17 Marathas at that time, recalls how he and his men were successful in pushing back the Chinese at the Nathu La pass when they were attacked. "I was on cloud nine! The newspapers described me glowingly as the young, short and robust officer who walked around Nathu La with the pugnacity of a Bantam Cock. I was eventually awarded the Chief of Army Staff Commendation Card for gallantry. I remember returning to Sikkim from the front as a hero who had just fought the Chinese army. A group of film stars were performing in Sikkim to entertain the troops." With this state of mind full of adulation and celebrations, Col Thapar was sitting in the front row with a gentleman flashing a pleasant smile. "I presumed he knew who I was. After sometime I asked him his name to which he either replied Talat or just Mahmood. I did not register who he was at all. So I asked him what he did in films. He told me that he is a singer." Talat politely expressed, "Aap ne iss nacheez ka koi to gana suna hoga?" (You must have heard some song by an insignificant artist like me?)

"Oh my god, that soft voice and his charm. To not recognize him there hit me like a ton of bricks", said Col Thapar , while narrating this incident to me in his animated style. "There has never been a greater embarrassing moment in my life since I was sitting next to one of my favourite voices but for some reason I had blanked out", adds Col Thapar. That day, Talat sang his latest hit for the troops apart from a few other popular melodies. Top of the list which got the loudest cheers was, of course, 'Hokey majboor' from the war film Haqeeqat (1964).

FANS FROM ASIAN ROYALTY

1964 was a significant year for the neighbouring country of Afghanistan. King Zahir Shah had just introduced a new constitution which made his country a modern democratic state by introducing free elections, a parliament, civil and political rights, women's rights, and universal suffrage. It was during this historic time, that Talat was invited to sing for the King to mark the annual celebrations for his Coronation Day. Other artists from across Asia were invited to perform as well. "That's where I met the famous classical singing duo of Pakistan, Ustad Nazakat Ali and Ustad Salamat Ali. I was amazed to hear from Salam saheb (sir) that he loved my song, 'Yeh hawa yeh raat yeh chandani'. Imagine, a classical-music Ustad paying a compliment to a film playback singer", gushed Talat.

Before he arrived at the hall to perform, a protocol aide gave him a long list of Do's and Don'ts. "We were not to do salaam with our right hand, we were not to sing more than one or two songs. Under no circumstance, we were to ask for a picture with His Royal Majesty. He hated posing for the camera. I was dumbfounded but dared not question the authority of the protocol man!" Talat continues to describe the scene with his tongue-in-cheek humour. "I went in saluting in the prescribed manner and took my seat. Then came the shock. King Zahir Shah got up from his seat (or was it his throne) and walked towards me. Now this was certainly not part of the protocol. I got up and braced myself for a nasty shock. The King handed me a list of nearly twenty of my songs and said that he and his family wished to hear me sing all these. I wondered about the protocol man", laughed Talat.

After he had finished singing all the songs, the King once again walked towards him, this time, to thank Talat. Since all protocol had already been broken, Talat decided to break the last one and asked the King for a picture with him. "To my amazement, he happily agreed. A round of photos were taken and to this day, some of these pictures stir some very happy memories in me", recalled Talat. He was gifted a large carpet by the King which became a centre piece in Talat's spacious living room. It was the iconic Khal Mohammadi rug which is exclusively hand knotted and comes in its signature combination of deep red undertones with a hint of dark blue and black.

It's fascinating how Talat's name would resonate at home with the latest news headlines. In 2002, King Zahir Shah returned back to Afghanistan after 29 years in exile. I had just started working as a newsreader for the Overseas Services at All India Radio. When I came back home, my mother asked me, "You know about King Zahir Shah?" I replied, "Yes, he was in my headlines today. What happened?". She casually responded, "He was a huge fan of your grand uncle." At that time, I didn't pay much attention to that fact. I was too busy with other aspects of the news. But now, in hindsight, I marvel at what a rockstar he was!

Talat had also ended up enchanting another royal of another neighbouring country of India. He was visiting the Himalayan Kingdom of Nepal for a concert tour when King Mahendra Bir Bikram Shah Dev invited him for an evening of music. "I learnt from someone that King Mahendra also writes poetry. So I bought a book of his poems and sat with a Nepalese friend to perfect my pronunciation. During my performance at the Palace, I suddenly burst into a Nepalese number amidst my Urdu songs. The reaction was electrifying. The King suddenly jumped from his seat", recalls an amused Talat. King Mahendra was undoubtedly charmed. "From where did you get this song?", he asked.

"Sir, I knew you were a wonderful poet so I bought one of your books and composed this number especially for this evening", replied Talat. The King was visibly moved and paid handsome compliments to Talat's pronunciation in Nepalese. He gifted the singer a replica of the famous Taleju Bell which is located in the Patan Durbar Square under a Pagoda roof. This replica was made of bronze encrusted with turquoise and coral. On a thoughtful note, Talat adds an interesting insight to his mind as an artist, "During my career as a singer, I have sung for all kinds of audiences. I have sung thousands of times inside a recording studio where I can only imagine my audiences. I love my audience and enjoy a concert program much more than I enjoy a recording. I have had my share of contact with the great. But I love to sing for the ordinary men and women of my land, for I am one of them and with all due respect to royalty, I shall any day prefer a loving heart to all the glory and majesty of a durbar."[30]

SUNBEAM, THE DREAMHOUSE

(Talat's glorious bungalow was called Sunbeam)

While Talat continued to be a popular name, his recordings for films were beginning to witness a decline. He translated this as a temporary lull as most artists in the film industry are used to. Some years, the work is great and some years it can face a brief dwindle. There was nothing alarming about it, Talat thought. He was always a dreamer. Nothing deterred him from having his dream bungalow in the Queen of Bombay Suburbs, Bandra. It was one of the poshest localities of the city (and still is) which boasts of homes owned by actors, singers, directors and other members of the creative field. A lot of these homes were old bungalows from the British Era with distinct architecture and design. The suburb is along the coast of the Arabian Sea and the big attraction is to have a sea facing bungalow.

When we talk about superstar Shah Rukh Khan's much celebrated purchase of his Bandra bungalow 'Mannat', it is a beautiful reminder that this has been the dream for most film stars two generations before, since the start of the Golden Era. And many had realized this dream in the 1950s. They all came from outside Bombay and made the city of dreams their home. Many of them settled in this queen of suburbs. The list includes stars like Dilip Kumar, Nargis, Gulzar, Naushad, Raj Kapoor, Pran, Rajesh Khanna, Rekha, Siddharth Malhotra, Deepika Padukone - just to name only a few across generations.

Talat Mahmood had set his heart on a bungalow named 'Sunbeam'.

It was one lane behind the sea front and before the current trend of high-rise buildings, Talat would often enjoy a clear view of the beautiful sunsets at the sea from his terrace. His wife Nasreen, who was an excellent homemaker, had tastefully done up their dream house. It was a typical English-style villa with marble flooring. The manicured front lawns had a bed of seasonal flowers with tall palm and Ashoka trees providing a cool shade to the house. The drive-in through the lawns led you to the main entrance which opened into a guest lounge. This further extended into a large living cum dining room which was divided by a three-paneled screen made of carved walnut wood. The living room was an inviting space with three sofas upholstered in deep maroon coloured velvet with multi coloured throw pillows. The curtains were usually in floral patterns with pastel colours. This large living cum dining room was flanked by two bedrooms on each side. On the left was the master bedroom and the kids bedroom was across the other side on the right. The outer walls of these rooms were constructed in a semicircular shape and the three long windows on these curved walls would open into the front lawns. The corridor behind the living room had the kitchen which further opened into the backyard kitchen garden.

Next to this was the all-important music room for the great singer. The waves at the seafront would create a beautiful rhythm through the day bouncing through the lawns and whispering into the windows of Sunbeam. The monotony of this rhythm was broken every morning by Talat's soft alaaps (vocals) and sounds of the tanpura (string instrument), as he sat at the break of dawn for his daily 'riaz' (vocal exercises). The side pillars ran up the ceilings with pointed roofs and wooden rafters. This was a double- storied bungalow and both floors had an identical structure. It was the perfect heritage house befitting the style and class of the Shahenshah of Ghazals.

Talat and his family stayed downstairs while the floor upstairs was rented out to celebrity ornithologist Humayun Abdulali. "It's a pleasure being his tenant. He leaves me at peace with my study and observations of birds. The house is always spruced up annually with impeccable maintenance. And as a landlord, Talat sa'ab would never delay any impending repairs", he would often say.

Had the house survived today, Sunbeam would have surely been one of the heritage beauties mentioned on Bandra's list of must-see bungalows. But alas, it was broken down and rebuilt as a multi-storey apartment in the 1980s and Talat was handed over the penthouse on the top floor. Down the years, he was an important resident of Bandra and became one of the first members of the popular Otter's Club.

Meanwhile, the number of his Hindi film recordings was showing clear signs of a decline. For the first time ever in Talat's career, 1965 was the year in which he had just one film recording. That film was 'Ek Saal Pehle' (1965), a murder mystery starring actor Sujit Kumar in the lead role. Talat had a duet in the film with Asha Bhosle called 'Nazar utha ke yeh rangeen sama' (Lift your eyes to see this joyous moment). His niece Romana who was 12 years old at that time has a very special memory about this film. "Children were never allowed to go for film premieres but this time, I had picked up a huge fuss to go. I remember wearing a *sharara* with light pink flowers. I was all dressed up and waiting to hear the distinct sound of the horn of Talat uncle's black Hillman car. He had come to pick up my mom but I insisted that I should be taken instead. He came dressed up in a suit and tie. We went to the Neptune Talkies near our house in Bandra."

When she got down the car with her Talat mamu (uncle) at the red carpet, the crowd that was gathered on both sides, started clapping. The little girl with stars in her eyes looked up and asked her uncle why is there such a huge applause? To which, the adorable Talat replied, "Arrey, jab film ki heroine aayi hai to taali nahin bajayenge log? (You are the film's heroine who has just arrived, won't people clap for you?)"

It's not difficult to understand why he was Romana's favourite uncle. Unlike his film persona as a singer who could move your soul with his melancholic voice, Talat as a person was full of vivacious fun and pranks. "Our families had gone out for a picnic to Powai lake. After lunch, we decided to trek around the lake but I was feeling very full after eating. I was walking very slowly, so Talat started to sing loudly just to pull my leg. He sang 'Jaane wale sipahi se puchho woh kahan ja raha hai' (Ask the soldier where he is going). He didn't realise there was another group of people who suddenly recognized him and waved out", recalls a giggling Romana.

If the Bombay film industry wasn't calling him for songs, there were others in regional cinema who wanted him. He sang for two Bhojpuri films in 1965. One was a duet with Lata Mangeshkar, 'Phulwa mein phool hai, gulab sabse aala' (The garden has flowers but the rose is the most unique) for the film 'Bhouji'. And the second was a duet with Suman Kalyanpur, 'Ka boli saiyyan batwalo na jaaye' (Can't express what you said to me) from the film 'Hamaar Sansaar'.

His friend since their New Theatres days in Calcutta, the composer and singer, Hemant Kumar, had an interesting single for him to record in 1965. "I enjoyed Hemant Kumar's company tremendously. He was such a nice and talented person that one could not resist his influence", Talat would fondly recall. He wanted Talat to sing a Bengali song which had the speaking voice of film star and actor Rakhee Gulzar. She puts forth philosophical questions while Talat answers them by singing to her. This was just a couple of years before her debut film.

Rakhee : 'Eto thuku aadharey mon aar eyi thuku aalor poroshey Eyi li aakash'
(The mind is so dark and the sky is beyond this little light)

Talat : 'E jodi akash hoye tomay ki bole ami ḍākabō boley
Bhulēy java naam dhorey ḍāak bina keyno
Betha hoye chirodeen roye geylo jeno
Kuley eshe baar baar kānnaaẏ bhengey jaava
Ei ki shagore
Ei jodi shagore hoye tomaye ki boley ami daakbo boley'

(If this is the sky, tell me what will I call you?
Why is it called by a forgotten name,
Why does the pain remain forever?
The sea that comes to the shore,
Breaks over the edge again and again
What is this sea?
If this is the ocean, tell me what will I call you?)

It was an exclusive single released by HMV in 78rpm and written by Mukul Dutta, a multi-talented lyricist and film director who played a major role in Modern Bengali films and songs.

The next year, in 1966, a new album of 12 Bengali songs called 'Vintage Glory - Talat Mahmood' was released by the Gramophone Company. This included a mix of his old hits. All of these have become classic songs like 'Ei rimjhim jhim', 'Ruper oi pradeep', 'Bou katha kau' and 'Shono go sonar' to name a few.

Throughout the 60s, Talat's non-film recordings kept him busy, with an LP or EP (extended play) record of his being released virtually every year of the decade. Some of these were re-recordings of his earlier hits that were released in the late 40s and early 50s sung for old-timers like Kamal Dasgupta, Chitta Roy and Khayyam, but many were newly-minted numbers by contemporary composers of that time, like C.K. Chauhan, Yunus Malik and Murli Manohar Swarup. An EP released in 1965 featured this particular Ghazal (composed by Shyam Sharma, written by Prem Warbatoni), which is a challenging composition and now a rare gem. Enjoy.

'Phool ki aankh mein aansoo hai
Aur naseeb ki kok mein moti
Kash mere bhi man mandir mein koi to moorat hoti'

(The flower has tears in its eyes
And pearls in the womb of fate
I wish I too had an idol of perfection in my mind)

It's one of the toughest compositions sung by Talat, in my view. It's impossible to replicate his drop and climb in pitches. This is the sole reason why his voice has been an original entity without any clones. None have been able to copy his style or voice. To date.

The year 1967 saw the release of a very popular LP record titled 'Spring Blossoms', which featured eleven new recordings. Listeners have appreciated for many years ghazals from this album, such as –
1. Gale lagake jo sunte the (The one who would hug me and hear me out)
2. Unke aage gham-e-dil chhupana pada (Hide my broken heart from her)
3. Aankhon aankhon ki hai jo baat (The way our eyes speak to each other)
All of these were composed by Yunus Malik.

Let's be very clear that for those who mislead music lovers by saying Talat's music career ended after 1964, they come with a mistaken view. We should appreciate that a skillful and popular singer's music is not limited to only film recordings. The 1960's was Talat's most busy decade for his non-film recordings. Talat ended this decade with a bang with the release of another EP record in 1969, simply titled 'Ghazals'. This featured ghazals composed by C.K.Chauhan, like 'Falak ki god sitaaron se khali hai' (The stars are fading away from the sky) and 'Mujhe kuchh khabar bhi na ho saki' (I could never say), which have enthralled fans for generations. Enjoy my favourite ghazal from this album, with poetry by Raaz Allahabadi –

'Mujhe kuch khabar bhi na ho saki
Meri zindagi pe woh chhaa gaye
Kabhi ashq banke rola gaye
Kabhi dard banke samaa gaye'

(I could never say
How she overpowered my life
Sometimes she rolled down my cheeks
Sometimes she became a part of my hurt)

SETBACKS BY VERSION SONGS

While the reduction in recording Hindi film songs must have surely got Talat worried, he was more hurt by the deceit he was beginning to face by music composers and filmmakers. Finding his voice replaced in the final version of songs that he had originally recorded for was a bigger emotional setback for him. But such has been the fate of many successful singers where the demand for another voice begins to sideline your potential despite a successful track record. This malpractice has existed since several decades in Bollywood and has only intensified today, with more number of singers available at hand. Today, this practice is callous to the extent that there could be about 6-8 version recordings of one single song till the director or actor decides which singer to keep!

In Talat's case, the late '60s was particularly the worst time for these circumstantial setbacks. Music composer Naushad had co-written the story for the film Palki (1967), starring Rajendra Kumar. When he composed the music for this film, it was perfectly suited to Talat's style, given that Rajendra Kumar played a poet from Lucknow. So Naushad recorded two songs with Talat. But here's where we understand the importance of the right timing; or the wrong timing in this case. These two songs for Palki were recorded by Talat much earlier in 1963. They were -

1. Kal raat zindagi se mulaqat (I met my life last nite)
2. Chehre se apne aaj to parda uthaiye (Unveil your face)

For reasons unknown, the shoot for the film was put on hold and it was a project long forgotten till 1967. In these intervening four years, Mohammad Rafi had been established as Rajendra Kumar's main singing voice. Alas, both songs of Talat were re-recorded in Rafi's voice.

The next year, the film Aadmi (1968) was released. Naushad recorded a duet of Talat with Rafi. The famous duet called 'Kaisi haseen aaj baharon ki raat hai' (How beautiful is this night, the night of blossoms) was picturized on Dilip Kumar and Manoj Kumar. With Dilip Kumar having Rafi's playback, Manoj Kumar was lip syncing to Talat's voice. Since the flavour of the season was a different style of voice, Manoj Kumar wanted a change. He had been happy with his previous hits in Talat's voice but this time he insisted on Mahendra Kapoor's vocals.

And so, the duet was re-recorded.

Co-incidentally, in both films, the music director was Naushad. Unlike Madan Mohan who argued and fought with film directors in support of Talat, it is alleged that Naushad chose to go silent on him. It would have been foolish for anyone not to see the winds of change. But Talat was no fool. He was the original star of concert tours. Being wiser than most, he decided to start touring again.

TALAT-MANIA AKIN TO THE BEATLES

(Talat (centre) with his troupe members Van Shipley (left) and Enoch Daniels (right) take the West Indies by storm)

Rock and roll music was taking up the music space. Even though Talat had successfully broken the mould of traditional Ghazals by using the guitar and violin in his non-film recordings, louder beats were influencing the tastes of the youth in full speed in India. These beats didn't suit Talat's gentle voice. And quite frankly, nor did he like the sounds of rock. The influence of this new genre was unstoppable, especially when The Beatles themselves came visiting India in 1968. Their much-publicized meditation retreat in Rishikesh created a media frenzy with daily press updates. After all, they were the biggest rockstars of the world. Would you believe me if I say that Talat faced equally frenzied crowds that same year but in another part of the world?

Unfazed by the setbacks in Bombay, Talat didn't mope around knocking on doors of directors and composers begging for new songs. He decided to cater to his fans overseas. Picture this. A photo studio abuzz with singing star Talat Mahmood doing a special shoot of promotional stills. But it all looked very different and unexpected. These promotional stills didn't seem to be for a film poster. Nor did it seem for the cover of an album. Why was Talat wearing a straw hat with a cigarette casually pressed between his lips? Flanked by two of his musicians, Van Shipley and Enoch Daniels, who were also wearing straw hats, one holding the Hawaiian guitar, the other holding the accordion. This was a photo shoot for an upcoming tour, with the three men having some fun, looking like the three musketeers.

Acutely aware of his demand for LIVE shows which he had already witnessed in his debut tour of 1956, Talat packed his suitcase, gathered his team of musicians and organizers and set out for his West Indies tour in July, 1968. Talat performed in Trinidad & Tobago, Guyana, Surinam, Fiji Islands and Jamaica. The team worked at least 5 days a week, 16 hours a day. "The shows were always houseful! It might sound crass but Talat was really like the golden goose with us," says his tour manager, Nandi Duggal. Once again, Talat was the first Indian playback singer to tour Trinidad. The concert market for Hindi films had not been tapped earlier there. And to arrange a two way trip for the entire troupe had to be vetted with guaranteed returns of investment. So therefore, houseful bookings needed to be confirmed in advance. After that was achieved, Talat's grand welcome was organized in great detail.
He was given a thunderous reception in Trinidad. The hysteria started right from the airport. As the door of his aircraft opened, there was an open limousine waiting for him down the red carpet at the tarmac. Talat took a deep breath as he got down the stairs and greeted a sea of fans, waving at photographs. There were flowers and heart shaped badges made in his name. As a special gesture, the organizers decided to record a theme song especially composed for Talat's tour. This song was played at his arrival and across record shops, bus stops and cafes to boost ticket sales. A popular West Indian steel band sang this Calypso theme song in his honour.

'Talat Mahmood we are proud and glad
We have a personality like you in Trinidad
Welcome to our land
The land of Calypso'

'Talat Mahmood mubarak ho
Trinidad mein aakey humko gana sikha do
Talat Mahmood tere aaney se
Dil mein hai umang, gana suna do'

(Congratulations Talat Mahmood
Come, teach us how to sing in Trinidad

You are here with us
Our hearts are full, teach us how to sing)

Talat arrived at the capital city, Port of Spain. The road to Bretton Hall Hotel was peppered with welcome notes and posters of Talat Mahmood. Because of the tremendous popularity of Indian movies in the 1950s and 1960s, there were local shops such as Balroop's Record Shop in Trinidad which not only sold LPs and 78rpms of film songs but also printed a lyrics booklet of those songs. That's how everyone would learn the lyrics and sing along. Mind you, they did not understand Hindi film songs, but just mugged up the songs they liked. Since people hardly understand the language, what was it about Talat that appealed to them? "It's difficult to understand the music tastes in Trinidad. Top blockbusters of Hindi films didn't always do well here. In Talat's case, what mattered was the sound of his voice. It felt good and that was the key," recalls Vishnu Balroop, CEO, Balroop Group, when I enquired about Talat's demand. Talat had made a stop at the famous Balroop's Record shop to meet fans and autograph albums for them. "My dad was the distributor of HMV India in Trinidad. But I must let you in on a secret. The demand for Talat was much more for his non-film Ghazals as compared to his film songs. His Ghazal market was very popular here, so people recognized his voice with a niche specialty", adds Balroop.

What happened on the day of his concert at the Skinner Park in San Fernando was unprecedented. According to Nandi Duggal, this single experience with Talat left him spellbound. He had never seen anything like this in his entire professional life. "Skinner Park was an open-air location with a capacity of about 7000 people. We had the opening of our second show there. A space which could fit in 200 parked cars was packed with people. So many people had gathered that even I couldn't enter backstage. I got worried about how Talat would manage to enter the venue. The police on foot just couldn't manage the rush."

Duggal continues to describe the chaotic scene, "The mounted police on horses had to be called in. There were helicopters above which were guiding the mounted police with crowd management. Ghode mangwane padhey, poora pagalpan tha (The horses had to be called in, it was sheer madness!). This hysteria I have only seen with Talat"

Balroop further adds, "My father had arranged for the recordings of his LIVE concerts which were handed over to Radio Trinidad 7:30 AM. These recordings used to play until many years later. Even today, his songs play at 103 FM." He fondly recalls the night that Talat had dinner at his house with his parents and siblings after a super successful show. "My mother prepared dinner for Talat. Trinidadian food is very different from the spicy food of India. Our food is less spicy with a different flavour but it still has some Indian influence. I remember him enjoying the dal-poori (fried roti stuffed with a paste of pulses), mango talkari (green mango curry) and pelau (rice dish cooked with meat and vegetables)." Talat left behind memories for his family to date. Balroop can't remember ever seeing serpentine lines at his father's store when people waited for hours to get their record signed by Talat. It is only after his concert that other singers like Manna Dey and Lata Mangeshkar followed suit. But he feels that Talat created the biggest impression. "The immediate impact of the success of his tour was that it boosted record sales at music stores across the country and also kickstarted a new singing competition. This was called the 'Talat Mahmood Singing Competition' in which young singers would compete in singing Hindi songs and then the winners would be rewarded." I was amazed when Vishnu Balroop said this to me because there is a similar kind of singing competition that I had kickstarted in colleges across Delhi in 2017 as part of my youth outreach at Jashn-e-Talat.

Talat did a minimum of 30 shows in the West Indies including Surinam, Guyana, Jamaica and Trinidad before flying to the United States. There they had a brief stopover with a couple of shows, including in New York city.

THE FRANK SINATRA OF INDIA

In August 1968, Talat received an invitation for a recording at the heart of Times Square at 1481 Broadway Studio. But this wasn't for recording a song. He had been invited as a guest on the popular talk show called the 'Joe Franklin Show'. The channel where this show was aired for decades was called WOR-TV with its recording studio called STUDIO-4, on the upper floor of the art deco Rialto Theatre. Unfortunately the building is no more. It has been demolished and the new swanky office with a glass facade is called the Reuters building, which is the headquarters of the media company Thomson Reuters. But nothing can beat the historic importance of this place which is part of the charming past of old Times Square. The show host Joe Franklin is credited for having the first ever talk show who was a pioneer in inventing the format of these one-on-one chats on television. The formula he created was about a curious show host sitting behind the desk, quizzing a range of personalities from varied professional fields. His show had an uninterrupted run from 1951 to 1993, with stars ranging from Bing Crosby, Paul Newman, Al Pacino, Barbra Streisand, Michael Jackson and Woody Allen, to name a few. His envious list of guests also included Andy Warhol, Muhammad Ali and U.S. Presidents like John F. Kennedy and

Richard Nixon.

There's a picture of Talat standing with Franklin in his studio set with a background of abstract white and purple Mondrian-esque triangles outlined in strong, black strokes. The adjacent wall was inset with an arc that featured a vintage image of the famous dancing couple, Fred Astaire and Ginger Rogers. In the foreground of Talat and Franklin, one can see the video camera on wheels with the letters "WOR TV 9", the official channel for the talk show. As the opening shot of the show panned across Franklin's table with Talat sharing the frame with a big microphone in front of him. The audience immediately took note of this gentle legend from India when Franklin introduced him as the 'Frank Sinatra of India'. This was a comparison which stuck on for long, especially when both crooning legends passed away barely five days apart in the same year in 1998.

The recording time of this episode with Franklin was about one hour long. His studio team had purchased a record of Talat's songs to play out for the audience in between the interview. It was an amazing moment when an all American audience watched their favourite talk show host speak to a suave singer from India, while his songs in Urdu played out in between their conversation. Talat spoke about his music journey that had taken South Asia and the Indian Diaspora by storm! The show was aired on 29th August, 1968.

While in America, Talat heard about a new concept of film tourism that had gained popularity in the U.S. This was called the 'Universal City Studio Tours' which was a ticketed trip inside the Universal Studios in California. The initial years of this tour from 1963 onwards were a pivotal period that reinvented the success of Universal. This is that part of history in which tourism and cinema were linked together with ticket sales. Universal showed how a film tourist gaze can bring immediate commercial benefit.

The initial tour included a series of dressing room walk-throughs, behind- the-scenes during LIVE shoots. And later, there were specially staged stunts that the visitors would see from their tram ride which was called the 'Glam-Tram'. They would get a chance to visit film sets of famous sitcoms and movies that were constructed there; the most popular being Bates Motel and the house on the hill from Hitchcock's sensational horror film, Psycho. Actor, singer and radio artist Bob Hastings used to be a regular at the Universal

Studios. He was best known for his portrayal of Lt. Elroy Carpenter in the hugely successful sitcom called McHale's Navy that ran for four seasons. His set used to be an important stopover for the Glam-Tram.

Soon enough, Universal started paying actors during breaktime to be on the grounds and talk to tourists. Other notable tour guides have included a long list of celebrities like Ron Howard, Jimmy Fallon, Whoopi Goldberg, etc. It is believed that Hastings got along so well with people that he earned the nickname of the 'mayor' of the Universal Studios tour.

It was one such day that Hastings found out about a big star visiting from India. He was eager to talk to him about the workings of showbiz in India. He was delighted to know that Talat was a singer too and shared his newly released music album called 'Bob Hastings Sings for the Family'. Hastings recorded an impromptu chat with Talat about his career and some pictures of them were clicked together for the local press. This trip to the U.S. worked as a great teaser. There were bigger concerts by Talat coming up in America for the next decade.

ROYALTY RIGHTS - MIKE DOWN PROTEST

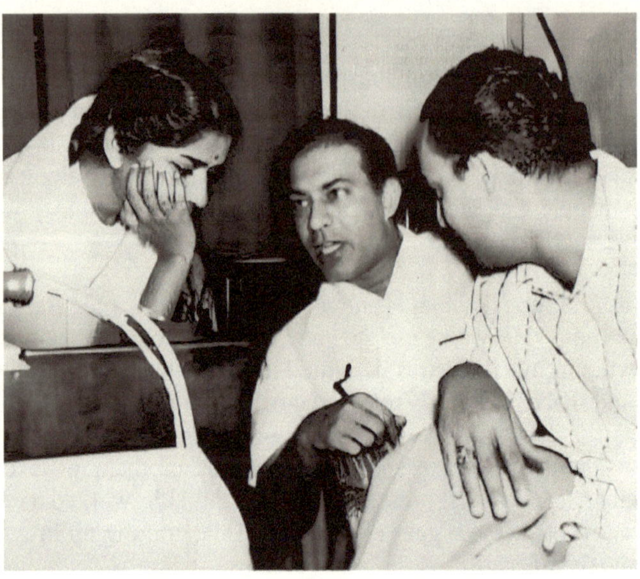

(Talat (centre) was Secretary of the Playback Singers' Association. Seen here with Lata and Mukesh in an intense meeting on Royalty Rights)

As an avid traveler, Talat was a keen observer of the international music industry. His global tours gave him an insight on how world music companies paid the royalty fees to their singers on the sale of each record. But this wasn't happening in India. The film producers were brazenly denying them this right by paying them only at the time of studio recording. The concept of royalty payment was existing in India but not for the singers. The music labels would pay a percentage of their record sales to film producers and music directors but not to the singers. Lata Mangeshkar was the only one to have raised it earlier and met with some success by convincing a few producers. But it still wasn't made a common practice for the benefit of all singers for all films.

One can't imagine a gentle and charming personality like Talat to be an activist. But he always believed in standing up for what's right. He took charge as the Secretary of the Playback Singers Association in the mid 60's and galvanized the campaign to get all big singers united for receiving royalty fees from the music companies. We must realize here, that unlike other playback singers in the film industry, Talat had a decent stream of income in his non-film recordings of Ghazals and Geets. The royalties for recording a non-film song directly with the music label was simpler. But in the name of justice, Talat decided to move ahead with this campaign for all playback singers. This campaign involved meeting with the stakeholders to negotiate a legal undertaking on royalty payment for playback singers. Lata Mangeshkar who was already vocal about this issue joined in. Other singers like Mukesh, Kishore Kumar and Manna Dey added to the force of this campaign. But soon these talks fell through. Film producers and music companies were not agreeable to their demand.

This led to a historic 'mike- down' protest. The singers decided to go on a strike and they stopped recording for film songs completely. It was the longest strike of singers that the film industry had seen for the cause. For 3 months, film song recordings came to a screeching halt. It became a defining moment for this cause, where music labels and film producers could no longer look away from this demand. Unfortunately, the protest weakened with two singers breaking away from the strike. As Lata Mangeshkar spoke about it in an interview, "Rafi Sahib and Asha (Bhosle) believed that once a song was recorded and the producer had paid us -- that was the end of it. Rafi Sahib didn't think that we should fight for royalties." [31]

Reportedly, recording for film songs resumed and the strike collapsed. Lata was so upset that she refused to sing with Rafi for almost three years! This became the basis of the most famous fall-out of two of the biggest singers, until they were brought back together in Jewel Thief (1967). The demand for singers' royalty fees went into the back burner. Decades later when the Copyright (Amendment) Act, 2012 was passed in Parliament, the singers were granted economic rights, independent of the composer and songwriter. This meant that once a singer had recorded an original song, for the next 50 years, everyone except the producer needed their consent and would have to pay royalty to play or perform their song in public. Today, no one remembers to thank Talat for creating the first big ripples for this cause in bringing together like-minded colleagues. But the fact remains, that Talat left his indelible mark on an issue which has come a long way in helping give singers their right to royalty. He was a mould-breaker with a foresight for an industry that he loved and belonged to.

REFRESHING MAURITIUS

In 1969, the Talat Mahmood Troupe was invited to the island nation of Mauritius. A special show of fireworks was put up for their welcome. This was a newly independent island nation marking almost a year of freedom from British rule. The Indo-Mauritians settled there are descendants from Indian immigrants centuries ago. The sense of belonging to India is still very strong. Many generations down, they have managed to retain some of their ethnic roots in terms of religion and rituals. The Hindi films and songs are popular amongst the locals there, with 65 percent of the population being Indo-Mauritians. This was similar to what Talat had experienced in his earlier tours to the West Indies and East Africa. The crowd in Mauritius avidly followed his songs but couldn't understand the language.

He was in a mood to rib the audience. With a receding hairline in his mid '40s, he looked different from what people in Mauritius were used to seeing him in the movies as a young, handsome singer-actor. "How do you know if I'm the real Talat Mahmood?", quipped Talat. "Your voice!!", the audience laughed and replied. "Well, let me sing my signature Ghazal for you and see if you recognize me then", replied Talat. He then sang the timeless hit 'Tasveer teri dil mera behla na sakegi'. Of course, what Talat perhaps meant was now they could see the real singer in person instead of his posters! At the prompt of an audience member, he was asked about the saddest song he had ever sung. Talat chose to sing 'Birhan baithi aas lagaaye', which left the hall stunned into pin drop silence.

Musician and accordionist, Enoch Daniels was part of this tour as well. "During our rest day, we were shown the remotest places where the oldest settlers of Indian origin are living. They were beautiful, pristine places. In one of the villages, they were having a family wedding where all the guests were dancing to Hindi songs. Their innocence was cute because they were enjoying a very tragic song for a happy occasion. The song that they were dancing to was 'Mohe bhool gaye saawariya' (My love has abandoned me) from the film Baiju Bawara (1952) . But they understood nothing of the language. They were only enjoying the music", laughs off Daniels.

The 60s decade ended with a melodious number by Talat which

belonged to the film 'Patthar Ka Khwab' (1969). The music director N. Datta fully exploited the nectar of Talat's voice to compose this bitter sweet melody. For music that had already become jarring in comparison, this song was a rare gem. Interestingly, YouTube has become an important testimony to the longevity and popularity of a song. It's a song which is not very well known in Talat's magnificent repertoire but it has curiously been turned into a karaoke track on popular demand! With lyrics written by Pal Premi, sing along…

'Yaadon ka sahara na hota, hum chhod ke duniya chal dete
Ye dard jo pyaara na hota, hum chhod ke duniya chal dete
Toota hua dil, tootey armaan
Teri hai amaanat paas mere
Ye dil jo tumhara na hota, hum chhod duniya chal dete'

(Were it not for the memories, I would have left the world long ago
Were it not for the sweet pain, I would have left the world long ago
With a broken heart and dashed hopes
Your precious love is under my care
Were it not for my heart being in your custody
I would have left the world long ago)

CHAPTER 7 - 1970'S - LIVING OUT OF A SUITCASE

(Talat (centre) with the Travancore dance sisters, actor Shashikala and comedian Johnny Walker at a concert tour to London)

BOOSTING TROOPS MORALE AFTER THE LIBERATION WAR

The popular practice of Hollywood stars going to army base camps to entertain troops was considered an important service to the nation by keeping their morale up and providing them with a much-required break from their rigorous duties. Everyone down the generations since the 1940's with Marylin Monroe, Bing Crosby, Jay Leno, Robin Williams to Jeniffer Lopez and Katy Perry today, have all performed for the troops. In India, to entertain Indian army troops in a similar manner was first started by the star couple Nargis and Sunil Dutt in the early 1960s. They formed the Ajanta Arts Cultural Troupe which took actors and singers to remote frontiers. In 1971, this film troupe travelled to perform in Bangladesh soon after their Liberation War. Talat was a dear friend of Nargis and Sunil Dutt, who had already gone with their troupe to Ladakh and Sikkim in the past.

"I promptly joined them and did shows all over India for their troupe. When China had attacked India in 1962, we prepared a number of patriotic songs and even went up to Ladakh in the extreme cold conditions to boost the army with our presence", recalls Talat.[32]. This time, the Ajanta Arts Cultural Troupe asked him to perform in Chittagong soon after the liberation of Bangladesh. There was a vacuum in the newly formed country. India was helping Bangladesh to settle in with a new administration and bring in a sense of law and order. Col Thapar was appointed the Civil Affairs Officer in the Chittagong Circuit House at the Military Headquarters. He was delighted to hear that he would be meeting Talat again after their previous interaction in Sikkim. He received the troupe in Chittagong which included Nargis, Sunil Dutt, Mala Sinha and Lata Mangeshkar, apart from Talat. "I took them on a city tour in Chittagong. They stopped over at relief camps where women were victims of genocidal rape and assault by the East Pakistani Army. As a measure of preventing them from committing suicide, their heads had to be shaved off. They would often hang themselves by their own long braids", recalls Col Thapar.

It was a disturbing insight for all the stars. But they knew they had seen only a fraction of what the Indian Army had seen on the systematic ethnic cleansing conducted by the Razakars (supporting militia of the East Pakistani Army). Rooms full of bodies and skulls had been found. Post war therapy in the form of music and art becomes a very important aspect in conflict zones and that's exactly what the film troupe intended to provide.

The Mukti Bahini which was later known as the Bangladesh Liberation Force were part of the audience along with the Indian troops. Talat's voice had a knack of pulling on the heartstrings and caressing your immediate sorrow. But this experience was very different for him. He had been to Chittagong before, for concerts and to meet his elder brother. He was a popular name here already, especially with his Bengali songs. But in context of the misery he had seen at the relief camps, Talat closed his eyes, took a deep breath and sang his heart out, "Tomar akash bhore alor madhuri" (Your sky is filled with the sweetness of light). The crowd with moist eyes broke into a thunderous applause. To lift the mood, he sang, "Ei rim jhim jhim baroshay" (Listen to the pitter patter of the rains).

With experience such as these, you tend to get hit not just with grief but also with an acute awareness of your own age and mortality. And Talat was always a sensitive man. Back home in Bombay, he would take his beloved terrier, Teddy, out for evening walks at Carter Road. But he observed something amiss in his own steps. He shared this with his brother-in-law and friend, "Iftekhar bhai, I seem to stumble on my own steps sometimes. It sounds strange but I get caught in my own legs while walking."

"Why don't you join the Bandra Gymkhana? It's right next to home and you can catch some good sports there too", responded Iftekhar. The idea of signing up for the Bandra Gymkhana worked well for Talat's mind and body. He got to hang out and catch up with his old friends Dilip Kumar and Johnny Walker there. They rekindled their old friendships and often started meeting at the gym, with each of them now having relatively more time at hand.

Meanwhile, an unexpected song came Talat's way. He was asked to playback for the young and handsome heartthrob, Sanjay Khan in a duet with Lata Mangeshkar. This was for the film 'Woh din Yaad Karo' (1971) with music by Laxmikant-Pyarelal (LP) and lyrics by Anand Bakshi. The song can be considered special because it's the only song that Talat sang for this young music duo, LP, and for actor Sanjay Khan as well.

Talat & Lata - 'Mohabbat ki kahaniyaan,
Sunane lagi hain jawaniyaan
Hamare tumhare pyar pe
Khuda ki rahen meherbaniyan'

(Moments of romance
Cannot be hidden by the joys of youth
May our love
Have the blessings of God)

For his next Ghazal album, Talat picked up poetry of his choice that he had never sung before and had musician Murli Manohar Swarup compose for the album. It was released by HMV titled 'Bazm-e-Talat' in 1973. There were a total of seven freshly sung ghazals. One of them included the poetry Sahebzadi Noorjehan Begum Nusrat. It was rare to have works of a 'shaairah' (Urdu poetess) acknowledged and celebrated, since this was also a world dominated by men. Talat chose to sing her work -

'Chhupaayi laakh mohabbat magar chhupa na sake
Hum apne daagh zamaane ko bhi dikha na sake
Karishma saaz ye ulfat na poochaye hum dum
Qareeb rah ke bhee apna unhein bana na sake'

(Try as much but love cannot be hidden
These wounds cannot be shared with the world
Look at the miracle of this instrument of love
Could not claim it despite the closeness of it)

SINGING FOR CHILDREN

As a person, Talat was very fond of children. His personality would liven up in their presence. He would love to play with them and pull pranks on them. With his own children, he loved to take them out for picnics, play in the sand at Juhu beach, lavishly celebrate their birthdays and travel around the world with them. As a gentle father, he deeply cared for them and lived up to every promise. "When I slept on his arm, he would not move it lest I wake up and inevitably he would end up in cramps. He would not eat unless I had eaten and would not sleep until I was back home", emotionally recalls his daughter, Saiby (Sabina Mahmood). [33]

One wonders what lullabies he would have sung to his children to put them to sleep when they were babies. In 1973, he shared this fatherly love for other children in the form of a new album. This was a 45rpm vinyl disc released by EMI titled 'Talat Mahmood - Lullaby' with four new songs composed by C.K. Chauhan and written by Zafar Goraphpuri. The cover of the record came in a beautifully designed case in the colour of baby blue with a drawing of white sparkling stars filling up the background and a rocking cot sketched in black in the foreground. Let's enjoy one of these lullabies –

'Chanda ki doli mein tujh ko baitha ke
Duniya ki nazron se tujhko chhupa ke
Le jaaon taaron ke paas
Phoolon ki yeh arzoo hai
Unki chhaya mein tu soye
Shabnam ki hai ye tamanna
Tera gora mukhda dhoye
Chanda ki doli…'

(Tuck you in the moonlight sleigh
Hide you from the prying eyes of the world
Ride you closer to the stars The flowers have this desire
That you sleep under their shade The morning dew is eager
To wash your bright face The moonlight sleigh….)

The euphonious voice of Talat would sweetly relax the babies and put them soundly to sleep.

As his own children were growing up to different tastes and preferences in music, he remained a large-hearted artist. The 1970s was the time when Kishore Kumar was at his peak and was the singer in most demand. His daughter Sabina wanted to attend his concert at the Shanmukhananda Hall. "He agreed immediately. Instead of asking for free passes, he went to the auditorium, bought tickets incognito and sat in the audience with me. Halfway through the concert someone recognized him and told Kishore Kumar", the proud daughter recalls her father's humility.

(Talat's children Khalid and Sabina)

Kishore Kumar always had the utmost admiration for Talat. "He called Daddy on stage and introduced him to the audience, 'Aapki jagah wahan nahin, yahan hai, aap mere saath baithiye' (Your place isn't there, it's here on stage, pls come sit with me). Such was the humility of this great man",
adds Sabina. [34]

SETTING THE TEMPLATE FOR THE AMERICAN TRAIL

In the early '70s, Talat already had an agent in New York to help chalk out his tour across the United States of America. This was the time when music venues in the U.S. were featuring the world's biggest rock musicians of the time such as Led Zeppelin, Rolling Stones, Rod Steward, David Bowie and other icons like John Lennon, Elton John and Elvis Presley. In the middle of this music calendar, a gentle and shy singer from India enthralled the audience in equal measure. And boy, did he grab those headlines with the Asian diaspora. He did around 20 shows in the United States of America and Canada, including Montreal, Atlanta, Chicago, Minneapolis and New York.

Kumar Saxena, who is now a film producer, used to be a part of Talat's troupe for 17 years as his music arranger and accordion player. He recalls fondly, "Talat would always get mobbed and we would get mobbed along with him. He had a bigger fan base with the ladies who would surround him completely. He was truly the most handsome singer I have ever seen." He remembers how the opening piece of one song would be a favourite with the audience. "The song 'Aye mere dil kahin aur chal' would always get an encore, especially when I played the catchy opening notes on the accordion. Talat would instruct me to play it at least three times before he would sing the first line." Saxena continues, "Despite his stardom and stature, Talat had no starry tantrums. He was always so warm towards us. In fact, I was shocked that once he picked up my suitcase in the hotel to help me with the luggage!"

"Talat was the top touring singer from the film industry in the 1970's. He would wrap up maximum shows in a year with an average of 8 shows in a month. And that's why musicians like me preferred touring with him on a better pay scale instead of the lower remuneration that they got from recording film songs in Bombay studios. His concert tour to the United States of America was packed with 16 shows", further informs Saxena.

At this point, it will be relevant to mention the importance of the uncharted path that Talat was treading on and how the ground research for his shows helped establish a concert circuit for other

Indian playback singers. For each city, Talat's team would conduct ground research on the potential demand of his music amongst the Indian diaspora. Venues and sponsors would then be identified to make these concerts possible for both the singer and the audience. This nature of research was helpful for the rest of his colleagues to follow suit. The ticket sales of his concerts were an encouraging sign for other singers to try out these cities for their own tours, if they wished.

The state of Minnesota had faced a huge influx of Indian immigrants after the Immigration and Nationality Act of 1965. Many Indians came for higher education and eventually settled into professional jobs. This was another state where there was a demand for Talat to perform. The Indians in this state officially formed a cultural club in 1973 called the India Club (renamed India Association of Minnesota - IAM), in order to officially be able to invite Talat.

One of the founders of this club, the late Jagdish Jack Desai, was a big fan of Talat. He had heard him at a concert at his hometown in Ahmedabad, Gujarat had since then, always wanted to meet Talat. He had spoken about how he planned his show in Minnesota. "We had a big drought in India, and there was a relief fund that the Government of India was raising. Talat Mahmood was touring the U.S. at the time. We invited him to perform for our club and help raise money for the relief fund. We got in touch with his agent in New York. They were willing to have him stop by in Minneapolis. That was in 1973. So, we signed up, and we formed the India Club at that time. Our first program on May 7, 1973 was Mr. Talat Mahmood's concert." [35]

India was facing an unprecedented crisis of water shortage because of an acute drought. The tallest waterfall in the world called the Jog Falls on the Sharavati river had dried up to a mere trickle. Even in Bombay, residents were warned of water supply shortages and were asked to wake up at 3 a.m. in the morning to fill up buckets and drums for the day's requirement. Talat was mindful of this crisis and was happy to raise funds for the aggrieved back home. The club made sure that everybody purchased tickets without any exceptions, including the organizers themselves. The invitation card read "India Club proudly presents - in aid of drought relief fund - An evening with Talat Mahmood."

Talat's concert for the Asian diaspora in the Twin Cities of Minneapolis and St. Paul was a raging success. Talat started with addressing the audience, "The nature of songs that I present need a commentary in Urdu. I don't mind speaking to you in English at all but you will enjoy it more if I talk in Urdu. So, first of all, 'Adaab' to all of you. Or let's just 'Hi', as is prevalent here." The hall broke into laughter. After a few songs there was thunderous applause to which Talat quipped, "Indeed, this is the best audience I have had out of all the cities in the U.S. My heart swells with joy."

The concert was a condensed recapitulation of the brilliant and nuanced light he brought to the stage, his voice that glittered and shimmered like a river of gold. It was his first time visiting Minnesota, so he dedicated his first Ghazal to the city by singing 'Main tere sheher mein aye dost pehli baar aaya tha' (I was here in your town, my friend, for the first time). He had divided his performances into three parts. He first sang his non-film Ghazals, followed by his film songs and later, the special requests by the audience. In his endearing wit, he reminded the audience that some of the song requests that he was asked to sing were actually songs sung by Mukesh. "I will keep these requests safe and hand them over to Mukesh. He will sing them for you when he comes here."

Looking at Talat's success in world tours, Mukesh had also started touring. Talat was happy to see his friend's busy calendar but in the late 1970's, he was also concerned about Mukesh's health. In 1976, just a few days before Mukesh went abroad with Lata Mangeshkar for a concert, he had been advised by Talat not to take a long distance trip to the USA as he had already suffered more than one heart attack. Touched by Talat's concern, Mukesh said, "Death is inevitable. It can come any time at home or abroad."

On August 24, 1976, Mukesh complained of a cold and sore throat during a performance in Montreal, Canada. On August 27,1976, hardly ten minutes before the concert, Mukesh suffered a fatal heart attack. This was Talat's worst fear about Mukesh's passing away but no one can control destiny. Talat was distraught with the news. It was a reminder of the poignant poetry of Jigar Moradabadi which he had sung together with Mukesh in their 'Hum-Radeef' Ghazal -

'Woh jo roothey to manaana chahiye

Zindagi se rooth jaana chahiye'

(An upset friend should be consoled
Else it is akin to being upset with life)

It was a friendship which had sweetened like old wine. Talat would have liked to have Mukesh by his side much longer but he left too soon. Talat's songs were a lot like old wine too. The re-runs of his old songs and Ghazals felt smoother and deeper with time. HMV quite literally labelled their next album of Talat with the same name, 'Sharab- e-Kohna', which means 'old wine' in Urdu. This album had 12 Ghazals, which were all non-film with Urdu poetry and couplets written by Jan Nisar Akhtar, Jigar Moradabadi , Mirza Ghalib and Shakeel Badayuni.

WHEN BEGUM AKHTAR WARNED TALAT'S FATHER

As we know, Ghazals remained Talat's original passion that had first brought him to singing, right since his childhood in the 1930s. Famous Ghazal singers of that time, including the legend Begum Akhtar would often perform in music gatherings held at his beloved aunt Mahlaqa's home. It is worth mentioning at this point that when Talat was trying to persuade his father to allow him to join professional singing, it was Begum Akhtar who had added to his father's apprehension and warned him against it. Her concern for the family meant well when she said, "Manzoor bhai, Talat ek khaandaani ladka hai. Film aur gaanon ki jagat aapke bete ke liye theek nahin hai. Woh nahin sambhaal payega (Manzoor sir, your son Talat is from a good family. The world of films and the music industry is not right for him. He won't be able to handle it)."

But we know how Talat tread this path and accomplished being the top most singer of the country, keeping his dignity intact. His friend Dilip Kumar always called him the 'perfect gentleman'. Talat absolutely admired Begum Akhtar's style and stature in Ghazals and it was poetic justice when things came full circle in 1975 when he won an award constituted in her name, barely a year after her untimely death. Well known historian and friend of the doyenne, the late Saleem Kidwai had set up an organization for her in her final years called 'Bazm-e-rooh-e- Ghazal'. This became the official body that booked concerts and mehfils for her. A year after she died, this organization constituted an award in her name. It was called 'Rooh-e-Ghazal (Soul of Ghazal) Begum Akhtar Award'. And the first singer to be given this award was Talat Mahmood on 24th March, 1975 in New Delhi. The award plaque read 'Mumtaz ghazal nawaz (Ghazal singer par excellence) - Talat Mahmood'.

Today's popular Ghazal singer Pankaj Udhas, explains what an impact Talat has had on him. "When I was in college, I went to his concert in Bombay. This was in Bhartiya Vidya Bhawan in Chowpatty. I was so excited because for the first time in my life, I was going to listen to him LIVE in concert. As I kept listening to him, I said to myself, this is the King. There is absolutely no doubt about it. In the real sense, the King of Ghazals. The way he projected this form of music was something else." [36]

His fan mails were also getting more creative with time. In 1977, the July issue of the film magazine 'Star & Style' had a contest for their readers. It asked them to write the most interesting letter to their favourite film star which would then be ranked and printed in their magazine. People had written to Dilip Kumar, Waheeda Rehman, Rajesh Khanna, Dimple Kapadia, etc. But guess who's letter won the first prize? It was a letter written to Talat Mahmmod by his die hard fan Meeta from the city of Agra, where the monument of love, the Taj Mahal stands. She wrote, "Talat, my sweetheart. I was 16 when I fell in love with you and now after a decade, the situation is still the same....I prepare 'kheer' (sweetened milk and rice) on your birthday and pray to Allah to give some years of my life to you....I wish I could hear 'Aye gham-e-dil kya karoon' while leaving this world....My husband gets cheesed off but I wish at least in the next birth that I will be your 'begum' (wife) and hear your voice straight from the heart, resting my head on your 'dil' (heart)."

Today, decades after this letter was printed, the concerned fan, Meeta, got in touch with me on the official page of 'Jashn-e-Talat'. Through my public announcements, she knew that I was in the process of writing his biography and excitedly informed me about this fan mail by sending me some pictures of it. Experiences such as these have led me to believe that this biography had already been blessed by Talat's fans even before its completion.

ROYAL ALBERT HALL

(Talat waves to his fans at the Royal Albert Hall in London)

It was the unstinting love and accolades that kept Talat going. Refusing to rest on his laurels, he was still on the move. He was touring and performing and winning hearts, gaining new fans across the globe. His tour to the United Kingdom was landmark, just like the United States. The highlight of this tour was performing at the esteemed Royal Albert Hall (RAH) in London in 1979. Ever since its launch by Queen Victoria in 1871, it has remained a coveted venue with a seating of more than 6,000. Leading artists of different genres from across the world wait for a chance to be approved for the venue, the calendar of which remains packed every year. Speeches have been given by Albert Einstein, events by boxer Muhammad Ali, performances by Eric Clapton, Pink Floyd, Andrew Lloyd Webber's Phantom of the Opera, Beth Hart, Adele, PlayStation music concert, 60 years of James Bond, Hollywood film premiers, awards nights, just to name a few from a very long list of prestigious events.

On 27th May, 1979, as Talat walked down the maroon coloured carpeted and circular corridor backstage, looking at all the framed images on the walls of previous performers, he was aware of the historicity of this moment. It is a dream come true for any performing artist worth his/her salt. The majestic interiors of the amphitheater under the glass dome designed in Italian Renaissance style has been witness to the world's most significant cultural events. To date, there are only a handful of Indian musicians and singers who have performed at the RAH. Talat stepped on stage to a thunderous applause, waving to the crowd which was occupying the maroon swivel seats and balconies with little arches clad in maroon velvet curtains. All of this grandeur was placed 180 degrees around the singer while his back faced the grand pipe organ in the hall. Talat was always there to help his friends however possible. Work had entirely dried up for popular comedian actor Agha. Many would recall his roles in old films like Patita, Jugnu, etc. He decided to take Agha along as part of his troupe who became a popular presenter with the crowd for all his shows in the UK. After being introduced on stage by actor Agha as the King of Hearts,

Talat stepped in and addressed the audience with a warm note, "Aapse mera purana rishta hai. Aapke saamne main ghair to nahin hoon. Aap ka purana gaane wala hoon jisko aap ne hamesha pasand kiya hai, shukriya (I have an old connection with you. I am no stranger to you. I'm a singer familiar to you, whom you have always liked, thank you)." He gave an interesting insight on how he connected with different generations through his stage concerts. He reminisced about the audience that he had met during his East Africa tour in 1956. After their forced exodus from Uganda and Kenya under the Idi Amin dictatorship, many of them settled in the UK. Many children who were part of his audience in East Africa were today attending Talat's concert at the RAH as adults. One wonders, could Britain's youngest Prime Minister Rishi Saunak's parents have been in this audience? Quite possibly, yes!

He started the show with one of his favourite songs to set the mood, 'Hain sabse madhur woh geet jinhe' from the film Patita (1953). Incredibly, despite all his film songs which were iconic hits and had become timeless classics by the 1970s, his foremost and first ever blockbuster of his career was a non- film ghazal which never failed to give Talat the loudest claps. Talat said, "This Ghazal was released in 1944 and it still sells like hot cakes to date". This ghazal was

'Tasveer teri dil mera behla na sakegi'. The audience at the RAH wanted an encore after the ghazal but Talat apologized in order to move on to other songs. The restless audience always had to be pacified by Talat that their 'farmaaish' (requested songs) would be sung by him as well but he would be unable to accommodate an encore for any song. But then guess what? The persuasive audience eventually got their way! Amidst the whistles and claps, Talat repeated the stanza of this song from the film Dil-e-Nadan (1953), which was also his film as an actor in the main lead.

'Bekhata tune mujh se khushi chheen li
Zinda rakha magar zindagi chheen li
Kar diya dil ka khun
Chup kahaan tak rahun
Saaf kyu na kahun
Tu khushi se meri dar gaya
Zindagi dene wale sun'

(Why have you snatched away my happiness
I'm alive but breathing without a soul
My heart swims in blood
To what avail is my silence
Isn't it crystal clear
You are envious of my happiness
O, Giver of Life, hear me out)

As the ovation for him thundered down, he had just launched the musical equivalent of a grand slam. The audience joined in with a fresh jolt of delighted cheers. In the alchemy that a great performance can produce, Talat had united a houseful of strangers into celebrants in the borderless nation of music. His final song for the evening was 'Jhoome re, neela ambar jhoome' from the film 'Ek Gaon Ki Kahani'(1957). As Talat hummed away the last line of this peppy song, the applause didn't stop. The crowd cheered louder for an encore. The British official from the RAH took over the mike, profusely apologising to the audience that the time is up, thanking Talat for the brilliant success of his show. It is believed that tickets to this concert were entirely sold out two weeks in advance.

THE UK TOUR

After his massive success in London, he continued with his UK tour to other cities including Manchester, Birmingham, Liverpool, etc. While speaking to popular presenter Dick Hatch on BBC Radio Manchester, Talat was asked about the mass hysteria that he often sees in his concerts. In his typical tongue-in-cheek humour, Talat responded, "Well you see I have no hair on top", to which both men started laughing. "No, no, my hair and clothes haven't been pulled off but sometimes I do get mobbed in India. I notice that people are stirred with emotions when I perform. This sort of response I face wherever I go. Especially amongst the ladies who come and cry to me. I am popular but it's because of my listeners, they've made me what I am. I should be humble about my popularity."

This was a telling statement put across with dignified subtlety by Talat. The power to make you cry and touch your inner most emotions is huge. And Talat managed to move your absolute core with such gentle charm that you wouldn't even realize it till you hear yourself sniff! Magically, people love being stirred that way, leaving them wanting for more. His daughter Sabina recalls being there at one of his shows in the UK and a unique insight given to her by one of his musicians. "His musicians would say that it would be difficult to listen to the words he sang because it would make their eyes moist. He sang with so much emotion that they would find it hard to concentrate." [37]

BBC's Hatch asks another interesting question to Talat about the difference between being a film star and a singer. "Yes, there are lots of differences. I have acted too, but I don't feel very free in front of the camera. I am very free in front of the mic."

On a final note, Talat added that he's been very satisfied with the promotions and the response to his tour in Manchester, Leicester and Birmingham, "It gets a bit cold here without the sun. My voice gets a little affected but I simply love this place. Many Westerners come to listen to me. I am a typically Eastern singer. But many Europeans and English speakers come to listen to me."

During this tour, Talat revisited his songs not just while performing them at concerts but he also re-recorded six songs especially for the

BBC's Pebble Mill Studios in Birmingham. This used to be the thriving hub for BBC in the Midlands between 1970s-2004. The Pebble Mill Studios had spaces that boasted pioneering technology and style in both television and radio production. Many signature shows of the network like Top Gear, Gardeners' World, The Archers, etc. used to be produced here. Global celebrities like Cliff Richards, Roald Dahl, Sophia Lauren, BeeGees, Christopher Lee, etc. have all shot at this iconic place.

The BBC 1 Channel wanted to cater to their growing South Asian audience from the first generation of immigrants across the UK. A brand new national programme was launched for the first time called 'Nai Zindagi, Naya Jeevan' (New life, new experiences). This was a show of iconic interviews, music and dance performances of stalwarts across the world of classical and film music in India, Pakistan and Bangladesh. The show ran between 1968-1982, all episodes were recorded at the Pebble Mill Studios and played out on BBC 1 every Sunday morning.

"It was our first special community show on TV and the highlight of the week for all our parents and grandparents. That's where my father would record the songs and performances from a variety of artists on our VHS tapes at home", reminisces Talat-Farooq Awan. He is currently working at BBC Manchester as a journalist and presenter on the radio. He says he was named after Talat Mahmood by his parents! They were avid followers of 'Nai Zindagi, Naya Jeevan' every weekend and would never miss a single episode of it.

In keeping with the cultural focus of the show, Talat Mahmood was invited with his eight-piece orchestra and musicians. He himself played his harmonium while singing and recorded a total of six songs for them. This was shot at the main studio of Pebble Mill called 'Studio A' which was 6,500 square feet in size. It had three separate control rooms looking onto the studio floor. It had a production gallery, a joint lighting gallery and a sound control gallery. Talat's team was given a generous four-camera set up with one jib camera that would glide in from the top to take Talat's close up shots while establishing the whole studio. The audience from the Midlands was called in to watch him LIVE while the songs were being shot. Once again, actor Agha, who was part of Talat's troupe in the UK, introduced him to the audience, "I have no other words to describe him best but quite simply, as the King of Ghazals."

Out of the six songs that Talat sang, one was an unknown song. It was 'Aye meri jaan-e-ghazal' from the unreleased film Nigah-e-Karam. Before Talat begins to sing this song, he says, "This song is from my upcoming film." Eventually, the film was never released but thanks to this recording at the Pebble Mill Studios, the song could be enjoyed by all Talat fans on BBC 1 in 1979. Now of course, it is available on YouTube, posted by his son Khalid.

'Aye meri jaan-e-ghazal
Ab to chilman se nikal
Shokh jalwon ki qasam
Yun nigahen na badal'

(O' my beloved poetic love
Emerge from your veil
With your lively presence
Don't look away from me')

The walls of the Pebble Mill studio gently changed colours and dissolved from peach to azure, as effortlessly as the flow of the legendary crooner's voice who sat crisply dressed, as always, in a black suit with a striped tie and white shirt. All through his career, people from across the professional spectrum have been enchanted by his personality, including journalists. "He was always delightfully charming and forthcoming. I had met him for the first time in the 1970s when he had come to Nagpur along with actor Shashi Kapoor for a music show. It was a lovely winter evening but his presence brought out all the warmth," recalls renowned author and journalist Sathya Saran who used to work for an English daily in Nagpur called 'The Hitavada'.

As a true fan of the crooner, she draws a unique analogy to my absolute delight, while speaking to me. "It's hard to imagine the impact of his voice in these times when WhatsApp and emojis speak of love in stereotyped formats; but in his time, the song swayed many a maiden's heart, making her yearn for just one such lover. The only parallel in the new millennium is perhaps the emotions evoked in even much-married women's hearts by the eternal romantic played by Shah Rukh Khan in his films."

Perhaps that explained his growing demand across the world, beyond the recording studios in India. Despite the dip in his film recordings, his concert calendar was swelling up. He established a tour circuit in the U.S.A. and the U.K. along with tapping new listeners in the Western world. This outreach proved to be much wider than the radius of the Indian film industry. He managed to enthral a new set of music lovers who belonged outside the network of the Asian diaspora and were alien to Urdu, Indian films songs and Ghazals. That was the impact and influence that his gentle voice enjoyed.

STRIKING GOLD IN MALAYALAM

The tail end of this decade had Talat recording a few songs in Malayalam, Assamese and Bengali. When he sang in the Malayalam language of Kerala, it struck gold. His song was from the blockbuster film Dweep (1977) which tells the story of a young man from a poor family who struggles to earn a living. When he finally gets a job as a teacher in the island of Lakshadweep amidst the brilliant blue waters, he feels lovesick about the village girl he left behind. It makes for the perfect situation to introduce Talat's sensitive touch in this song.

'Kadale...neelakkadale...
Ninnaathmaavilum Neerunna chinthakalundo
Kadale neelakkadale

Oru penmaniyude ormmayil muzhuki
Urangaatha raavukalundo
Kadale neelakkadal'

(O sea.. O blue sea
Do you carry any burden on your soul?
Do you have nagging thoughts?
O sea.. O blue sea)

Immersed in the memory of a woman
Are there sleepless nights?
O' sea.. O' blue sea)

Noted journalist from Kerala, P. Mohan recalls how his father introduced him to the music of Talat Mahmood. "I remember my father telling me that he had come for a concert there and had the privilege of meeting him personally. One of the first 78rpm records he bought was a collection of Talat Mahmood's hits of Hindi film songs. Even at a young age, I was smitten by the sheer silkiness of his voice, which was a stark contrast to the other great voices of the time." He further adds that Talat had a huge following in North Kerala, in the region of Kozhikode to be precise. That could be one of the reasons why the music composer M.S.Baburaj decided to take Talat for the song 'Kadale... neelakkadale'. Baburaj was born in Kozhikode and one of his greatest achievements was the introduction of Hindustani strains into Malayalam popular music. Talat's voice and fan following made him the perfect candidate for this song.

Just a few months ago, a young influencer and singer on Youtube, Rosepriya Kannath, had posted a cover version of this song, using the sounds of the guitar. It was well received by the listeners including Baburaj's family who felt that it added a new dimension to the original. As a youngster, Kannath has always loved this old hit as a deep, up-close and personal work of art. "The way this song evokes despair, longing, grief, heartbreak & pain through Talat Mahmood's mellifluous voice is brilliant. This song belongs to the era of single take recordings. He has sung it with so much ease that I am still amazed by the fact that it doesn't sound like it was sung by a non-native speaker of the language."

Before wrapping up this incredibly eventful and busy decade of his life, Talat recorded one Assamese song 'Niob Kareng' (The Silent Palace) for the film Megh (1979) and one Bengali song 'Kichhu kichcu katha acche' (The story goes on) for the Bangladeshi film Rupali Saikate (1979).

CHAPTER 8 - 1980S - INSPIRING AND PROMOTING THE YOUNG

(Talat, the legend, the mentor. Photographed by his son Khalid)

EMOTIONAL ROLLER COASTER

This decade started with a significant day that comes in every father's life. The wedding of his daughter. Saiby (Sabina Mahmood) had started seeing a young handsome man named Riki Rana. Soon enough Talat found out. "Daddy asked me just one question, 'Do you love him?' When I answered yes, he asked me to invite the boy", she said.[38]. They were straight out of college and the only condition that a simple father like Talat put forward was to ensure that Riki had a job before he married Saiby. They waited till Riki could fulfil that one and only pivotal condition. Their wedding was a star studded affair where Talat's happiness knew no bounds. He invited all his friends, young and old from across the film industry. Dilip Kumar, Mala Sinha, Nimmi, Lata Mangeshkar, Asha Bhosle, Naushad, Manna Dey, Mahendra Kapoor, Agha, Nitin Mukhesh, etc.

The night ended with Talat singing one of his songs especially for Saiby. It was from the film Shahenshah (1953) and he dedicated it to his daughter. In Indian homes, the happiness and celebrations of a daughter's wedding suddenly turns into an extremely sombre and sad affair when the rukhsati (departure) happens. Suddenly, the parents feel the impending emptiness of their home after the daughter leaves for marriage.

'Naazon ke pale, kaanton pe chalen
Aisa bhi jahaan men hota hai
Taqdeer ke zaalim haathon se
Dil khoon ke ansoo rota hai'

(Raised with care, walking on thorns
This can happen in the world too
With the brutal hand of fate
The heart bleeds in sorrow)

Talat was always an emotional person and he had no qualms in openly showing what he felt. When he sang this, he was expressing his own sorrow at his daughter leaving home.

Apart from his gentle manners, part of his appeal was being transparent. What you heard in his voice is what he felt in his heart. His emotion could also be seen during the most devastating news for the world of films and music. The singer who was the undisputed king of all musical notes, unattainable pitches and an unparalleled range - Mohammad Rafi, passed away. In July 1980, the country saw a huge outpouring of emotion with the Government of India announcing two days of national mourning.
Thousands of mourners, including friends, family, colleagues, celebrities and admirers, all walked in the rain to the burial ground, Juhu Kabristan. Talat Mahmood was one of them. He was as devastated as anyone else. In an extremely touching moment, Talat sat on the floor, bent down and kissed Rafi's forehead as his mortal remains lay immobile.

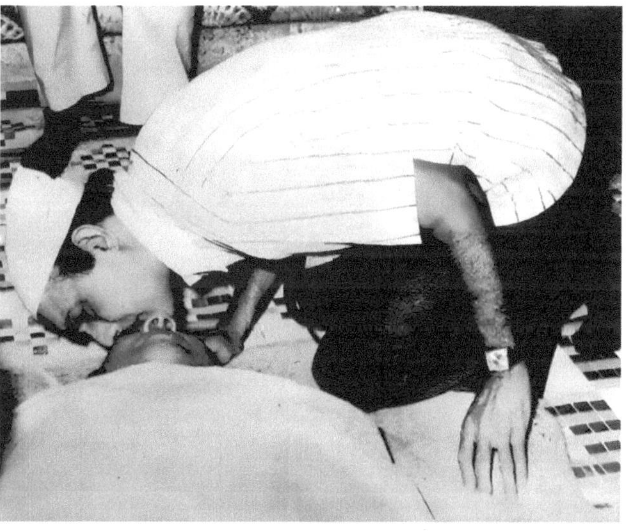

An inconsolable Talat said, "The world needed Rafi more than me. For everyone's sake, I wish Allah had taken my life instead of Rafi." That stunning admiration for a colleague would have surely demolished all talk of any rivalry between the two men. They were both gifted with a special talent and Talat knew how to admire Rafi without any malice. Their duet together was a consolation for Talat in this hour of grief. From the film Sushila (1966), the song was about one friend encouraging the other to look beyond grief and find happiness.

‘Gham ki andheri raat mein
Dil ko na beqaraar kar
Subah zaroor aayegi
Subah ka intezaar kar’

(In this night of despair
Don’t make the heart restless
You will see the light of day
Wait for the light to come)

Rafi’s passing away felt like a personal loss to Talat. But the news that came from home offered him the much-needed peace. The birth of his grandson. Samir was born to Saiby and Riki. Talat was ecstatic to have someone call him ‘naanu’ (gramps).

THE ADVENT OF NEW TECHNOLOGY - STEREO SOUND

Samir's birth marked the third generation of his family. The start of a new generation also meant that the world around him was moving ahead with new trends in music. Technology was moving ahead even faster in the music industry. A new technology was showing signs of a sound revolution in films. Talat recognized those signs. It was called the stereophonic technology, popularly known as 'stereo-sound'. While it had been there in India for a while, film songs were still being recorded in mono-sound.

"Stereo sound means that you can feel the orchestra and the singer in front of you. The sounds of music get distributed in the left and right speakers while the singer's voice seems to come from the centre. It's very much like listening to a LIVE concert", explains Enoch Daniels, music arranger.

Talat was always a singer ahead of his times. Just the previous year (1979), he had cut an album with music composer C.K. Chauhan. It was titled 'Sham-e-Talat : New love songs by Talat Mahmood'. The album had four brand new songs. This was Talat's first ever stereo-sound recording but it was a non- film album. After the release of Shaam-e-Talat, the singer suddenly had a brainwave. He envisaged the need of his old film hits to be re-recorded in stereo-sound because the old records were in mono-sound and were not available in the market anymore. So, he sat down with HMV to ascertain a short-list of these songs that he wanted re-recorded.

Daniels was in charge of this new project. He conducted the orchestra for these songs and re-imagined the arrangement of instruments. Some of these songs have a refreshingly new input with added string and percussion instruments suited to the newer listeners of the 1980s. Talat's shortlisted songs from the Golden Era were originally sung by him in his youth when he was in his 20s and 30s. Could re-recording these songs in 1980 prove to be a challenge for the legend because he was 56 years old now.

"Fortunately, his voice did not differ. Talat could sing well for many years. The tonal quality did not change and he sounded the same. Talat could sing all his old pitches and we could maintain the original pace", add Daniels.

This turned out to be a good idea for global outreach as well since stereo- sound records were available to the worldwide market. His decision added to reviving his songs of the Golden Era. The stereo album was titled 'Melody - The Queen, Talat - The Prince'. It had a total of 11 songs and was sold in the market as audio cassettes and LP discs. Was Talat one of the first singers in Bombay to re-record his old songs in stereo? Yes! The technology caught up first in the film industry of South India but it was only being used for new film releases. These were the 11 shortlisted songs that Talat re-sang in stereo-sound :

A1 Wohi Chandni Hai Wohi Aasman Hai (Film: Rishta)
A2 Nazon Ke Pale Kanton Pe Chale (Film: Shahenshah)
A3 Bechain Nazar Betab Jigar (Film: Yasmin)
A4 Mera Jeevan Sathi Bichhad Gaya (Film: Babul)
A5 Mera Qarar Leja (Film: Ashiana)
B1 Koi Nahin Mera Is Duniya Mein (Film: Daag)
B2 Aaja Tujhe Mohabbat Awaz De Rahi Hai (Film: Caravan)
B3 Andhe Jahan Ke Andhe Raaste (Film: Patita)
B4 Hai Yeh Wohi Aasman (Film: Char Chand)
B5 Berahem Aasman (Film: Bahana)
B6 Jayen To Jayen Kahan (Film: Taxi Driver)

The back cover of the LP described Talat as "There was a time, not so long ago, when singers were dreamy, soft and handsome. Their voices soothed and calmed even as they sang of passion and romance. When melody was queen, the sensuous voice of Talat Mahmood was always near. His voice personifies romance and poetry, dim lights and sensitivity." Daniels adds how this album caught the fancy of listeners, "People liked Talat's vibrato even more. Each nuanced sound becomes brighter with stereo, so the vibrato became more distinct. The details of his voice were heard more lively." It was a well calculated decision by the genius of Talat who was continuously finding new ways of staying connected with his listeners.

BOUNCING BACK FROM THE HEART ATTACK

Destiny brought in a brief lull in his journey. A heart attack in 1981. "When he was getting chest pain while waiting for a doctor, he asked me to press my head against his chest, saying, "It's hurting a lot my dear, pls keep your head on my chest", recalls his daughter Sabina Rana.[39] It was a grim situation but Talat was a fighter. "He was rushed to the Breach Candy hospital and was declared clinically dead for a few seconds. The team of doctors had to walk his body to revive a heartbeat. Later, they operated upon him to place a pacemaker that would help regulate his heart beat. He had become very thin and weak. But like an injured soldier, he would proudly and happily talk about the machine placed under his skin on the left side of his chest. He was always cheerful and strong", remembers his niece, Romana Zaman.

He was certainly feeble after this jolt but that didn't stop him from going back to the studio after regaining some strength. He bounced back within a few months in 1982 with a brand-new song. This was the coming together of a winning team - Talat Mahmood and music composer Salil Chowdhury. Talat has praised him often as one of his favourite composers, "He was a class apart. Most talented but sadly couldn't rise to the heights he deserved." The song was recorded in both Hindi and Bengali. In Hindi it was 'Tup taap boondein barsen' and in Bengali it was 'Tup taap brishti podche'. It was from an unreleased film 'Artap' (1982).

A very considerate Chowdhury composed a gentle and low-pitched song with minimal orchestra that wouldn't strain Talat's vocals soon after the heart attack and highlight his USP of mellow numbers. It's a melodious whisper on the gentle patter of the rains written by lyricist Yogesh. Once again, the two legends score an ace but the destiny of this song was unfortunate. It remained a hidden and lost gem for about 20 years till it was discovered and uploaded on the official website of both men. Now, it gets a fresh lease of life on YouTube.

'Tup-taap, tup-taap, tup-taap
Boondein barse re barse
Chup chaap, chup-chaap,

Khoyi khoyi do aankhein hai tarse re tarse
Tup-taap, tup-taap…'

(Pitter patter pitter patter
Listen to the falling raindrops
Silently, softly
With two lost souls aching to meet
Pitter patter pitter patter)

Another rare gem for music lovers which is also a special treat for fans of lyricist Nida Fazli. The song is believed to be written by him since there is an image which shows Fazli, Talat and music composer C.K. Chauhan sitting together for the recording of this song 'Jaoon kahaan aye aasmaan, koi nahin mera' (Where do I go in this world, alone). The song was for an unreleased film 'Sawaal' and the recording took place in 1983. The music included a combination of jhankaar (heavy bass) beats with Talat's vocals. How do you think it sounded? The verdict is out there. Once again, YouTube comes to the rescue for making these hidden gems available to the world. Comments by listeners on the post indicate that the jhankaar beats added a new flavour to Talat's voice.

MORTAL MEN IMMORTAL MELODIES

1981 was the year that the film industry marked 50 years of the advent of sound and music in the Indian film industry. India's first talkie, Alam Ara was released in 1931 and its biggest USP was that it had talking, singing and dancing! It was India's first talkie. It not just performed well at the box office but is considered to be a major breakthrough in the film industry. Members of the film industry came together to celebrate this anniversary with a music show dedicated to singers and musicians. It was a celebration of the 50th Anniversary of Sound in Indian Cinema.

Legendary television anchor and producer, Siddharth Kak, who ran the most successful culture show on Doordarshan called 'Surabhi', was the producer of this tribute concert. His company, Cinema Vision India, put together the entire show. "Cinema tributes are mainly for actors. People behind the scene for music such as singers, composers, lyricists, composers are not remembered very often. I have my deep appreciation for my friends, the late Pamela and Yash Chopra who helped me with this show. Pamela took one- and-half years to compile the list for the best of 50 years of Indian cinema music. This was a sentiment with an academic purpose too. We had multiple sessions at Yash ji's house and shortlisted the final songs to be performed. What emerged is the history of our film music", fondly recalls Kak. It was a laborious process of finding people who had heard the early songs, the recordings of which were not available. For other songs, they searched for available LPs. They got in touch with those who were still alive such as Rajkumari, GM Durrani, etc. It became the biggest show of its kind with singers across generations singing on the same stage. The list included Ashok Kumar, Hemant Kumar, Lata Mangeshkar, Alka Yagnik, Mahendra Kapoor, Kavita Krishnamurthy and of course, Talat Mahmood.

"When I met Talat ji, I was a young man of 30 years old. I remember him as a courteous and dignified gentleman who spoke so politely and with so much respect even to a young fellow like me. I was totally taken up by his personality. I think it was soon after his heart attack, so he expressed a concern during rehearsal whether his voice had lost some of its elasticity", remembers Kak. But under the safe hands of his mentor Anil Biswas on stage, Talat was comfortable singing his old hit 'Aye dil mujhe aisi jagah le chal'.

He was presented on stage by young actor Shabana Azmi who called him a voice that reminds us of the softness of muslin, the sliding of dew drops on leaves and the tenderness of the morning breeze. After his performance, there was a thunderous applause by the audience of more than 2500 who filled up the Shanmukhananda Hall beyond full capacity. As a special goodwill gesture, the Mallika-e-Tarannum Noor Jehan was invited from Pakistan to sing on stage. She had sung many songs in films during British India but migrated to Pakistan after Partition. This was her first visit back to India after 1947 and she was introduced on stage by thespian Dilip Kumar as the guest of honour. When she met Talat backstage, she warmly said, "Talat bhai, aap ki awaaz mein wohi kashish ab bhi hai (Your voice still has that enduring charm)!" [40]

I am also informed by Kak that it took them a few months to edit the entire concert and give it to Doordarshan as a TV show in 1982. That's when the entire country got to enjoy this remarkable feat.

ON TOUR AGAIN

By this time Talat was fit to travel again. Carrying the pacemaker in his chest along with the desire to conquer new territories. In 1983, he went back to the United States of America on popular demand. Nearly 400,000 Asian Americans live in the state of Ohio with Indian Americans being the largest ethnic group.[41]

Of course, there was huge anticipation for Talat to perform there. His international concerts were attended by the entire Asian diaspora rather than just Indians. The Pakistanis listened to his Urdu Ghazals as much as they appreciated his film songs. The Bangladeshis could not get enough of Tapan Kumar's Bengali hits. Looking at the huge footfall of his shows, he was given special state honours in Ohio. The Mayors of two cities in the State - Cleveland and Euclid - conferred on him a special citation for his contribution to music and bringing their Asian American communities together.

By this time, Talat also added the Middle East countries to his tours. He performed across the United Arab Emirates, Saudi Arabia, Oman , etc. The absolute humility of this living legend at the age of 60 was on display when he apologized to his audience in Dubai for his concert starting late due to some unavoidable delays. "It's late but I promise you that I will make sure you hear the best from me and you will feel no loss of time." This show was at the newly launched Al-Nasr Leisureland in 1984 which was sold to full capacity with about 12,000 people. The sponsor of the show, Cathay Pacific Airlines, headlined Talat as "the greatest name in Indian music history".

Popular and award-winning singer Kavita Krishnamurthy fondly recalls her experience of working with him. "I used to wonder what made him so great. Even if he missed a note, every word had so much emotion and truth. We have learnt since childhood that truth should be there in your music. And these legends showed it to us. God made them for this purpose. They could not get into any rat race. The only purpose was to sing and God took care of the rest. No politics, no hassle, just sing. Don't worry about anything else", she says insightfully.

She was introduced to Talat by his friend and fellow singer Manna Dey at his house. During the initial days of her career, she used to do concerts as the accompanying woman singer for legends like Hemant Kumar, Manna Dey. From the late 1970's onwards, she started touring with Talat Mahmood as well. "In 1984, we had a big concert in Holland. This was with Hemant Kumar, Manna Dey, Talat Mahmood, Rajkumari and myself. We were all together, I think. There was a very tricky duet of his that I sang with Talat sa'ab, 'Aha rim jhim ke ye pyaare pyaare geet'. I would walk in like a student when he called me on stage. And with his soft voice, he would ask, 'Kaisi hain aap?' We always met on stage with hardly any rehearsals. My interactions with him were also less because he was a very quiet man. He put all his expressions into his songs", recalls Krishanmurthy.

This performance of theirs together has caught up with great fervour on YouTube. It is one of the most challenging songs to sing and is often described as a musical marathon for its continuous swing in pitches. It is really endearing to watch a young and skillful Kavita Krishnamurthy standing on stage, with her head shyly bent towards the microphone. Apart from the song above, they also sang one of his first hit duets from the film Babul (1950), 'Milte hi aankhen dil hua deewana'.

SUMMER BREAK WITH BAMBAI NANA

(The author when she was just a few months old with Talat (left) and family)

I remember meeting him in 1985 during my school summer holidays. He had seen me when I was barely a few months old but of course, I have no recollection of that. I used to live in Kuwait during my childhood and travelling to India meant catching up with family across Bombay and Delhi. I was 5 years old then and I didn't know what to call him. My elder brother reasoned with some serious logic of a 9 year old and said, "See, he lives in Bambai (Bombay) so we will call him Bambai Nana". That name stuck on and decades later, it made it to the national headlines when I started the Jashn-e-Talat series.

(The author at age 5 clinging on to Sabina with Talat (below) and family at their Sunbeam penthouse in Bandra, Mumbai)

We stayed at Bambai Nana's Sunbeam penthouse which overlooked the Arabian Sea. By that time, his beautiful bungalow had been broken down and built into a multi-storied apartment. Since he was the original owner of the place, he was given the penthouse. We would catch sunsets together at his terrace. I would tell him this is the same sea I have next to my home in Kuwait and I never realized that we were neighbours by the sea. He would mostly chuckle at everything I said. I was an impish five-year old with the most outrageous questions to which he would just squint his eyes and laugh away. His wife, Bambai Nani, my grand-aunt, showered me with toys and dresses, including a tricycle. Their son, Khalid uncle was asked to meet every demand of mine. Like a sweet chaperone, he would take me for ice creams, drive around the city and most importantly, try to have me meet the love of my life, 'Eetabh Bachan' (Amitabh Bachchan). He dutifully took me to the gates of the actor's newly built home Jalsa only to be turned away by his security guard, "Sahab baahar shoot pe hain" (Sir is out for a shoot).

I happened to be unabashedly friendly with Bambai Nana's close friend, legendary singer Manna Dey. We visited him at his house in Bandra for evening tea. I plonked on to his lap and called him 'dost' (friend) and chatted away to glory. The Otter's Club in Bandra was the family's hangout place ever since it launched in the 1970s. Well known residents in the neighbourhood, including Talat, supported the club's progress in being Founding Members and promoting it. Our special dinner at Otter's Club was a spread of the best seafood and Bambai Nana's favourite roasted chicken. These were lovely family memories I took back home as Bambai Nana was getting ready for some "outside trip". I obviously had no idea what he did for work or who he was. To me, he was just an old, funny gramps whose eyes sparkled just like mine.

ENCOURAGING YOUNG TALENT

That outside trip was probably the one he was taking to Calcutta (now Kolkata) for a performance at Birla Hall. "I had introduced Alka Yagnik to Talat sa'ab in those days. She was a very new and young singer at that time. So this was one of the shows that he had called her on stage to sing with him. He was always very encouraging to youngsters", recalls Kumar Saxena, his accordionist. Alka Yagnik went on to become one of the biggest singers of the 1990s. Talat carried an aspirational value not just for young singers but also for many young music directors of the 1980s. They had the desire of using his mellow vocals in their musical notes. These were special compositions away from the demands of the market but reminiscent of the gentle times left behind. Fresh from the success of his blockbuster music in 'Ram Teri Ganga Maili' (1985), music composer Ravindra Jain recorded Talat for his song 'Aao main tum ko bataoon' in the same year. He put his voice on echo effect as the legend crooned into the microphone about teaching love.

'Aao main tumko bataoon ki mohabbat kya hai
Aur is lafz ko insaanon se nisbat kya hai'
(Let me teach you what love is
And what the word means for people to love)

Talat believed that Jain was one of the most talented composers of the 1980s. "Ravindra Jain is certainly one of them. He is a writer and composer. And what a composer!" [42].

In 1983, when late Pankaj Udhas was a young singer, he had come out with his ghazal album named 'Mehfil'. "I insisted that Talat sab'ab be the Chief Guest for the launch of my album. He gave me time to meet him at his home and that's where I played a few of my ghazals for him. He was impressed to see a youngster interested in this niche genre despite its shrinking market," Udhas tells me, in fond remembrance of Talat. He reasoned that his album launch turned out to be great for both of them. "I feel that Talat sa'ab also got to see first-hand that people in India still wanted to hear new recordings from him." As an admirer of Talat, he believed that it was 'Mehfil' which galvanized the old legend to work on his next album.

THE FORMIDABLE COMEBACK ALBUM

(Dilip Kumar releases Talat's comeback album 'Ghazal Ke Saaz Uthao')

1986 was a celebration year for Talat. One being the wedding of his dear 'guddu', his son Khalid. And the second being the release of his comeback album.

Khalid's wedding was a close-knit affair at home with just immediate family and very close friends. He fell in love with Reena Pande (Isha Mahmood) and told his daddy about it. Talat was always supportive of his children's choices. All he wanted to know was if the love was true. Going by his own choice of life partner, he knew every other happiness would follow once there is sincere love in the marriage. Unlike Saiby's wedding, Khalid chose for his wedding to be a low-key affair with only close family members and very few friends.

His old friend Dilip Kumar who couldn't be there for the wedding made sure to support Talat at the release of his comeback album by

HMV. It was called 'Ghazal ke saaz uthao' with all eight ghazals being freshly composed and sung. Two ghazals were given music by Talat himself, including this peppy one mentioned below, with the delightful use of the santoor and violin with a fast rhythm. The poetry was written by Khumar-Barabankvi -

'Kahin sher-o-nagma banke, kahin aansuon me dhalke
Wo mujhe mile to lekin mile suratein badal ke
Ye vafa ki sakht rahein, ye tumhare pa-e-nazuk
Na lo inteqaam mujh se, mere saath saath chal ke
Kahin sher-o-nagma banke, kahin aansuon me dhalke'

(As a couplet in melody, or trapped in my tears
She met me but in different circumstances
This is a difficult path of loyalty for your delicate feet
Don't test me by walking along with me
As a couplet in melody, or trapped in my tears)

At the release function of the album, the HMV banner splashed "The Ghazal King Returns". Dilip Kumar released the album along with his beautiful wife and top actress Saira Bano. They unveiled the first LP and disc. Dilip Kumar was full of praise in reflecting on the kind of mental disposition that is equally important to be a good Ghazal singer. "Talat has always been a very popular personality. A very rich culture reflects in his voice, full of dignity. He is not just a good singer but a very refined gentleman." [43]
The press was out with gushing reviews, saying "The Ghazal rejoiced that night. Talat Mahmood, the King of Ghazals, the singer who breathed new life into the ghazal so many years ago, the voice that worked wonders for one whole generation, came back to soothe a generation brought up on sound and fury."

He had gifted us an autographed LP of this album with a special handwritten message by him in Urdu. He wrote three lines from the poetry of Himayat Ali Shair who was the first poet to break out from the format of couplets. He started the format of three lines of poetry which was called 'salaasi', derived from the Arabic word 'salaasa' which means three. The salaasi style was inspired from the Japanese forms of three-lined poetry, haiku and senryu. In inspiring us to remain informed about trends in Urdu, Talat wrote these lines by Himayat Ali on his brand new LP,

"Ye ek patthar jo raaste mein pada hua hai
Isey mohabbat taraash le to yahi sanam hai
Isey aqeedat nawaaz de to yahi khuda hai"

(Consider this stone lying on the way
If love finds it, it takes the form of a beloved
If faith finds it, it takes the form of God)

The comeback album was a runaway hit. His listeners included old, loyal followers and the newly tapped young generation as well. It was little wonder that the weekly Chart-Toppers list of 10, released by Mid-Day newspaper that week, featured Talat's comeback album on No.1 while other non-film albums by younger artists of that time including Jagjit Singh, Pankaj Udhas. Peenaz Masani, Talat Aziz, Shobha Gurtu and Anup Jalota were listed after his album. What brought Talat back was not just the desire to connect with the new generation but also his helplessness with what he felt was the erosion of Urdu poetry in Ghazals.
"Why, may I ask, this stress, in the ghazals today, on 'saaqi' (female wine server) and 'sharaab' (wine) all the time, to the virtual exclusion of finer feelings? Is there no place, any longer, for the gentle caressing style of ghazal I made famous in the shape of `Nigahon ko chura kar rah gayi hai' ; or `Gham-e-zindagi ka yaarab na mila koi kinaraa' ; or `Dil ki duniya basa gaya hai kaun'? And remember, I compressed each one of these ghazals into the bare three minutes permitted by a 78rpm record. Today, we have LPs and cassettes and all that technology by which a singer can spread himself out. But to what poetic end?'

Talat goes on to argue that poetry was always integral to his music. And it was this intrinsic poetic content in his vocalizing that elevated a mere film song as well. "At one time, I was singing for such divergent heroes as Dilip Kumar, Raj Kapoor and Dev Anand, on the one hand, Bharat Bhooshan, Shammi Kapoor and Ajit, on the other. Yet I always insisted on a certain standard of poetry in the music that they created for me, no matter what the budget of the film. In fact, it was to give nuanced expression to such poetry that music directors sought me out. When `Mirza Ghalib' was made by Sohrab Modi, it went without saying that I was going to sing for Ghulam Mohammed", explains Talat who remained dedicated to a quality of Urdu poetry which can no longer be heard in popular cinema or non-film Ghazals. [44] He had achieved the stature of a

Ghazal icon for whom poets and music directors would give an arm and a leg to compose. They knew his inimitable aesthetics would further add finesse to their composition. His formula was to keep it simple. "My request to young Ghazal singers is to keep the focus on the meaning of the poetry that you are singing. It is okay to add your inflections and style while singing a couplet but please don't stretch it to the point of losing the essence of the words. Even the poet will frown and wonder what he has written. You can't stretch a poem and take one hour to sing the whole thing." [45]

(Talat celebrates the success of his comeback album with new talent)

But Talat managed to have his last hurrah with his comeback album. The success party of his comeback album being a runaway hit was celebrated in the Taj Palace hotel in Bombay with all newcomers of that time. There's an image from that party which has a visibly satisfied and smiling Talat standing in the centre flanked by ghazal singers Jagjit Singh, Chitra Singh, Pop singers Gary Lawyer and Alisha Chinai on one side; and Ghazal singers Bhupinder Singh, Talat Aziz along with Ila Arun, Mitalee Singh and Nandu Bhende on the other side. It was a significant moment in the history of our music industry where the legend was happily handing over the baton to the younger talent.

THE LAST FEW FILM SONGS

At this point, it will be important to mention Talat's association with the iconic filmmaker K. Asif who had made the magnum opus Mughal-e- Azam. He had started the production of his next film, Love and God, in 1963. Knowing his style and ambition, this was also being made on a huge scale. The plot was about the love story of Laila-Majnu, a costume drama set in the desert of Arabia. But multiple impediments caused many delays. Firstly, actor Guru Dutt, playing the role of Majnu, passed away in 1964. He recast the second actor to play Majnu, the young and dashing Sanjeev Kumar. K.Asif's own death in 1971 was the biggest blow to the production. The final death knell to the film was the passing away of Sanjeev Kumar in 1985. The main lead actress Nimmi was progressively looking older in two decades of playing the role of Laila. The film was finally released 23 years after the first shot, by painstaking efforts of the filmmaker's widow Akhtar Asif. It was released in 1986.

Talat had one devotional song in the film which brought together other greats on record like Mohammad Rafi, Lata Mangeshkar, Manna Dey, Mukesh and S.Balbir. Composed by Naushad, all voices of the singers were used for multiple devotees taking blessings at a Sufi shrine. Neither of the singers had a full stanza to themselves. They were given a single line to sing solo and the rest was sung along with the others as chorus! Naushad's favourite singer, Rafi was given the final stanza to sing solo for the playback of the main lead, Sanjeev Kumar. Only the stature of Naushad could have convinced other singers to be heard as chorus voices. This was a feat in itself. The song was -

All singers in chorus - 'Rahega jahaan mein tera naam
Banenge tere bigde kaam
Humein kuch rahein khuda de de (2)'

(The world will know your name
Your prayers will be answered
Show us the way, o'Lord)

Talat - 'Gham ki ghatayen chhat jayengi'
(The clouds of distress will wash away)

Manna Dey - 'Sab zanjeerein kat jayengi
(All shackles will be broken)

Talat and Lata - Dil ko chain aankhon ko ujala'
(With peace of mind, hope in the eyes)

Balbir - 'Sab kuch dega dene wala'
(You will be blessed with his bounty)

Talat - 'Jisne tujhko dard diya hai'
(The one who brought you this pain)

Chorus - Dega wohi aaraam
(Is the one who will bring you relief)

With the delayed release of the film and a sea change in the tastes of audiences after two decades, the film unfortunately bombed at the box office. For Talat, the song, despite its brilliance, was at best a fond memory of singing for the greatest filmmaker, K. Asif's film.

It was time for Talat to be on the move again and he headed to the West Coast in the U.S.A. in 1987, including Chicago. This was a unique treat for music lovers when Talat took along his close friend Manna Dey and Kavita Krishnamurthy. They did a minimum of six shows with back-to-back weekends. But this was also a time when the fragility after a heart attack and age was beginning to affect his voice. Krishnamurthy defends Talat about this argument. "Despite him slowing down, his words and notes were on point when he sang on the mic. Understanding words was in his blood. In his soft volume, words were like clear pearls. There was emotion in every song. It felt like he was the poet. He embraced the poetry completely." That same year in 1987, Krishnamurthy struck gold in the film industry. Her first commercially hit song was from the film Mr. India (1987) called 'Hawa hawaii' and the rest is history. There was no looking back for her but she did always look back with utmost cherished memories about Talat. "My favourite song of his is 'Phir wohi shaam'. I heard him sing that LIVE for the first time in the Shanmukhananda Hall as an audience member when I was in college. It was a 45 minute performance. He ended the show with 'Raat ne kya kya khwab dikhaye'. He added another infliction to it which is not part of the original song. He brought us all to tears."

While Krishnamurthy raced ahead with a hugely successful career in films, Talat recorded his last released Hindi song for the film industry in 1987. This was from the film Vali-E-Azam. Composed by his old friend Chitragupta, it's a duet with singer Hemlata.

'Mere Shareek-e-Safar, ab tera khuda-haafiz
Main tere saath rahoon, yeh mera naseeb nahin
Main chahta tha ki mar jaoon tere dar pe magar
Mere janaaze ko kandha tera naseeb nahin'

(Goodbye, my soul mate
It is not in my destiny to be with you
I wanted to breathe my last with you
It is not in my fate to be buried in your presence)

The song feels as if Talat is kissing goodbye to what has been his most constant companion in life, his music. The lyrics written by Ahmed Wasi epitomized the sentiment of what can be called Talat's swan song in the Hindi film industry. "When I reduced my film recordings, I did it out of choice. I wanted to preserve my style. I thought I had set a particular standard of singing which would have gotten destroyed had I compromised like my other peers. If I am remembered till today, it's because I sang in a particular way", says a defiant Talat. [46] He was grateful to the film industry and his fans for having treated him well. He considered himself a child of an era when soft and sentimental songs were made. He fit the role well and when the world was wanting a different taste, he respectfully left without regrets.

MEHDI HASSAN - HIS BIGGEST FAN

(Talat with his biggest fan and admirer, Mehdi Hassan (Courtesy: Rishad Mahmood)

In 1988, Talat made a personal visit to Pakistan for a family wedding. No one from the music industry there was told about this visit. But somehow, his biggest fan in Karachi, legendary Ghazal singer Mehdi Hassan would always come to know. Talat's nephew and senior journalist in Karachi, Rishad Mahmood recalls, "I was astounded by how he found out. He reached home and told me, 'Talat sa'ab (sir) ko main yeh gulab ka phool unke kurtey mein pehnaoonga' (I've brought this rose for Talat sir, to pin it on his shirt). He would meet Talat uncle and bear his heart out. Things that you would never get to hear."

He often spoken about what got him into singing Ghazals, and it was Talat's voice that inspired him to be a singer. He spoke about a music competition that he participated in Karachi in 1957 where he was given a chance to sing two songs on stage. Both the songs that he sang were Talat's famous hits. The first one was 'Ek main hoon ek meri bekasi ki shaam hai' (An evening full of my loneliness and helplessness) from the film Tarana (1951). The second song that he sang was from the film Babul (1950), 'Husn walon ko na dil do (Don't lose your heart to a beauty). He received such a huge applause from the crowd that Mehdi Hassan felt that the claps would never stop. He was then showered with money by the crowd. By the end of it, he ended up collecting an enormous amount of around fourteen thousand rupees! After that, there was no looking back for him. But this appreciation came after almost four years of putting himself to a strict schedule of unforgiving training.

Rishad says that in a rare moment of self-criticism, Mehdi Hassan told Talat, "I was not a born singer like you. I used to listen to you and then I started singing myself. When I recorded my first song, someone passed a snide remark to me to go sing in the women's section. After that insult, for 4 years I heard only you and practiced how to sing by emulating you. From 1953 to 1957, I remained underground. Then I resurfaced to record for Radio Pakistan again."

Indeed, it was a rare moment of one legend bearing his heart out to another legend who was his ideal. One is reminded of what Talat had once told Saigal of listening to him and wanting to sing like him. Even for legends, life comes full circle.

UP IN THE AIR, EXCLUSIVELY

Talat ended this decade on a high note, quite literally, up in the sky. In 1989, the national carrier, Air India had newly acquired and introduced the Airbus A320-200 aircraft. Part of the new offering in these planes was a brand-new IFE (In-flight Entertainment) program. Talat was requested by Air India to host a special two-hour music program which was part of their exclusive IFE. It was called 'Romance in the Air'.

This was a unique compilation of all-time great Hindi film songs presented and hosted by Talat. In this show, Talat not just played his own songs but also the songs by all his colleagues from the bygone Golden Era. He offered personal insights on music composers like Madan Mohan, Roshan, S.D. Burman, to name a few. And added special notes on his colleagues Mohammad, Rafi, Mukesh, Kishore Kumar, Lata Mangeshkar, Geeta Dutt, etc. It was heartening to listen to a legend speak in fond remembrance and high praise of all his colleagues who were often pitched against each other in the news as bitter rivals.

"In the 1940s-50s, we all came with our own signature style. And that became our distinct point of recognition. Like I was known for my softness, Rafi was known for his range, Hemant Kumar for his sweet and deep voice. Mukesh for his folk style and Manna Day for his classical prowess."

It was the generous spirit of artists of that time to speak well of their colleagues and rivals in absolute admiration. It was clear that in Talat's mind that these were all fellow artistes without whom it will be difficult to fully appreciate the greatness, success and legacy of our Hindi film music.

CHAPTER 9 - 1990S - BIGGEST HONOUR IN THE FINAL DECADE

(Talat was content with life in his twilight years. Photographed by his son Khalid)

INEXHAUSTIBLE DEMAND

DAILY NEWS

PRESENTS

The Melody King of India

Talat Mahmood

LIVE!

Along with his talented son

Khalid Mahmood

Produced by Yash Paul Soi

HEAR ALL OF YOUR FAVORITE GAZALS, GEETS AND WINNING "FILM FARE AWARD" SONGS.

Sunday, April 28, 1991 - 7:00 p.m.
Colden Center, Queens College, Flushing

Exit 24 at the intersection of Long Island Expressway and Kissena Blvd.

TICKETS: VIP $100, $50, $35, $25 & $15
Charge by phone: (718) 793-8080

In the last decade of his life, Talat continued to tour across Europe, Asia and America. This was a man, an artist who knew not how to rest. The legacy newspaper of New York called the Daily News was one of the main sponsors and presenters of his concert at the Colden Centre in Queens College, Flushing on 28th April 1991. This is a 2,085-seat concert hall and the largest indoor venue space within the borough of Queens. The hall was full with members of the Asian diaspora from across New York. This time his son Khalid was performing along with him for a few songs. He often toured with him through the 1970s to 1990s and sometimes sang his own songs too. Khalid would often talk about how much his father used to love travelling and exploring new cities, especially in the U.K. and U.S.A. Khalid's music and voice was very different from his father. He defined his genre of music as Pop Ghazals. He also released a few albums but unlike contemporaries of his time, such as Talat Aziz and Pankaj Udhas, he couldn't make a big mark in the music scene. But as a son, he was always there, standing by his father and supporting him during these world tours while the world noticed the legendary star age and slow down before their eyes. "I have travelled with him everywhere and I have seen how the audience would be stumped into silence by his voice. Wherever he went in America, the auditoriums would be fully packed. He had this aura about him."

[47]

This was one of his last international tours to America. He also performed for a charity fundraiser in North Carolina at Chapel Hill. The organizers of the concert, the HSNC (Hindu Society of North Carolina) were worried if they would be able to recover costs. They were expecting music lovers of the Asian diaspora to come from the three main cities of North Carolina, called the Triangle area. This included Raleigh, Durham and Chapel Hill. Arvind Shah, who is on the Board of Trustees at the HSNC informs me, "It was a great show. We organized this concert with the help of the Indian classical music society. The show was underwritten by 10 members in case HSNC loses money. But it was hugely successful, we made money and there was no need for underwriter's money."

Talat looked back at his decision of taking up concerts full time as a huge boost to his music. "In the past two decades, I have come closer to my fans than ever before. These shows not only pep me up and keep me going but have tested my talent time and again. It's a LIVE experience and you get to know your worth instantly", explains Talat. [48]

It seemed that there was an inexhaustible demand for Talat to perform. The love and anticipation from his fans was unlimited. But The travel schedule was beginning to get very tiring for Talat. He wondered if it was time to hang his boots for LIVE concerts as well?

THE PADMA BHUSHAN AWARD

(Talat receives the coveted Padma Bhushan award by the Government of India in 1992 by the hands of the President of India, R. Venkataraman)

Telex No. 1 -
Date: 25th January, 1992 Department of Telecommunications, Government of India

'The President of India has been pleased to award the Padma Bhushan to you in recognition of your services in the field of music playback singing. Congratulations.'
From,
S.B.Chavan , Home Minister

=======================

Telex No. 2 -
Date: 25th January, 1992 Department of Telecommunications, Government of India

'Congratulations on the conferment of Padma Bhushan in recognition of your contributions in the field of music playback singing.'

From,
Madhav Godbole, Home Secretary

============================

The Mahmood household was elated when they received this message. Finally, there came the announcement of what every professional waits to hear. An honour that seals the ultimate success of your work. The final icing on the cake. The national award and recognition by the Government of India.

Prime Minister Narsimha Rao in 1992, was a well-known multi linguist and a connoisseur of music and arts. Born in Andhra Pradesh, he was deeply interested in Urdu and Ghazals. It wasn't surprising when it turned out that he was a great admirer of Talat Mahmood. He was very happy to receive the recommendation of Talat's name by the Padma Award Committee and soon approved of the honour along with President Venkatraman. Talat was conferred the country's third highest honour, the Padma Bhushan award in 1992, in recognition of his artistic contributions in the spheres of cinematic and ghazal music.

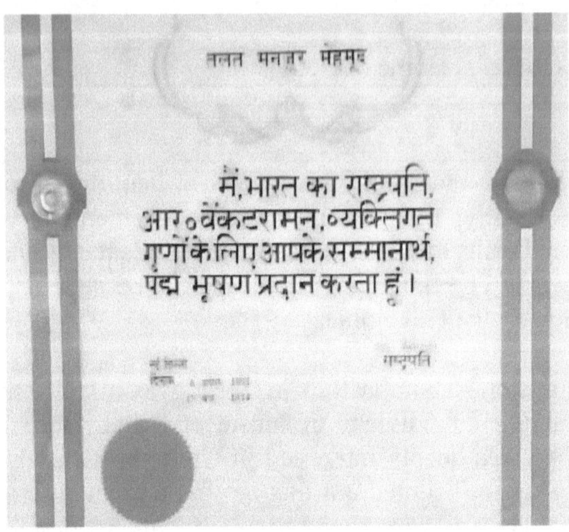

(Talat's Padma Bhushan was framed on the wall of his living room)

In April, 1992, Talat travelled to Delhi along with his son Khalid, to receive the Padma Bhushan. It was undoubtedly the pinnacle of his career. "I was almost in tears", Talat told us. A day later, we met him at his room in Janpath Hotel in an absolute state of jubilation. His old comrade and sister, Laila, was in town too. It was an emotional moment for both of them. All those decades of supporting his choice of career and cheering for him had been a rewarding journey. She was there for him in the most crucial initial years of his singing profession when he was struggling to persuade his father and would help gently slip in records sung by him into the house. The award brought in a rush of memories and unknown emotions as they hugged each other.

But for how long can two strong-headed siblings remain calm together? They ended up in a childish brother-sister tiff which had all of us in splits and giggles. It was a scene of two siblings forgetting that they're all grown up. Incidentally, the Padma Bhushan came a few days after the festival of Eid. Amidst the celebratory mood of the award, it slipped Talat's mind to give me and my brother some traditional Eidi (small amount of cash given to children as a token of love). Of course, this custom is purely traditional and out of affection for children of your family but followed very seriously in families of Lucknow. Talat asked his son Khalid to treat us to some ice cream and caramel custard at the hotel's cafeteria downstairs. Meanwhile, the two sparring siblings were cooled down by my mother who treated them to home cooked *sewaiyan*. It became a twin celebration of Eid and the Padma Bhushan for all of us.

My family had recently moved to Delhi, disturbed and uprooted from Kuwait during the 1991 Gulf War. I remember this evening being one of the first happy moments we got to experience after coming to Delhi. That same evening, the national broadcaster Doordarshan was showing his film 'Sone Ki Chidiya' on television. This was the film in which he acted in a romantic role opposite Nutan. The lead actor was Balraj Sahini. While watching the movie with us, Talat started remembering moments from the shooting of the film and couldn't stop praising his colleague Sahini as an actor par excellence.

(The author was 12 years old (centre, below) when she met Talat (above) with family in Delhi after his Padma Bhushan)

My brother, Samar, who is a research analyst by profession but has always been a Golden Era aficionado since childhood, remembers that evening with a crystal clear memory. "It was remarkably special. Bambai Nana (Talat) was explaining how a Padma Bhushan is a rarity for singers. It's important to understand at that time, he and Lata were the only two singers in the country who were conferred with the Padma Bhushan."

Senior journalist Sathya Saran adds an interesting insight from that moment. “When Talat Mahmood won the Padma Bhushan, along with music composer Naushad, I spent the day meeting Naushad first, and Talat Mahmood, second. Naushad had lashed out at the film industry which he insisted had deteriorated to din. Talat, on the other hand, spoke with wistfulness and nostalgia of the glorious days. If he was remembered during his lifetime, despite his retirement, he was happier for it. He was gratified by the fact that his concerts, at home and abroad, had kept him in public memory.”

On the request of his fans in Delhi, who wanted to celebrate his award, he obliged for an impromptu stage show. It was to thank them for their unstinted support in all these decades. I attended this show and I was touched by how painstakingly he tried to sing most of the requests from the audience. Sitting in the front row, I looked back at those shouting out his name. Some were wiping their tears, some were too overwhelmed to say anything at all. In a packed hall, the requests for songs wouldn’t stop, till he apologized that he couldn’t stretch his time any further.

No trip to Delhi was complete for Talat without meeting his mentor and Godfather, the legendary music composer Anil Biswas. As Talat always said, “Aasman pe hai khuda, aur zameen pe Anil da” (I have God up there in the sky and Anil brother down here in this world). Talat was always like a son to Anil Biswas and this was a moment of great reckoning for all the trust that Biswas had always placed in his talent. The two legends celebrated Talat’s Padma Bhushan by giving the go ahead to veteran journalist and award-winning documentary maker Sharad Dutt to make his next documentary on the life of Talat Mahmood. “When Anil da introduced me to Talat sa’ab that day, he promised to meet me in Bombay and give me all the required details and contacts. It was really special to meet him right after his Padma Bhushan. We later had a couple of sittings where I filmed him talking about his life story. He then helped me get access to Dilip Kumar and Khayyam.” The documentary faced some delays and was released several years after Talat’s death. It was called ‘Ek Makhmali Awaaz - Talat Mahmood’.

TALAT GEET KOSH - THE SONG ENCYCLOPEDIA

Back home in Bombay, there was another significant development on a much-awaited project. Just as the Padma Bhushan was the final seal on his music legacy, this project was the biggest testimony to his legacy. It was the launch of a special book which, for the first time ever, compiled all the songs of his entire career that he had sung and recorded in 45 years. This included recordings for All India Radio, Hindi films, regional cinema films, non-film geet, non-film ghazals, unreleased films, Bangladeshi films, Pakistani films and some government advertisement spots.

Dr. Rakesh Pratap Singh was a Kanpur-based academician and a die hard fan of Talat Mahmood. He had collected and bought several records and cassettes of Talat's songs. In the 1970s, as a hobby, he started jotting down details of these songs in his diary, including the lyrics of entire songs. By 1987, when the diary started getting thicker, he realized this was a unique compilation on his favourite singer. He had about 200 records of only Talat Mahmood songs in his collection. Around the same time, Talat was visiting Kanpur for a performance at the Lajpat Bhawan auditorium. He stopped over at Dr. Singh's house to see his collection. That's when they spoke about this unique book.

The idea was to compile all his recordings in a book in chronological order, with all information of the songs including the year of release, name of film/name of album, director, producer, writer, composer and lyrics. It would serve the purpose of an encyclopedia of songs sung by Talat. It would be called the "Talat Geet Kosh". Talat was delighted with the idea and immediately offered him all the support and help that would be needed for Dr. Singh to complete this herculean mission.

Dr. Singh was a professor of Zoology at the DAV College in Kanpur, who would spend the first half of his day teaching students and keep the rest of the day dedicated to his music mission. His wife, Professor Kirti Nidhi, who taught political science at the same college, recalls how the whole family supported this mission. "I would come back from work and get into the kitchen to handle the whole house in order to leave him absolutely undisturbed during his research. I would say that ninety percent of his life was completely dedicated to music. He was in touch with music clubs across different cities and people would come home to check his collection of records, books and diaries - all related to the music of the Golden Era, especially Talat Mahmood. Guests would come home and sit till 1 am in the night, discussing music and singing songs."

One must appreciate that to do this work from the 1970s to the 1990s was doubly difficult. Firstly, the songs had to be played, rewound and replayed several times before he listened to each line and finished writing all the lyrics of the song by hand in his diary. Talat had recorded almost 780 songs in his entire career. While it was easier to find information on film songs and popular ghazals, the task was to locate all the non-film songs, non-film ghazals, naat & bhajan (devotional songs) and regional cinema songs. This soon became a multi-city project where Dr. Singh had to check with recording studios, film productions to cross check dates. The biggest challenge was the help required for the lyrics of Talat's songs from regional cinema. Talat has sung in about 16 different languages including Bengali, Telugu, Assamese, Marathi, Punjabi, Sindhi, Malayalam, Gujarati, to name a few. To understand and write the lyrics of these, Dr. Singh had to take help from language experts from across the country. A lot of it was voluntary help that people lent for the love of Talat. Often, one collector based in another city had a copy of one particular song which had to be recorded into a copy and posted to his home in Kanpur. This was the age of typewriters and postal mail much before the advent of computers, emails, internet or mobile phones. Cross checking and doubly verifying information would take weeks and months.

"He would travel across the country to Delhi and Calcutta to complete this book. And would be in touch with other music collectors in Ranchi, Ottawa, Gujarat, even England and America. After his passing away in 2015, we have preserved everything in his music room in top condition. We have been so emotionally attached to his passion." adds his younger brother, Professor Adesh Pratap Singh. In fact, he was the one who sent me a copy of the Talat Geet Kosh which was required for my research in this biography. The music room of Dr. Singh is full of endless cabinets and shelves of 78rpm records, 45 rpm records, CDs, cassettes, gramophone players, published music books, encyclopedias, diaries and film memorabilia.

The Talat Geet Kosh also contains innumerable testimonies by singers and musicians, who had given their quote in support of the song encyclopedia. It also features a hand written note by filmmaker par excellence and Academy Award winner, Satyajit Ray. Dated 29th December, 1991, he wrote, "Talat Mahmood was a singer of treat, talent and popularity. I am glad that a book is being completed which includes all the songs he had sung."

Finally, in August, 1992, the Talat Geet Kosh was ready to be released. In the strained love-hate relationship that Naushad had for Talat, he seemed obliged to come for the launch of this significant book. This happened on the request of common friend and veteran film journalist Raju Bhartan. He felt that it was only Naushad's stature as music composer from the Golden Era who could do justice to this occasion. We must be reminded here that this was after the bitter experiences that Talat had had with Naushad where his voice was replaced in the songs of Palki (1967) and Aadmi (1968) without his knowledge. After much coordination and cajoling, Bhartan managed to get both legends on the same page, for the larger good of music.

The behind-the-scenes of this launch was not without the climax of a thriller. As Bhartan had described in his own words. As the goodwill liaison partner to this, he was getting ready to pick up Naushad from his apartment and take him for the launch. That's when he received a frantic call from Talat, "I've just spoken to Naushad as a gentle reminder for today but he gave no assurance that he would be coming for the inauguration of the Talat Geet Kosh." Bhartan rang Naushad to which he responded, "I will be there within half an hour. Not to worry. You drive straight there and I will join you at Talat's place directly." [49]

When all men finally arrived, the book was released at Talat's penthouse in Sunbeam Apartments at Perry Cross Road with a few invited guests, including those who had helped the researcher and author Dr. Singh in his decades long journey of compiling the legend's varied list of songs.

It was a simple and close-knit occasion, almost like a very small family wedding. Dressed in a crisp, white traditional kurta-pyjama of Lucknow, Talat was garlanded with orange marigold and red roses amidst claps and cheers. That day what Naushad said was in

(Talat's (left) Geetkosh was launched by Naushad (centre) in the presence of journalist Raju Bhartan (right) & author Dr.Singh (extreme left)

effect trying to mend bridges as well. “It gives me great pleasure to pay my humble tribute to the Ghazal King, Talat Mahmood saheb, whose human qualities as a gentleman of character and calibre far exceeds his outstanding accomplishment in Hindustani film music. His songs have left a mark not only on our minds but our hearts and souls”, expressed Naushad.

MORE AWARDS IN THE TWILIGHT YEARS

The last few years of his life were spent without recordings or tours. It must have felt dull for an artist who spent his life in breaking new grounds and finding new avenues for sharing his music. But this was also the time when the world was busy bestowing upon him with more awards.

In 1994, the EMI Records marked his 70th birthday by presenting him with a special Silver Disc. This made Talat the first ever singer from Asia to receive this honour.

In 1995, the State Government of Madhya Pradesh honoured him with the 'Lata Mangeshkar Puraskar', which is a national level award given for exemplary work in the field of music.

The same year, EMI Records released an album called 'Once More - Rare Songs of Talat Mahmood'. The CD had 16 songs which were indeed forgotten gems, including some from his first few films in Calcutta like Raj Laxmi (1945), Samapti (1949) to films in the 1950s in Bombay which had gotten lost in the crowd of other bigger hits by Talat.

LAST HOLIDAY WITH BAMBAI NANA

In 1996, as a teenager, I went with my mother to Mumbai to stay with Bambai Nana and the family. Of course one didn't know that this would be the last time that we ever met but he was already lost in a manner. Lost in his thoughts, as it happens with most people in old age. He would be sitting in his recliner bed, staring at his TV screen as some sitcom blared out jarring sounds which would have hurt his gentle tastes and sophisticated aesthetics during his prime. I looked at his daughter-in-law, Reena aunty, who effortlessly handled all his requirements of old age. She was there to attend to his every need. Khalid mamoon (uncle) understood the horror on my face after seeing him in this condition. By this time, I had heard and seen enough of his films to know what a great artist he was. Not just an old and funny gramps but a vivacious, beautiful star whose voice and face jumped out of the airwaves to charm you, to comfort you and bedazzle you. Everybody grows old but when a handsome star degenerates in old age, destiny feels crueler. Till a few years ago, Khalid would respond to some of his father's fan mails and requests to meet the legend at home. Khalid allowed it sometimes but it left a lot of fans with mixed reactions. Some were delighted but some were shocked to see him grow old. It's one of those things that you can never understand. Don't celebrities have the right to grow old?

I sat in the living room of the Sunbeam penthouse tastefully done up by Khalid, with peach-coloured walls and mirrored walls donning huge photo frames of Talat's studio images in his prime years. Khalid created a photo gallery of portraits at home, surrounding his father with happy memories of his stardom. He handed over some old photo albums to me from the 1950s, to make me feel better. These were family albums and some professional studio albums too. "See these, you will enjoy them. There are more in that cabinet, if you want", Khalid said.

Many of these pictures I had seen before since they were at my home as well but some were new to me. What we effortlessly share with our families on Facebook today with a magical click, required much more work in the yesteryears. Multiple copies of family pictures used to be printed and then posted by mail to the extended family across cities and countries. This is how families kept up with capturing moments of growing children and family functions. As I flipped through these black cardboard pages which had corner frames to slip on the pictures, I carefully peeled away the butter paper sheets used between each page to protect the pictures from leaking on to each other. These were pictures of Bambai Nana's youth as a young father, a doting husband and a charming star. His vibrant presence jumped out of these old and faded black and white images. In one image, Talat is hanging out with his friends Madan Mohan, Enoch Daniels and Shekhar at Khalid's 4th birthday party. Many images of actress Mala Sinha and Nargis feeding the indulgent birthday boy. Other images from what seems like a housewarming party with Talat and his sisters sitting with Dilip Kumar and his sisters in a family get together. A few poignant moments from Saiby's wedding album where father and daughter were seen hugging each other.

(The author (left) as a young teenager with Khalid and his wife Reena in Mumbai)

The later years captured his world tours showing him on stage and some behind-the-scenes with his sponsors and hosts. I kept aside the albums and walked towards his Padma Bhushan which I was seeing for the second time, years after I had first seen it rolled up as a scroll, freshly handed over to him in 1992, by the President of India. It had now been spread out and framed in glass and hung up on the wall right opposite the entrance door. An uncomfortable question crossed my mind in despair. What do awards and accolades mean at this stage in life when the only concerns left are the basics of how to eat your food, digest it well and have a normal stroll across the house?

Maybe I was reeling from the shock of seeing him in this helpless condition but I knew the answer at the back of my mind. How many people become legends and live life to the fullest? His journey has certainly been worth the while, worth every accolade, worth every award, worth every heartbreak.

I peeped into his bedroom where he was still sitting up on his bed and had fallen asleep. I quietly stepped into the adjacent guest room and sat next to the terrace window where nature had put up a light and sound show for me between the shadows of the trees and the parrots outside. “You should spend more time at this window. You will see a whole family of parrots on this tree,” said my cheerful Nasreen nani (granny) from behind. “What do you want for lunch today? How about chicken mayo rolls?”. Sure, I replied with delight. She was known in the family as a fabulous cook, especially with her Bengali dishes, like doi maach, alur dom and chholar dal. But with a teenager at home, she wanted to try something different that she had just seen on her favourite TV show, Khana Khazana by Chef Sanjeev Kapoor. The show was staple viewing every evening at the Talat household. You couldn’t miss it, you couldn’t talk during it and you certainly had to agree with Bambai Nana’s insistence that “Yeh Chef mera bahut bada fan hai " (This Chef is a big fan of mine). To which Nasreen nani would argue, “How do you know? He never told you!!” The singing legend would retort with uncanny clairvoyance, “Mujhe pata hai" (I am certain). So, there.

CHAPTER 10 - BAMBAI NANA IS NO MORE

'AB AKHRI HAI SALAM' - THE FINAL GOODBYE

There was a song that Talat sang for the film Mera Salam (1957). It was a poignant reminder to everyone that from dust you came and to dust you return.

'Salaam Tujhko Aye Duniya, ab Aakhri Hai Salaam
Chhalakne wala hai ab meri zindagi ka jaam'

(My last and final goodbye to you o'world
My cup of life is full, it is about to spill over)

In 1998, on the 9th of May, the phone rang at our home in New Delhi. My mom took the call and started crying. We got worried and my brother took the receiver from her. It was Khalid uncle calling us from Bombay.

"Bambai Nana is no more."

He passed away at the age of 74 by a heart attack at around 8 a.m. His sister Laila (my grandmom) was with us and she broke down when she heard the news. She had visited him in Bombay just a fortnight ago and I remember her saying that she felt this would be the last time that they will get to meet. How true was her hunch. The two siblings had spent hours reminiscing about their childhood and Lucknow home. Meeting Laila had triggered old memory flashes for Talat which he got to revisit after years. She was surprised how far back in time his mind would wander and remind her of almost forgotten people and places from their childhood in Lucknow. "We had kept meeting and separating all our lives but during this last visit of mine, we both sobbed like children", expressed Laila.

The news of his death spread fast. He left behind distraught fans all over the world. His son Khalid had been continuously getting calls from London, West Indies, Holland, Lagos and America. His friend Manna Dey, Naushad Ali's family, the Mangeshkars, singer Anup Jalota and actress Shyama were some of those who immediately came home to console his family, after hearing the news. Meanwhile, at my home in Delhi, there were some media crews knocking at the door. Zee TV and Star News (NDTV) wanted to take our comments for their 9pm news and weekend special shows. The two were not 24x7 news channels back in 1998. They used to run only one single news slot of 30 minutes at 9pm every night. We provided them with some old photographs from our family albums for them to run in their news report. In those days, general public access to the internet was provided barely a few years back, so there was hardly anything available online.

When they came home, Laila spoke to the press, saying, "He was always very active in singing for school and college functions. He wanted to make it big as a singer. The first step towards professional singing was when he signed up for Marris Music College (now called Bhatkhande Music Institute). Soon enough, he became a well-known radio voice in AIR Lucknow. In Bombay, his talent was tapped by Anil Biswas. They were always very fond of each other", she added, before rushing to Mumbai for his final burial.

(Talat with his friend, guide and mentor Anil Biswas)

When the Zee TV crew gave the news to Anil Biswas at his home in Delhi, he broke down and was unable to speak for a while. He needed a few moments to recover. "The velvet voice is no more", he sobbed. "I was not prepared to hear this news. I am shattered. Talat was like my son. There have been hundreds of singers who managed to copy the styles of Mukesh, Kishore Kumar and Mohd Rafi but there can never be another copy of Talat Mahmood", he added, emotionally.

In Bombay, his wife Nasreen and son Khalid were inconsolable. The Star TV team was at home in the midst of Khalid uncle making all arrangements for the burial. "He wasn't suffering from any ailment but was generally weak and slow because of his age. He was almost 75 years old. He suffered from a heart attack in the morning and passed away within 10 minutes. I'm grateful to God that he was given a peaceful death. You can imagine the love and blessings of thousands of his fans that must have surely helped Daddy in the final moments', expressed Khalid Mahmood. [50]

Since only a few close friends and family were informed, a major part of the film industry found out later, through the media. It was kept as a very private affair. There were several who complained later as they believed that the legend deserved a grand final adieu by his fans. But this was the son's personal prerogative for his own father. The legend's daughter, Sabina was distraught for not having had a chance to see her father for one last time. She was rushing on a flight from Europe but the burial could not be put on hold. "My greatest regret is not being by his side when he was breathing his last. I would have hugged him and begged him to stay on. A still bigger regret is being deprived of seeing his face for the last time and hugging him before he was buried and left me for eternity." [51]

I had just finished my Class 12 Board Exams and was barely out of school. My friends noticed me on television and called up. They were surprised to know about my connection with Talat Mahmood. It was something I was taught not to flaunt about and eventually, my closest friends and later my media colleagues, never knew about it.

In the television news reports and tributes, it was as much about celebrating the work of a genius in remembrance. Doordarshan and AIR played out his recordings and interviews from their archives. The newspapers were full of half page obituaries, remembering a legend who was spoken less about but remained close to hearts. His songs were played, replayed and revived.

Almost like a second birth. He had not been in the public eye for the past many years yet the outpouring of emotions that flooded in newspaper obituaries was testimony to the fact that he had continued to live silently in people's hearts. My mother's collection of all those newspaper and magazine cuttings, which is almost like a mini booklet, is today a great source of information for me.

Incidentally, I built my own archive. In those days, it was my hobby to build a video library of films, songs and documentaries which I would record directly from television. So, I also ended up recording anything that was aired across different TV channels on his passing away. Today, while writing his biography, my VHS tapes are an integral part of my research to revisit who said what while reminiscing about Talat Mahmood.

THE PERSONA

The national broadcaster, Doordarshan (DD1 channel) played a special tribute show of one hour, speaking to various stalwarts from the film industry reminiscing about their experiences with Talat Mahmood. The tribute show was titled 'Ek fankaar, ek insaan' (The artist, the persona), throwing equal light on how Talat's warmth and personality touched people , apart from his work as an artist. It was hosted by popular actress and TV host, Tabassum, who was also his neighbour in Bandra. She was almost in tears when she was recording the show.

Dev Anand, actor, friend and co-star for whom Talat sang the famous 'Jayen to jayen kahan', was distraught. "I'm very emotional to hear about his death. I will be unable to say much. It's similar to what I felt when my brother Chetan Anand passed away. I couldn't say much even then. But I would like to convey my heartfelt condolences to his family and fans."

Legendary filmmaker, often called the architect of the Golden Era, B.R.Chopra, called it a hurtful loss. "He was as beautiful as his voice. His face always had a radiating smile reflecting on his face. A rare civilized and cultured person in the industry. After meeting him, one felt that you had met a genuine friend. And such a special voice that even poetry would applaud in admiration. He has left behind an unparalleled impact in the industry. I am reminded of his song 'Mera jeevan saathi bichhad gaya', we have lost a great friend. But I am confident that his voice will stay alive forever."

His long term friend, admirer and singer Manna Dey was equally shaken. "It's a personal loss for me. I was his fan first and friend later in life. I remember when I heard his Ghazal 'Tasveer teri dil mera' in the 1940s, I was bowled over. No one had ever sung in that style before. I was honestly envious of the soft, velvety romanticism in his voice. Later when I met him in Bombay, I was bowled over once again because he was so handsome and charming in his manners and style."

Music director Naushad Ali showered him with praise. "Talat's voice and his specialty in presenting the Ghazal was in such a manner that I have no hesitation in saying that he was himself a

'Taghazzul-e-Ghazal'' (the very embodiment of Ghazals). And unless you have that singular quality, you can't evoke those profound emotions."

"For Ghazals, he was put on the pedestal as equal to Begum Akhtar. And in films, he created a unique identity of singing songs that were *makhsoos* (respectful and intimate). He was never interested in loud or over the top songs. And as a person, he always had a smile on his face with a gentle disposition", added Naushad.

The final word came from his friend and musical soulmate, the thespian Dilip Kumar, "Talat had a beautiful personality. Much more than his songs, I would like to praise his nature. The kind of ghazals and songs sung by him carried a unique style. That style was very popular with people. Even when I would lip sync his songs, I would enjoy it a lot," he recalled.[52]

CLOSE TO MANY HEARTS

The next generation of film and Ghazal singers equally felt swept by a wave of sadness on hearing about his death. Pankaj Udhas was backstage for his concert when he got news of his demise. When he greeted his audience on stage, the first song he sang was 'Jalte hain jiske liye' as an immediate tribute to an artist who had inspired and supported him. Talat had launched one of Udhas' earliest albums in 1983 called 'Mehfil' and sealed a place in his heart forever.

Similarly, singer Kavita Krishnamurthy reflects on what Talat meant to the music industry. "Mehdi Hassan was a big fan of his. Talat was iconic for him. Both him and Jagjit Singh felt that if Talat had taken Ghazals to such a successful height, they could try to do it as well. They were truly inspired."

Jagjit Singh had himself spoken often about this inspiration and firmly believed that there had been none to rival Talat Mahmood. "Talat Mahmood is THE ghazal original and all who followed, including myself, were inspired by his style and idiom."

Just as Talat's songs and career was being revisited in multiple tributes on TV and radio, within the same week, I saw the same happen with Frank Sinatra who died 5 days later on 14th May, 1998. The BBC replayed his concerts and interviews on loop. And that's how I discovered my love for Sinatra. It was like his second birth triggered by his death! It is the biggest truth that an artist never dies. These two singing stars remain on my playlist forever. Both Sinatra and Talat were crooners of another kind that the world has not had again.

As an interesting observation, I would like to add that this was the time when the upcoming music label T-series was flooding the Hindi music market with cover versions of songs from the Golden Era. This was being done under the essence of *shraddhanjali* (tributes) to legends gone by. It upset a lot of original music labels. Songs of Kishore Kumar, Mohammad Rafi and Mukesh were being sung by new singers and churned out. When I had the chance to ask someone from their team, "Why not Talat?", pat came the reply, "It was difficult to copy his style or voice. His songs didn't sound good in any other voice."

But someone who did sound good singing his songs in a tribute show was a young and upcoming Ghazal singer Sudeep Banerji. The first *shraddhanjali* performance in the form of a LIVE concert had taken place in the India Habitat Centre (IHC) in New Delhi, soon after his passing away. Sudeep was intellectually invested in the deep meaning of Urdu poetry. It was something that the Ghazal King would have been extremely happy to know about. While singing the legend's songs, Sudeep added some couplets by Firaq and Faiz. These were couplets that were similar in sentiment and sounded good when threaded into Talat's original Ghazals.

It was the first time I shared the raw grief of his passing away with strangers. While I was receiving guests for the concert, I didn't know that I would end up consoling them since they would start sobbing as they met me. His name Talat has many meanings, one of them being, the appearance of the rising moon. His persona and quality as an artist truly lived up to his name. With the enchanting rise of the moon every night, how can Talat ever be forgotten?

The beauty of Talat's journey was that he lived his dream with conviction without any regrets. "I have been most satisfied with what life has given me. Life in Bombay has been most fulfilling and I have received my share of recognition and appreciation." [53]

His son Khalid's biggest contribution to his father's legacy has been in managing an active website on Talat's life and career. For decades, his fans have been able to get a glimpse of his life through images and information that Khalid posted on this website. But with Khalid's recent passing away too in 2023, preserving this rich legacy faces fresh challenges.

Undoubtedly, he was a son who unstintingly dedicated his life to promoting his father's music, and his loss would be keenly felt by all Talat lovers globally.

CHAPTER 11 - 20 YEARS LATER : 'JASHN-E- TALAT BY SAHAR ZAMAN'

(The author speaking at the Jashn-e-Talat concert curated by her)

"Madam, I like Talat Mahmood a lot, pls listen to this", a fan wrote on the official Facebook page of Jashn-e-Talat. It was a video clip of the fan singing one of Talat's songs. He was singing out of tune with a few wrong pronunciations. But it was still endearing to hear because of the passion and respect with which he decided to send this video to me. Another fan met me at our Jashn-e-Talat concert in Hyderabad. She gushed, "Shaking hands with you is like I have touched Talat Mahmood. I am so fortunate". In Lucknow, an old gentleman said, "Oh, he used to be my uncle's neighbour. They spent a lot of time together." I had no way of verifying that but creating this tribute platform opened up a whole new world to me.

I started receiving all sorts of fan mails. Interestingly, I humbly admit that some of them were my fans from television news who then became Talat Mahmood fans. Many of my young followers would see posts about Talat on my social media feed and listen to his songs out of curiosity. This reverse fandom has been a unique experience. It made me wonder how Talat Mahmood handled those heady days of his fame. I remember my mom telling me that there used to be letters written to him in blood. Women wanting to marry him, signing autographs on crowded crossings outside his home at Bandra, hiding in the car, stepping into the cinema hall only when it's dark - never being able to watch the start or end of any movie.

A lot of it seemed inconvenient but he didn't mind at all. In fact, he was once asked on BBC radio during his UK tour in the 1970s on how he handled this hysteria. He said, "Well, my hair hasn't been pulled out by anyone yet. But somehow my fans keep a very respectful distance. I appreciate that."

THE CREATION OF 'JASHN-E- TALAT'

20 years after his death, the first ever Jashn-e-Talat concert took place in 2018. The name of the concert literally means a celebration of Talat. It was a smashing hit in the Delhi circuit of LIVE music events but it took many years of sweat and toil to make it happen. My personal journey of actively digging through Bambai Nana's archives started sometime in 2014. A serious process of retracing his professional milestones and understanding his contribution started in a moment of gratitude while waiting at a traffic light. It came to me in a flash. I remember driving to my office on a wretched Monday morning. My toddler son at the time was running a high fever and I didn't want to leave him behind at my mom's. But my studio bookings were confirmed and I just had to go handle my news shows for the day. I put on the radio in my car and there it was. His voice. Talat Mahmood was singing to me, 'Shaam-e-gham ki qasam…' I felt like he was singing especially to me because his soft voice soothed me like a balm over a burning heart. I had always known that his voice had this unique quality of comforting your mind but I deeply felt it now for the first time in my life. I immediately had an immense sense of gratitude. That very moment, I decided to organize a musical tribute in his name.

It was a decision I made unbeknownst to me what an uphill task this would turn out to be. My expertise lies in journalism and television. Curating a music event or organizing a LIVE concert is something that I knew nothing about. But as his grand-niece, I took upon myself the task of creating a brand-new tribute platform. I decided to call it 'Jashn-e-Talat by Sahar Zaman'. It is designed as a unique multi-performance platform which is dedicated to his music, his films, his personality, his unparalleled contribution to Ghazal *gayaki* and his pioneering efforts in introducing this genre to mainstream film music. My curatorial skills were up for the litmus test.

I painstakingly worked out a formula for involving the youth in his music and celebrating his legacy not just with vocal performances but also with dance, theatre and visual arts. The proposed concert was nothing like what has been seen in other tribute concerts where the stage is filled up with the orchestra and a few singers stand and sing songs in remembrance of a legend. Therefore, pitching my show to potential sponsors became a huge challenge. Very often, the straight jacketed marketing world refuses to understand anything out of the box and is unwilling to take the 'risk' of a new formulae.

For three years, I had to put Jashn-e-Talat in cold storage!! I always believed that it was only a matter of the right timing because there was nothing wrong with my curatorial formula. I got extremely busy juggling the quintessential work-life balance of being at work as the prime-time news editor-anchor and bringing up a young child.

Things began to look up in late 2017. The idea was to re-introduce his songs to the younger generation and make them realize the beauty of his music and his voice. This also meant that the demographics of the audience for this show would change. Instead of an audience age of 35+ onwards, we would now be looking at an age of 18+ onwards. I happened to mention this to a PR professional, Sudesh Chawla, who was taking care of my other projects. As luck would have it, she turned out to be an ardent fan of Talat Mahmood and offered to help me work out something for Jashn-e-Talat. We ideated on the youth factor and decided to launch a singing competition at a few colleges in Delhi.

The criteria for the students was to sing only Talat Mahmood songs or Ghazals. Many of them Googled up his top songs and spent a week rehearsing the right notes and expressions. The big catch of this competition was that the shortlisted winners would get to share the stage with established artists on the day of the main concert, which was due in a few months to mark his Birth Anniversary. These college competitions would create the much-required buzz on ground in the build up to the anniversary. Sudesh selflessly did the job of visiting different college campuses across Delhi to convince their music clubs to participate in this competition. The 18–20-year-old students had not even heard his songs. I was about to engage an over-stimulated bunch of millennials with a kind of music that was created in the days of their grandparents. The challenge was immense.

These kids had playlists that ran into hundreds of songs. And none of these were anywhere close to the kind of offering that I had in mind. Why would they want to hear Talat's soft, caressing voice? He was a star of their grandparents' generation or at the most some of their parents were fans of his. But nothing to do with this present Gen Z. But here's what changed to my delight. Once they tried out his hits, he stayed on their playlist forever. They had never experienced the power of lyrics in this manner and how his voice emulated every essence of the poetry he sang. It was a new experience for the youngsters and soon we had a cue of short-listed winners who were vying to participate in the main show. RJ Devika Dutta and singer Sanjeev Choudhury from the All India Radio were invited to judge all these competitions in the following weeks. They marked the students on the criteria of vocal expression, rhythm and tempo. To my utmost surprise, some students picked his rare non-film Ghazals and a few unreleased film songs as well to sing at these competitions. It reflected their process of research of going through his popular hits and then settling with some rare gems to perform on stage. To hear what these students said after being introduced to Talat, is my biggest reward :

"I was baffled by the lyrics 'Teri aankh ke ansoo pee jaoon' and the way he sang it so tragically. It was a wonderful experience for me to sing this song. I had only heard of his name before but never paid attention to his songs."

- Sourav Mukherjee, Taleem Society (DU)

"I took one full day of hearing his songs on YouTube to decide which song to sing. There is such intensity of emotions in his voice. I feel that his songs should keep playing on and never end."

- Shritama Jha, Sri Aurobindo College (DU)

"He does so much justice to the lyrics. Such sweet songs like 'Jalte hain jiske liye'. If you hear them in solitude, you will find so much peace."

- Nidhi Pandey, Dyal Singh Morning College (DU)

"Singing his songs felt like I've lived the most beautiful part of music. The happiness and sweetness that his voice gives cannot be felt from hearing today's music."

- Jatin Sharma, Dyal Singh College (DU)

Their views and insights were precious. It made my resolve firmer that this is a treasure which has neither gone out of style nor expired. It shines up when it is revisited and re-introduced to the current generation. Talat's voice has stood the test of time. Testimonies of the youth are the greatest gift on the relevance and creative prowess of an artist.

My husband Dhiraj Singh who has remained my staunchest support in this madness of mine, got down to designing the 'Certificate of Recognition' and signature trophies for the winning students. Jashn-e- Talat now had its branding in place with a specific look and feel, both physically and in the Social Media world. Initial help for ground execution at colleges was provided by Sanjiv Saraf from the Rekhta Foundation, who believed in the cause. The All India Radio came on board to help publicize the college competitions. Time and again, I was reminded of how much love there was for Talat Mahmood. The news media like The Pioneer, Education Times, Times of India, The Statesman, etc. were generous in their print coverage in listing out these college competitions with gushing responses for their novelty.

TALAT MAHMOOD FLASH MOB

My next step in sync with the youth outreach was to do a flash-mob dance in a shopping mall. This grabbed the headlines as the first-ever flash mob on vintage music. But this also brought along a fresh set of challenges. This generation is used to dancing on beats and certain dance styles but not vintage music, or ghazals or melodious tracks. I tied up with the largest mall of the country, the DLF Mall of India under the dynamic leadership of Pushpa Bector, Executive Director for DLF Retail, who was truly excited about this experiment. The super talented dance-troupe of Delhi called StepKraft, were willing and happy to step-up their game and venture into a music genre not attempted earlier by any contemporary dance company.

This was in December 2017 and the mall was decked up for the Christmas and New Year fervour. It was in the spirit of festivities that Talat became part of this celebration. I created the soundtrack for the flash mob with a mix of Talat's peppy numbers that could add some zing for the young dancers. On the day of the performance, there were so many visitors who were pleasantly surprised to have a young bunch of 20-somethings dancing to the pure melody of Talat's timeless songs. His hits such as 'Itna na mujhse tu pyar' or 'Yeh hawa yeh raat' were brilliantly made to fit the moves of Rock-n-Roll, Salsa, Tango and Bachata. The flash mob ended up being performed thrice that day, repeated on popular demand. It made an otherwise shopping-crazy crowd to stop and take notice, cheer and furiously clap and take videos and selfies around the dancers. This sealed the identity of Jashn-e-Talat as a contemporary platform for his timeless music.

The dancers spread across the atrium space of the mall which is approximately 8000 square feet. The footfalls on the day of the flashmob were an average of 70,000 visitors. Which means that our flash mob was watched and experienced LIVE by at least 6000 visitors in that given hour. As I looked up across the top floors, standing on the ground floor, I could see hundreds of people thronging the glass railings to get a glimpse of this flashmob with a curious melody. The Times of India reported about how Talat Mahmood set GenZ dancing to his tunes. It's worth noting what the dancers said after their performance. "We were wondering how we can do a flash mob to such soft music but Talat Mahmood's voice is so amazing. It creates a dreamy image of flowers, birds and all things lovely", said Ankit Shikhar. Another dancer, Gaurav Maini expressed, "I had never heard of Talat Mahmood before. But when I googled up his name, I was so shocked to learn that he was the first singer who started his world tours and performances abroad in the early '50s. It was an honour to dance on his songs. Slow but meaningful songs." Aashmiin Kaur was the biggest surprise for me. "I'm the youngest in the troupe. I'm 10 years old and I didn't know about Talat Mahmood at all. But my grandparents were so happy that I would be dancing on his songs. And now I'm going to tell my friends about him as well", she said. The chief choreographer from StepKraft, Jigyasa, was more philosophical about it. "This gives us an idea that a flash mob on such music is a possibility as well. Because these songs don't have beats.

It's just melody and beautiful lyrics. Choreographing this was difficult but for the audience, it's an intriguing concept." Once again, this was covered in the Delhi press as a unique offering. It added an impetus to our ongoing plan for the main stage show with the participation of other established performers.

FIRST CONCERT IN DELHI

(A galaxy of top performers - Talat Aziz, Radhika Chopra, Amit Srivastava, Vidha Lal, Moving Souls (clockwise) for Jashn-e- Talat, Delhi)

In 2018, the first proper Jashn-e-Talat concert inside a big auditorium happened in the heart of Delhi. The support of a venue was provided by the India Islamic Cultural Centre (IICC). This concert was the culmination of all our work in the past three months and it also set the ball rolling for more such concerts across the country in the future. The IICC has one of the most sought-after auditoriums in the prime of Delhi. And they opened up the doors of their auditorium to leave me and my team undisturbed for one dry run and final performance. The Raag Mantra Music Foundation, founded by Sitarist Azeem Ahmed Alvi came on board to help provide musicians and orchestra. If all this help wasn't enough, my dear friend from hotel Le Meridien, COO, Tarun Thakral, was there to provide accommodation for visiting artists. My colleague and friend from the news industry, Kartikeya Sharma, Founder of ITV Network, was providing publicity and reportage of the event across his print and television channels. An existing anthology on Talat Mahmood printed by the Manipal University Press and written by well-known musicologist Manek Premchand, was distributed to our performers, generously donated by my friend Prof. Madhav Das

Nalapat, the Honorary Director of the university. There are so many partners to name and thank, who stood by me only because they appreciated and acknowledged my efforts in these past years to make Jashn-e-Talat a reality. I mentioned this joint effort by all in my opening speech that night, "All of these partners and logos that you see here on our poster, on the left of the screen, they're all here for the love of Talat Mahmood. Nothing else. You are also here for the love of his music. Nothing else. So thank you all, for this love."

From my family, my mother Romana made sure to add personal insights from his life to add a touch of warmth. My brother Samar was vigil with all the required chronological details of Talat's career. My husband Dhiraj functioned as the executive producer for the platform. "Our first concert was a dream. It came together in perfect harmony with all the performers, supporters and audience. I was truly astounded to see such a packed hall. I remember it being extremely hectic backstage because we had lined up so many artists. I've never been to a show where the audience felt responsible to make this a hit. The amount of people pouring in to congratulate us in the green room was very touching."

(Author's husband Dhiraj Singh backstage with a portrait of Talat Mahmood)

The evening was threaded together with a lively anchoring and presentation by another friend, Red FM's popular RJ Sachin. It was a three-hour evening show. And as I mentioned in the beginning of this book, the show had to start half an hour early because it got packed to the isles before time. The anticipation and footfall were landmark, as was informed to me by the IICC team. My first set of performers were four young singers who were our winners from college. They sang Talat's foot tapping romantic duets which suited their youth.

Popular dancer and Kathak exponent Vidha Lal agreed to dance on two songs of Talat. I am hugely grateful to her for making an exception to my request because Kathak dancers don't perform on film music. She reinterpreted 'Jalte hain jiske liye' through her Kathak mudras and lent more classical gravitas to the traditional song, 'Ghir ghir aaye badarwa kaare'. "Songs of the Golden Era had a lot of classical compositions which were beautifully incorporated into popular film music. I am truly honoured to justify his songs through my dance. I believe Jashn-e-Talat is a benchmark show for the manner in which it has involved the youth. They will be inspired to carry on this concept ahead", explains the Guiness Record-holder dancer.

After Vidha's graceful presence, the audience gasped in surprise when the runner up of Dance India Dance (a popular dance competition reality television series), Dipasree Chatterjee along with Ravi Rastogi hit the stage for a Bollywood Salsa on an original Talat soundtrack, 'Bechain nazar betaab jigar'. This was an unthinkable interpretation of a vintage song. The Salsa dancers received the loudest applause.

There was a part of the audience who were at their feet for all three hours of the show because the hall was packed and there was no place to sit. It was heartening to see that no one left the hall midway. Eventually, the IICC minders at the entrance had to stop more people from getting in. But there was another person who was at his feet, momentarily bending down, sitting and standing back for those three hours. At one corner of the stage, visible to the entire hall. With an easel and brush, tirelessly bringing alive a remarkable life-like portrait of Talat Mahmood. Three feet by four feet in size, painted in sepia tone. It was one of the most life-like portraits I had ever seen. I was lucky to have the support of an extremely skillful artist, Amit Srivastava, to realize this dream. He painted the crooner's face in a classic style, bringing alive the sparkle of his eyes and the warmth of his smile on canvas by the end of the evening. My request to him was to listen to Talat's songs in his studio and experience his music to understand what kind of personality needs to reflect in the portrait. "I heard his music for the first time and appreciated it. Honestly, I had not anticipated such a huge response to the show. I wasn't aware of the extent of Talat Mahmood's popularity. This is truly an eye opener for me", expressed an awe-inspired Srivastava. But never did I realize that I would be creating dedicated new fans of Talat Mahmood who were more fascinated by his s mile than his voice! After his stage portrait, Amit wanted to revisit more of Talat's studio pictures to create more portraits in the future. He said there's something very soothing about his eyes and smile which inspires him to study his face in more detail.

The three hour concert was not just experimental and unconventional . I had promised a healthy mix of traditional too. The Ghazal darling of the Delhi circuit, Radhika Chopra and the superstar maestro Talat Aziz were part of this magnificent line up as well. "I'm here as Talat Mahmood's fan and admirer. There was such a uniqueness in the intoxicating quality of his voice with the vibrato. And if the voice and music of Talat Mahmood has reached the youngsters through Jashn-e-Talat, its really a big deal", said a congratulatory Chopra, who is admired for her own sweet, nectar filled voice. Her rendition of 'Meri yaad mein tum na aansoo bahaana…' and 'Sab kuch luta ke hosh mein…' was received with pin drop silence and moist eyes in the audience.

Ghazal maestro Talat Aziz entered stage to a thunderous applause. For someone who has his own dedicated following of ardent admirers, he believed in the cause of Jashn-e-Talat right from the start. He sang his favourite song, 'Phir wahi shaam..' which left the audience with an encore. But he engaged them further by urging them to sing along with him in the next song 'Tasveer banata hoon…'.

"I know Sahar has been working on this for the last couple of years. It's a great effort and I am here to support her. But she also has a very hard-working husband Dhiraj, who does all the running around along with her. So please give him a big hand as well. I wish them both all the best to do more such shows because there's a vast treasure of Talat sa'ab that needs to be re-explored, since it's already there for us."

He fondly recalled that he had met the legend at least four times in his lifetime, starting from Hyderabad, where Talat Aziz was brought up. “Talat (Mahmood) sa’ab had come to perform in Urdu Hall in 1961. There were around 400 people and I must’ve been four years old at the time, sitting right in front, on my mother’s lap. Of course, I couldn’t understand much. But hearing him was a very strong memory. He sounded very nice to me. Then when I moved to Bombay in 1978, I met him at his home for tea. He was so gracious, extremely soft spoken, tehzeeb-yaafta (refined) person because of his Lucknow background. The last time I met him was in 1986 at the Taj hotel where there was a celebration of his comeback album”, recalls the current maestro in fondness.

Soon after the success of this concert, it was spoken about in the concert circuit and Delhi clubs in gushing tones. Since I was not a professional in this field, people wondered how I managed to hit the ground running. The newspaper headlines described the concert as a festival of memories that evoked sensitive emotions.

HYDERABAD CALLING

(Clockwise - With Hyderabad's cultural ambassador, Khaleeq-ur-Rahman, cricketing legend Azharuddin, singers Tauseef Akhtar & Radhika Chopra, dancers Raghav & Mangala Bhatt)

The word spread fast. Soon after our Delhi concert, I got a call from Hyderabad, inviting me to do a similar concert there. The person on the other side of the call was a political leader by profession but a cultural ambassador of Hyderabad by passion. Khaleeq Ur Rahman was keen to showcase Jashn-e-Talat in his city. "I thought it would be lovely to take this tribute ahead to the youngsters of Hyderabad who are not acquainted with his music and talent. And the process that Sahar has started by re-introducing his music to today's generation is noteworthy. I am proud to present this in my city."

The venue for the show was at the auditorium of the famous Salar Jung Museum in the heart of the city. The show in Hyderabad followed the same formula of involving young college performers as well as established artists. When the young singers and dancers spoke on stage, they said they were amazed by the range of Talat Mahmood's romantic songs and are eager to explore more of his music.

Our established artists this time included London based Ghazal singer Tauseef Akhtar. While he performed most of the songs with the original composition, he introduced a fresh element to the song 'Ae mere dil kahin aur chal..'. He almost turned it into a slow waltz with the strumming of the Hawaiian guitar. "We will keep moving ahead in time but these old compositions will always keep touching our hearts. When youngsters are singing his songs today on the Jashn-e-Talat platform, they are getting exposed to great poetry and melody. It's not easy to sing Talat sa'ab's songs but his music remains timeless." opined Akhtar.

For Kathak, the renowned dance couple Raghav Raj and Mangala Bhatt graciously offered to perform. I was hesitant to ask them to dance on film songs but they agreed in just one single phone call that I made to them. Such was their generosity. They picked two classical numbers which Talat had sung, including 'Laage tose nain..', "I used to hear Talat ji's old songs every morning during practice sessions with my guru Pandit Birju Maharaj. He used to sing his songs all the time and I used to sing along too. A lot of them were classical based compositions. So, when Sahar asked me about dancing at Jashn-e- Talat, I readily agreed for the sake of Talat ji", recalls Raghav Raj Bhatt. Since these were classical numbers, they both kept their moves focused on facial expressions. Mangala Bhatt was spectacular in dancing to 'Ghir ghir aaye badarwa…' in which she brought out the mood of the rain song with her captivating eyes. "We have so much love for Talat ji since we have been listening to him since childhood and his voice always brought us so much peace. The songs of his time had beautiful rhythm and compositions", said Mangala Bhatt.

The finale in Hyderabad was by Radhika Chopra, on popular demand. "I'm very fond of Sahar and how she curates this festival to present Talat sa'ab's music in so many different colours, through youngsters, through dance, and paintings. I was there for the Delhi show and now I'm here for Hyderabad too. For me, as a female artist who has to sing the songs of a male artist, it is very challenging. It is out of my comfort zone but this is a special tribute in which I present some of my favourite songs of Talat sa'ab", added the contemporary queen of Ghazals.

The Chief Guest for the show was former Indian Cricket Captain, Mohammad Azharuddin who kept the best punch for the last. "Talat Mahmood is the Donald Bradman of music!!", he said. It would have been wonderful to have Bambai Nana hear him say that since he was himself a fan of Azharuddin and would eagerly wait to watch him play in the early 1990s.

The progress of Jashn-e-Talat was moving at break-neck pace. In the first 6 months of 2018, we had already done two concerts and were about to do the third one by the end of the year. At my workplace, things were getting equally busy. As the prime-time face for the evening debate shows at Times Network, my days would often start with editorial meetings with my team and end with the last roll of the show by 10pm. This is how I ended up distributing my life: Mon-Fri was dedicated to news and the weekend was kept aside for Jashn-e-Talat. Through the week, my mind was engaged in hardcore political news, raising citizen issues with aggressive accountability from the public servants and the government. The weekends would switch to soothing music of the charming Golden Era. In addition to that, the continuous demands of being the mother of a beautiful, growing up son.

A MUSICAL BIOPIC ON STAGE

(Kathak legend Shovana Narayan, theatre thespian Sohaila Kapur, singer Rashmi Agarwal and artist Anubhav Som (clockwise))

We ended 2018 with a bang by being back in Delhi for another concert. This time, at the India Habitat Centre, with the support of its Director, Sunit Tandon. As a theatre thespian and cultural aesthete, Tandon kindly agreed to partner with Jashn-e-Talat. The sentiment of the tribute and the music resonated with the profile of most of their members. For our latest Jashn-e- Talat show at IHC, I decided to add a fresh element of theatre to the performance. Could we try out an experimental mini biopic? For this, my friend Sohaila Kapoor was extremely happy to experiment about it. Sohaila is a popular actor in the OTT circuit and a well-known theatre director. She is also the niece of superstar Dev Anand. A tribute to a legend from the Golden Era immediately struck a chord with her. She took time out from her busy schedule to specially brainstorm on what her contribution could be in Jashn-e-Talat. It was decided that

Sohaila would perform a LIVE theatrical reading of Talat Mahmood's life. Sohaila incorporated some personal moments from their life that she was aware of. This was especially in reference to their film 'Taxi Driver' (1954) where Talat sang the famous song 'Jayen to jayen kahan'.

"My uncle and Talat Mahmood had brilliant songs together, especially 'Jayen to jayen kahan'. The film Taxi Driver will always remain special for me because it was on the sets of this film where my uncle and aunt (Dev Anand and Kalpana Kathik) got secretly married in between shots!" recalls Sohaila. The script enacted by Sohaila covered the highlights of Talat's life. It was like a musical mini biopic of a duration of 50 minutes interspersed with at least 8 of his songs, including Ghazals, Bengali songs and film hits.

The next challenge was to find a professional dancer who would agree to dance on eight diverse songs of different moods and styles. Who could do justice to such a variety? These were a mix of classical, modern and traditional songs. I braced myself up to broach the issue with Kathak guru Shovana Narayan. With a decades long illustrious career, she has always been open to sharing stage with different artists of diverse styles. She was one of the first to do a *jugalbandhi* (collaboration) with Flamenco, ballet and tap dancers in the early 1990s. I could think of no one else who could do justice to our script. And voila! She simply loved the idea. One of the most liberating things she said to me was to select any song from his career which I felt suited the script best and not be worried about how Kathak could be performed on that song.

Sohaila and I had a few meetings at Shovana's home with her warm hospitality of tea and snacks while we fine tuned the final performance. When Shovana came on stage, she added so much more beauty to the timeless songs, that I was amazed to watch her emote to perfection. On the mellow melody of 'Pyar par bas to nahin', she decided to keep away all the footwork and simply sit on stage, using only her eyes and hands to express the love in Talat's voice. In the peppy rain song of 'Aha rimjhim ke pyare pyare geet', she delicately sprang up to electrify the air with her happiness. And when Talat sadly sang 'Main teri nazar ka suroor hoon', she went up to hold his portrait on stage, conversing with it with her tearful eyes. At the end of the show on stage, the sweet danseuse honoured me with a touching compliment, "I wish everyone has a grand-niece like Sahar. The way she has strung this narrative together takes us through the highs and lows of his (Talat's) life and helps throw perspective on his journey. His songs had the beauty of the lyrics which I think we all need to revisit today."

The selection of the portrait artist for this show turned out to be a significant reminder of the Commemorative Stamp which was released by the Government of India in 2016. When I requested artist Anubhav Som to ideate about a large Talat portrait to paint LIVE on stage, he wanted a few days to structure the final look on canvas. What he showed to me as a rough draft was remarkable and thoughtful. He painted the exact image of Talat Mahmood's Commemorative Stamp painted over the background colour of khaki brown supposed to be the cover of an envelope. Over this khaki brown, he painted a red stamp on the bottom left corner of the canvas, bearing the birth date of the legend, 24.02.1924. This stamp is akin to the official postal stamps that one can see on envelopes. On the bottom right corner of his canvas, Anubhav painted a vintage metal microphone; the same microphone that one used to see inside radio studios which have come back in vogue for podcast recordings nowadays. "My ready reference for understanding the legend's personality are his songs. That's the only way I can get closer to him as a person, as an artist and as somebody who dedicated his entire life to a particular form of art. Whenever I hear his voice, I get the feeling of a train gently chugging up to the top of a hill. One can feel his passion", said an observant Anubhav. His beautifully composed painting also gave me a chance to speak about my efforts behind the Commemorative Stamp. It was a year-long process of first filling up the official form and sending frequent reminders to the office of the Minister of Information and Broadcasting in 2015. I was appalled as to why there was never a commemorative stamp issued in memory of Talat Mahmood when most other singers of the Golden Era had already been given that honour once before. Finally, in 2016, the Government of India did the needful. The Department of Posts released a set of ten commemorative stamps and a miniature sheet on Talat Mahmood, Manna Dey, Mohammed Rafi, Kishore Kumar, Mukesh, Hemant Kumar, Bhupen Hazarika, Geeta Dutt, T. M. Soundarajan and Shamshad Begum. This was released under the 'Legendary Singers Series' on 30th December 2016. Talat's image on the stamp was a fully smiling face dressed in a white shirt. The background of the portrait was a bright yellow colour. I was really happy with the look of the stamp because it oozed with his charm and his happy disposition.

The official release on Talat stated, "Talat Mahmood (February 1924 – 9 May 1998) is considered one of the greatest male singers in India. A born singer with an intuitive sense of beauty, charm and grace; a legendary Indian playback singer who created his own new style of ghazal singing which was to be followed afterwards. Talat Mahmood received the Padma Bhushan in 1992, in recognition of his artistic contributions in the spheres of cinematic and ghazal music."

After briefing the audience with this piece of information, I introduced them to the first performer of the evening, Rashmi Agarwal. She regaled the crowd with her top picks of Talat's most popular songs. As a well-known singer in the Delhi concert circuit, Rashmi took great care to understand which songs, apart from just the popular hits will be appreciated by the audience. She got loud claps for 'Yeh hawa yeh raat' and 'Jalte hain jiske liye'. There was one particular selection by her that surprised me. It was a lesser known song sung for Dev Anand from the film 'Kinare Kinare (1963). The song was 'Dekh li teri khudayi, bas mera dil bhar gaya...' (Your divinity has given me sorrow). The tone and pitch of the song suited her to the T and she sounded best in this soulful number. She painstakingly brought together the best orchestral team for the show who had a deep understanding of the original compositions and made sure to play all the hooks almost identical to the original. "When you hear him sing, it sounds very simple and easy. But when you try to sing his songs, you realize the amount of practice that is required. By listening to him, I have learnt some fresh nuances of Ghazal singing which I didn't know about earlier. And these new learnings will become a part of my singing. It's been an enriching experience for me because I will add this to my style now", informed Rashmi.

The Morning Standard newspaper creatively headlined it as "Portrait of Mahmood at a Multi-performance Show" while the New Indian Express called it "Moving to the Rhythm of Resilience".

LUCKNOW BOY'S HOMECOMING

(The author with singer Radhika Chopra for the performance of 'Jashn-e-Talat by Sahar Zaman' in Lucknow)

A couple of months later, we were approaching Talat's 95th birth anniversary in February 2019. I decided to take Jashn-e-Talat to yet another step ahead by starting the process of partnering with popular cultural festivals across the country. I was hoping that my next stop would be the city of Lucknow because it was the legend's birthplace and hometown.

This is when I pitched the show to the lovely team of the Mahindra Sanatkada Lucknow Festival (MSLF). The popular annual festival happens in February every year and they immediately warmed up to the idea. Their Director, Madhavi Kukreja, was certain that re-igniting the memory of his music in the hearts of Lucknowites would be great. After all, this was about bringing the music of Talat back to his hometown, the locality where he grew up, where his ancestral home was, where he studied and where he first became a recognizable radio singer. It was perfectly serendipitous to have

Jashn-e-Talat collaborate with the MSLF to pay tribute to the Lucknow boy.

"I am very happy to perform for Jashn-e-Talat for the third time, especially in his hometown, Lucknow, which was where he was born, where he grew up and where he started his journey of music", reflected Radhika Chopra.

The night of the performance was attended in full force at the lawns of Salempur House in the Qaiserbagh area of Lucknow. While Radhika Chopra sang the most popular songs of Talat Mahmood's career, I played the part of narrating the highlights of his life to the audience. I wrote my script highlighting all the places that mattered to his life - his house, his school, his college, places where he hung out, etc. Our concert was happening in the same area of old Lucknow where Talat lived with his family in Aminabad and later studied music at the (Marris College) Bhatkhande Music University. Each location that I mentioned in my script was a stone's throw away from where we were performing. Sitting outside the heritage Safed Baradari in Lucknow's Qaiserbagh, an audience of about 400 sang along to the song 'Tasveer banata hoon', one of Talat's most popular songs. It was a beautiful coincidence that this song was from a film of the same name as the venue, 'Baradari' (1955). Radhika Chopra added her own interpretations to his music while being true to his ethos. It was an experience of a mehfil (cultural gathering) in the city of nawabs. The local media in Lucknow headlined Jashn-e-Talat as the highlight of the MSFL festival. The Amar Ujala newspaper defined it as "Songs of Talat Mahmood Embellish an Evening of Awadh". The Navbharat Times was more expressive with stating, "The Ecstasy of Talat's Ghazals." After the show, I was surrounded by people from the audience who were eager to share their own story about Talat. Somebody's uncle's neighbour, somebody's classmate, somebody's grandfather's friend. It was like Talat's homecoming in his 95th year.

By this time, we had done an average of one Jashn-e-Talat concert every four months. The tribute in Lucknow was the 7th such ground event for us.

BOMBAY MERI JAAN

(Kathak dancer Shovana Narayan, Ghazal singer Sudeep Banerji and the author for the Jashn-e-Talat show in Mumbai (clockwise))

In February 2020, it was time for his birth anniversary again. And this time, I was interested in taking the show to Mumbai. This city was the most important in Talat's life. The city that made him the star of the masses and classes both. The city that catapulted him to being one of biggest singing stars of the Golden Era. The city of dreams, the city of films, music and romance!

Mumbai's signature festival called the Kala Ghoda Arts Festival (KGAF) was happy to receive my proposal. It was certainly something they wanted on their list of performances. This is a festival which is a legacy platform since 1998 dedicated to promoting music, films, books, food, visual arts and dance in the popular art district of South Mumbai. Spread over a duration of 9 days, the festival attracts about 150,000 people every year. The footfalls come from Mumbai and beyond. The crowd is a mix of discerning individuals, senior citizens, young arts practitioners and cultural connoisseurs. This is certainly the kind of eyeballs and attention that I wanted for Jashn-e-Talat.

Kathak Guru Shovana Narayan graciously accepted to perform for the tribute again. She looked mesmerizing as the spotlight shone on her while dancing to the duet 'Aha rim jhim ke ye pyaare geet'. Dressed in a bright pink *angarkha* kurta, she lit up the stage with her vivacious presence. She effortlessly danced to a song with two singers in a music composition which was non classical and fast paced. It was the work of a true master who accommodated her Kathak mudras to popular film music.

We added a new performer to the list of Jashn-e-Talat. Ghazal singer and music composer Sudeep Banerji. Yes, he is the same singer who had performed for Talat's first ever tribute in Delhi soon after his passing away in 1998. Sudeep was delighted to be part of another show dedicated to the handsome singer. According to him, Talat was the only Ghazal singer who romanticized the image of a crooner as a sensational heartthrob with his charming mannerisms and stylish suits. "He was always so crisply dressed in a suit. When I sing on stage today, it will be in front of the Jashn-e-Talat banner that features a handsome picture of him from his youth", added Sudeep. In the past few years, my experience of bringing today's artists and singers to pay tribute to his films and music has always been an eye opener on how people view his legacy. Sudeep was excited about altering a few songs of Talat to add newer elements for today's young audience. I was surprised to hear boom-box beats in his rendition of 'Itna na mujhse tu pyar badha'. The Mumbai crowd loved it. His orchestration of Talat's melodies was refreshing and unheard. The drums and guitars added to classics such as 'Tasveer banata hoon' and 'Seene mein sulagte hain armaan' were undoubtedly the work of a master musician, that Sudeep is.

It reminded me of an experiment Talat himself had done in 1967, in toying with the traditional sounds of the Ghazal. He daringly used the Hawaiian guitar and metal drums for the opening piece in a non-film Ghazal from his album called Spring Blossoms. The ghazal is about a love that has been lost, but its memory is celebrated in the happy mood of the composition.

'Unke aage gham-e-dil chhupana padaa

Ro raha tha magar muskarana padaa'

(The sadness of my heart had to be hidden
I was crying from within but I had to smile)

Some orthodox critics had frowned upon this experiment which seemed blasphemous to the pure form of Ghazal. The final verdict on Talat's experiment came with the record-breaking sales of that track. Sudeep further innovated with the classic hit 'Jalte hain jiske liye' by adding translated verses in Bengali. He smoothly transitioned from one stanza in Urdu to the next in Bengali. Thus, paying homage to his career in Modern Bangla music as well. The night at KGAF was an enchanting reminder to Mumbaikars of a legend who lived amongst them and was an ambassador of their city when he toured abroad. When I came on stage to tell them about the journey of his life, I mentioned his favourite places in Mumbai. The food at Sun N Sand hotel in Juhu and the Gaylord Restaurant in Churchgate, the bookstore in Ritz Hotel, recreation at Otter's Club and the sunsets at Juhu beach. The crowd clapped in delight as they could immediately relate to him as one of their own.

TURNING ONLINE DURING COVID

The show in Mumbai was the last Jashn-e-Talat festival in the physical world for the next two years. It was literally a month before the nationwide lockdown. The world was hit by an unprecedented pandemic and all festivals either shut shop or shifted to the online platform. In May 2020, Talat's death anniversary was marked with a full day of programming on the official Facebook page of Jashn-e-Talat. Nine hours of LIVE interaction brought together some fascinating partnerships to revisit the music of Talat Mahmood.

The first session started with various portraits of Talat painted by today's young artists. It was an interesting mix of styles from realism, fauvism, poster art to water colours. Old black and white portraits of the legend were given a fresh interpretation in colours and style that are in vogue today. The next session was about learning the nuances of Urdu by listening to Talat. His songs and ghazals are a repository of understanding how to pronounce and express in Urdu. The language of love and emotions needs to be spoken in a certain manner but how does one best understand its import? By listening to the poetry that Talat has immortalized in his voice. This was in partnership with a volunteer organization called Joy of Urdu, which aims to facilitate and enable the revitalization of the Urdu language.

One of the world's most popular karaoke applications called 'Smule' joined hands with Jashn-e-Talat to invite people to sing his songs all day long. We must appreciate that since this was during the lockdown, online engagements were showing a peak in activity. Karaoke recordings were showing a steep climb and the announcement on celebrating Talat's anniversary created a desirable buzz on the platform.

There is very little spoken or written about Talat the actor. Away from his towering career as a singer, Talat as an actor showed considerable demand amongst his fans which is why producers had begun to cast him on screen as well. The dozen films in which he starred as the main lead showed a progress in his range of emotions that could play on camera. Although he always maintained that soft romantic roles were all that he could manage and it always remained a side hustle. I wished to create a special documentary exclusively about Talat, the actor. This is where 'Cinemaazi' stepped in. It is an archive and research centre dedicated to document the rich history and heritage of Indian cinema and its people. Their team created this special feature and for the first time, a documentary on Talat was made which spoke only about his films as an actor. This was played out on the Jashn- eTalat platform as part of our LIVE programming.

Popular digital news media, The Quint, did a special episode on

Talat in their award winning weekly podcast series called 'Urdunama'. They spoke with me about his life long career USP - his inimitable voice and his unparalleled command over the beauty of Urdu. Soon after, we also played out a video version of my opinion column in the Times of India where I speak about the pleasure, and perhaps therapeutic benefits as well, of listening to Talat's voice during the stressful times of the lockdown. This was a time when people were going through unforeseen despair. The right music is always believed to calm your senses. But the right voice which soothes your frazzled nerves with the sweetness of honey and softness of velvet? That has to be Talat.

We concluded our programming in partnership with Hunar TV, Asia's first webchannel on arts, by creating a special mash-up of all our Jashn-e-Talat concerts. In hindsight, these nine hours that we spent online became one of the most fruitful engagements with a much wider outreach. But could this really replace physical interaction with humans? We were yet to learn.

SOFT LAUNCH - FIRST LOOK UNVEILED

(The author with Talat's colleague and friend, Enoch Daniels, launch the first look of the book)

By 2023, the world of culture and arts had bounced back fully and completely. A lot of festivals relaunched and many decided that the new formula of being hybrid was the best lesson learnt from Covid. Hybrid means the combination of doing a festival in both the physical space as well as a simulcast (simultaneous telecast) online. We were suddenly equipped with the power of technology that could no longer limit us to a linear path of physical shows. We could be all over the place, all the time, online across different cities and anytime! There was no way that this genie was going back in the bottle.

Meanwhile, I spent a little over a year researching and writing this book which is in your hands right now. From a television news anchor and concert curator, I became an author. I travelled to a few cities closely connected to his life as well as used the online benefits of the post Covid world. Even the octogenarian generation with whom I was mostly interacting with, were now used to the concept of digital meetings and video calls. Technology had truly been embraced by all. I reached out to his old friends, colleagues settled across cities, music clubs in the U.S., U.K., etc. - all of them who gave me exclusive insights into his professional life. After the first draft of the book was ready, I wondered that since films always have a series of publicities in the form of promos, first look, teasers, etc., why can't an upcoming book follow a similar promotional plan? So, I decided to bring out the first look of Talat's biography.

In May 2023, I was invited by the Royal Harmonica Orchestra in Pune to attend their special show marking Talat's anniversary in May. They are a team of professional musicians with the harmonica being the main instrument of the orchestra which is used to play the main rendition of the song while the rest of the orchestra plays the preludes and interludes. It was a marvel to watch them effortlessly play Talat's fast numbers as well the slow-paced ones, which can be a bigger challenge with the mouth organ.
But each song was distinctly recognizable without the need of any singer.

"What converts a tune into a song are the lyrics. So, playing the songs on an instrument requires bringing in lyrical values in it. It takes almost four rehearsals in a period of two months to get it right. But even then, we are just 60 percent close to his original songs. No instrument can do justice to his voice", explains Nandu Belvalkar, Director of the Pune Harmonica Orchestra. It was on this stage that we decided to unveil the first look of the biography. His old friend, the sprightly and active nonagenarian, Enoch Daniels was there to do the honours. As his accordionist and music arranger, Daniels recalled his time spent with Talat in studio recordings and their landmark global tours. With at least 300 dedicated Talat fans in attendance, the music hall broke into a thunderous applause as they got to see the first look of the book. The photograph which was chosen was from the film Waris (1954). Crisply dressed in a white shirt and striped necktie, it's an image from his romantic song 'Ghar tera apna ghar laage'. But this was just a teaser for the first look.

The final book cover has an equally charming studio portrait of the legend. Talat's smiling face epitomizes all that his persona stands for - warmth, generosity and gentleness.

The centenary year of his birth in February 2024 is a significant milestone in the legacy of an artist. I hope this definitive biography does justice to his contribution to cinema and music as well as lives up to the expectations of his die-hard fans whose unfailing love keeps his name afloat. While I mark the completion of this biography, the journey of his music doesn't end here. Talat Mahmood lives on. Jashn-e-Talat lives on. See you soon, somewhere, someday, celebrating the remarkable genius!

ACKNOWLEDGEMENTS

There are many people whom I am grateful to for being part of my journey of revisiting Talat Mahmood, my grand uncle. But first and foremost, I must thank the legend himself. More than 25 years after his passing away, his brilliance has continued to inspire me and give me strength to keep moving on. His magical voice, with its trademark soft nudges, has given me hope in the darkest of hours whenever I felt I could no longer face the many challenges involved in completing this biography. How I wish he knew what he means to me today. How I wish he could see what has been created in his name, with love. Bitten by the bug of re-discovering his music and career, this journey has been more than worthwhile. I have been most fortunate to have had him as my grand-uncle. In the course of the book, I would like to inform you that for the sake of easy readability, I have addressed him simply as Talat. this does not mean any disrespect to him at all.

I am hugely indebted and eternally grateful to our national treasure in the world of Hindustani Classical music, Padma Vibhushan, Pandit Hariprasad Chaurasia. His generosity in writing the Foreword for this biography has added layers of beauty and credibility to my work. I thank his daughter-in- law, the ever-so-gracious Pushpanjali, for patiently coordinating with Pandit ji and lending her support.

I am grateful to the family members of those who were crucial to Talat's career. Anil Biswas' daughter Shikha Biswas, Pankaj Mullick's grandson Rajib Gupta, Dilip Kumar's wife, actress Saira Banu, all of them spoke to me as their own, like family.

I have been extremely fortunate to get in touch with artists who worked with Talat Mahmood. I want to thank legendary accordionist and music arranger Enoch Daniels, India's most prolific concert manager, Nandi Duggal, and singer par excellence, Kavita Krishnamurthy, who have all enchanted me with their personal stories connected to Talat.

India's tallest and best-selling writer, Dr. Shashi Tharoor, was there to provide moral support right since the early days of the Jashn-e-Talat concert and the start of this biography. He especially took out time to endorse this biography with his gentle touch of kindness and sincerity. As a bonus, he wrote a special Foreword for the book too.

India's most talented and popular singer, Sonu Nigam, sprang a surprise on me by penning down a personal piece for the book. I am hugely grateful for his heartfelt insight and his sincerity in supporting my efforts in writing this biography.

I want to thank Adil Hussain, one of the most recognized names in international cinema today, who took out time in the middle of his travels and shoots to give a shout out to the world for reading about the fascinating journey of Talat Mahmood penned by me.

Eminent books editor and television news editor, Sudha Sadanand, trusted my skill to pen down this labour of love and always reminded me to never give up. Her early intervention on what was just a mere plan in my head was given the first thrust by her strong support.

It has taken me a little over a year of intense research and writing to complete this book. I managed to do this with my habit of working with tight deadlines in the television news industry.

Nevertheless, in hindsight, the concept of a book had been building in my mind for the past several years, ever since I started the series of tribute shows dedicated to him called 'Jashn-e-Talat'. So obviously, anyone involved with this series is part of my list of acknowledgements, apart from those who came along as I wrote this biography.

Leading performers of today such as legendary Talat Aziz, Shovana Narayan, Radhika Chopra, Raghav Bhatt, Mangala Bhatt, Sudeep Banerji, Rashmi Agarwal, Vidha Lal, Tauseef Akhtar, etc. have all lent their time and talent to Jashn-e-Talat. Many others who helped have been remembered in the last chapter of this book, including many young performers from different colleges.

I was fortunate to find the right collaborations for concerts with help from cultural ambassadors like Sunit Tandon, Madhavi Kukreja and Khaleeq-ur- Rahman.

My wonderful extended family members Zaheer Kidvai, Rishad Mahmood, Shehzad Mahmood, who dug into their archives, photo albums and memories to help reconstruct different phases of Talat's life.

Lastly but most importantly, my closest and dearest forever - my husband Dhiraj Singh, mother Romana Zaman, brother Samar Zaman and son, Kazuo Imad - who were there for just about anything that I required. I applaud them for keeping up with my highs and lows, my emotional outbursts and unpredictable mood swings that became part of the territory, considering the challenges involved.

BIBLIOGRAPHY

[1] Pandit Bhimsen Joshi, A Film By Gulzar
[2] Radio interview with Vividh Bharti
[3] Tribute show 'Ek Fankaar, Ek insaan', Doordarshan
[4] Shahenshah-e-Ghazal, article in Shama, 1981
[5] Shahenshah-e-Ghazal, article in Shama, 1981
[6] Jaya Ramanathan's column, Passages Lifespan
[7] Ek Fankaar, Ek Insaan: Talat Mahmood, Doordarshan
[8] Total Recall show, Times Now
[9] As told to Lata Khubchandani in Talat's obituary
[10] Interview to journalist Ranjan Das Gupta, 2013
[11] Total Recall show, Times Now
[12] Talat Geet Kosh, 1992
[13] Talat GeetKosh, 1992
[14] Sajjad Hussain's obituary by Raja Rajyadhaksha
[15] As told to Jaya Ramanathan, Passages Lifespan, 1984
[16] Interview to journalist Girija Rajendran
[17] TV series 'Shammi Kapoor Unplugged'
[18] Ek Makhmali Awaaz, film by Sharad Dutt
[19] Interview to journalist Girija Rajendran
[20] Filmfare magazine, 1955
[21] Interview to journalist V Gangadhar
[22] Total Recall show by Times Now
[23] Talat Geet Kosh, 1992
[24] 'Shahenshah-e-Ghazal' article in Shama
[25] 'Shahenshah-e-Ghazal' article in Shama
[26] Ameen Sayani presents Geetmala ki Chaon Mein
[27] Totat Recall show by Times now
[28] Legend Of Talat Mahamood-Savera Publication, 1979
[29] Total Recall show by Times Now
[30] The Legend of Talat Mahmood - Savera Publication
[31] Nasreen Munni Kabir's 'Lata Mangeshkar, In Her Own Voice', Niyogi Publishers
[32] Interview to Rishad Mahmood in The News, 1992
[33] An anthology titled 'Talat Mahmood - The Velvet Voice' by Manek Premchand, Manipal University Press
[34] An anthology titled 'Talat Mahmood - The Velvet Voice' by Manek Premchand, Manipal University Press
[35] India Club history from IAM, Minnesota
[36] Total Recall show by Times Now

[37] 'Ek Makhmali Awaaz', a film by Sharad Dutt

[38] 'Talat Mahmood : The Velvet Voice' by Manek Premchand, MUP

[39] 'Talat Mahmood : The Velvet Voice by Manek Premchand' by MUP

[40] Official website talatmahmood.net

[41] Official website of the Indian American Impact organisation, iaimpact.org

[42] Interview to Jaya Ramanathan in Passages Lifespan

[43] 'Ek Makhmali Awaaz' film by journalist Sharad Dutt

[44] Interview to journalist Girija Rajendran

[45] Interview to Akashvani All India Radio

[46] Interview to journalist Malvika Kaul

[47] 'Ek Makhmali Awaaz - Talat Mahmood', documentary by journalist Sharad Dutt

[48] Interview to journalist Malvika Kaul

[49] Naushadnama - The Life and Music of Naushad by Raju Bhartan, published by Hay House

[50] TV report on Doordarshan National channel

[51] 'Talat Mahmood,The Velvet Voice, an anthology by by Manek Premchand, published by MUP

[52] Tribute by Zee TV

[53] Interview to journalist Jaya Ramanathan in Passages Lifespan

ABOUT THE AUTHOR

Sahar Zaman is an award-winning television news journalist, author and cultural curator. She is recognized for her work in television, print and digital, for almost 25 years as political newscaster, news editor and features correspondent on prime-time news media across India's top networks. She is the Founder of 'Hunar TV' and the Chief Curator of 'Jashn- e-Talat'.

As her debut book, this is an extension of her journalistic work which required deep research, analysis of history, fact checks, interviews and the art of story-telling of an iconic life. Her insights as the legend's grand-niece and skills as a journalist give an edge to this voluminous tome that brings together an impactful narration to both personal and professional aspects of his life.

www.ingramcontent.com/pod-product-compliance
Lightning Source LLC
LaVergne TN
LVHW041011150826
845672LV00001B/47

9798896105534